THE NORTHERN FOREST CANOE TRAIL
THROUGH-PADDLER'S
COMPANION

Northern Forest Canoe Trail

An historic water trail through New York, Vermont, Québec, New Hampshire, and Maine

THE NORTHERN FOREST CANOE TRAIL
THROUGH-PADDLER'S
COMPANION

A guidebook to paddling the 740-mile water trail
from its western terminus in Old Forge, New York,
to the eastern terminus in Fort Kent, Maine.

KATINA DAANEN

THIRD EDITION

The Northern Forest Canoe Trail Through-Paddler's Companion, 2nd Edition
A guidebook to paddling the 740-mile water trail from its western terminus
in Old Forge, New York, to the eastern terminus in Fort Kent, Maine.

NFCTPaddler.com

Copyright © 2014 Katina Daanen

First edition, April 2014
Second edition, December 2014; revised October 2015
Third edition, January 2017

Cover design and layout: Katina Daanen/Indigo Design
Cover photograph: West Branch Penobscot River © Katina Daanen

All photographs © Katina Daanen except Grand Portage © Jim Cole; Moosehead Lake, Tramway Carry, eastern terminus and back cover author photo © Kay Glodowski; and Spencer Stream and Attean Pond © Kacia Kolstad

Any outdoor recreational activity is potentially hazardous. This book is not a substitute for outdoor skills or good personal judgment. Certain risks are inherent in any paddling trip and each user of the information presented in this book must accept personal responsibility for his or her own safety and orientation. The author assumes no liability for any accident, loss, illness, injury or drowning happening to readers who participate in the activities described in this book.

ISBN-13: 978-0996052504
ISBN-10: 099605250X

Table of Contents

PART 2

Mileage Segments

Overview..49

What Constitutes a "Wheelable" Portage: Definitions 50

------ ◆ ------

MAPS

The Northern Forest Canoe Trail
Segment Overview Map

The breakdown of the Trail into 35 *Through-Paddler Companion* guidebook segments and the corresponding official NFCT maps.

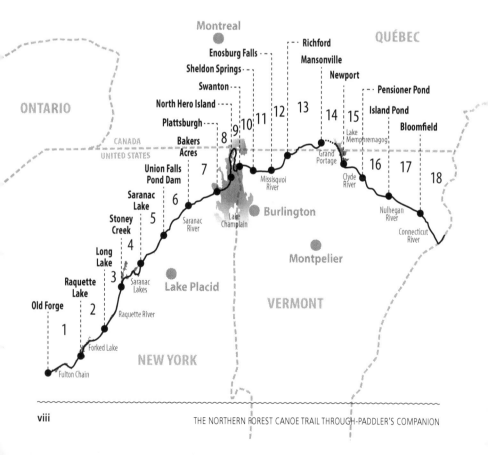

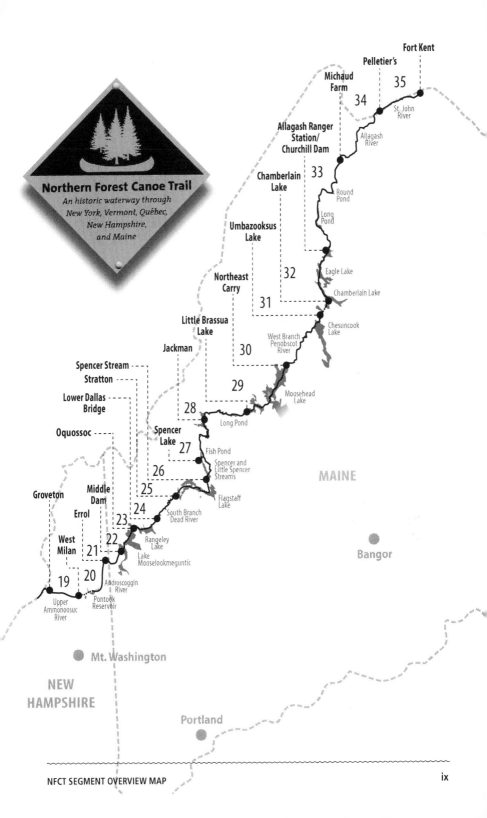

Northern Forest Canoe Trail

An historic waterway through New York, Vermont, Québec, New Hampshire, and Maine

Fort Kent

Pelletier's

35

Michaud Farm

34

St. John River

Allagash Ranger Station/ Churchill Dam

33

Allagash River

Chamberlain Lake

Round Pond

Long Pond

Umbazooksus Lake

32

Eagle Lake

Northeast Carry

31

Chamberlain Lake

Little Brassua Lake

30

Chesuncook Lake

Jackman

West Branch Penobscot River

Spencer Stream

Stratton

29

Lower Dallas Bridge

28

Moosehead Lake

Oquossoc

Long Pond

Spencer Lake

27

Fish Pond

26

Spencer and Little Spencer Streams

MAINE

25

Middle Dam

24

Flagstaff Lake

Groteton

23

South Branch Dead River

Errol

22

Rangeley Lake

West Milan

21

Lake Mooselookmeguntic

Bangor

19

20

Androscoggin River

Upper Ammonoosuc River

Pontook Reservoir

Mt. Washington

NEW HAMPSHIRE

Portland

NFCT SEGMENT OVERVIEW MAP

ix

Foreword

A **lifelong canoeist**, I've canoe-camped on several Midwestern National Scenic Rivers, but have spent the majority of my paddling trips in the Boundary Waters Canoe Area Wilderness/Quetico Provincial Park along the Minnesota and Ontario borders. I first heard of the Northern Forest Canoe Trail (NFCT) in March 2010, when I attended Canoecopia, an annual paddle sport show held in Madison, Wisc. Within the hour I was already scheming about whom I could recruit in order to spend the following summer heading to the Northeast to paddle this compelling trail.

On August 25, 2011, I successfully achieved my goal—following all 13 maps of the Northern Forest Canoe Trail in 53 days with friends and family members accompanying me for six "legs" of the trip. This included six days of paddler "swap days" or zero mileage days.

The year 2011 was an unusual weather year in both spring and late summer. Heavy snow and early spring rains created flood conditions in the upper Northeast. Lake Champlain rose to its highest recorded level, 103.2 feet above sea level, on May 6, 2011. Some of the first Through-Paddlers that year had to miss entire sections due to dangerously high river levels. Huge sections of banks ripped away in the Highgate Falls Dam area on the Missisquoi River in northwestern Vermont and shoreline erosion was experienced all the way to the Connecticut River in New Hampshire.

From August 20 to 28, 2011, Hurricane Irene rolled up along the Northeast coast and landed squarely over most of the NFCT. Rivers and streams, including Little Spencer and the Allagash, rose five feet overnight. Houses were destroyed and bridges and roads throughout eastern New York, Vermont and New Hampshire washed out.

By contrast, 2012 was a drought year. Several paddling trips were suspended due to exceedingly low water levels occurring throughout the Trail.

While there is nothing typical about any one journey or any given year, *The Northern Forest Canoe Trail Through-Paddler's Companion* reflects many common stopping points and organizes mileage goals into useful segments that work for both an aggressive schedule as well as for those traveling at a more relaxed pace. Weather conditions, stamina or interest will dictate your own daily mileage goals.

The 35 segments detailed in this guidebook were determined by my own experience as well as the collected experiences of more than two dozen other Through-Paddlers beginning with the first published accounts in 2006 and with interviews conducted of paddlers through the 2014 season. The guidebook is not intended to be a road map instructing you how to travel the Trail, rather it is assembled with details that will help make choices more informed.

Even on the most challenging days—passing between mountain ranges and across watersheds or pushing against headwinds on expansive lakes—you will experience moments of grace. Hardly a day will pass that doesn't impart some remarkable and unexpected experience—an evening breeze clearing away voracious bugs or finding yourself coasting along the current of a powerful river. You will amass an accumulation of fiery sunrises and sunsets while surviving drenching rains. You won't possibly be able to define exactly how it feels to be there, except to say there is no place you'd rather be.

The Northern Forest Canoe Trail is an outstanding environmental and economic asset for paddling enthusiasts and Northeast communities. In a time when border security and private land ownership threaten access to public waterways, the paddling community is fortunate to benefit from the efforts of visionaries who established this phenomenal 740-mile treasure connecting two nations, four states and one Canadian province.

Preface

You can study all the maps, read the guidebook and browse all the blogs, but the unique set of weather and water conditions under which you will travel have never occurred—and will never occur— exactly the same for you or any other paddler. Each day spent on the Trail is one that prepares you for the next.

It's not as simple, though, as just picking up your paddle and following the maps for a month or more of paddling. While the Trail is accessible to all levels of paddling skills, you'll want to be aware of what challenges—and pleasures—the trail holds.

The purpose of this guide is to complement the official NFCT guidebook and expand upon the maps, drawing a linear picture of the Trail from the perspective and needs of a Through-Paddler or any paddler looking for more detailed Trail information. Although *The Through-Paddler's Companion* currently lacks GPS-specific references, mileage and portage references correlate with the official NFCT guidebook and all 13 maps. However, you may be surprised to learn that the accumulated mileage of a through-paddling trip does not add up to a total of 740 miles. An explanation of this discrepancy can be found at the end of *Part II: Mileage Segments* on page 204.

The most efficient direction paddling the Trail in its entirety—and in a single journey—is traveling from west to east. Even though this means Through-Paddlers are required to ascend a total of 162 miles paddling upstream and against a current, this is considered preferable to paddling the last and longest downstream river sections, the 77-mile long Allagash River that next connects to the 17-mile St. John River, in their reverse directions. Undoubtedly there will come a day when someone attempts to paddle the entire trail from east to west.

Because the majority of Through-Paddlers treat the Trail as an expedition, most side trips detailed within the official NFCT guidebook have been disregarded. Additional routes that enrich the NFCT as a destination have not been included in this companion guide.

General packing tips and concerns specific to the needs of the NFCT Through-Paddler and information unique to the Trail have been included, but this guidebook is not intended as an inclusive canoe camping resource.

The content created for this publication is the result of the best efforts of the author using information obtained from personal experience, interviews, paddler blogs, trail data and facts available at the time of publication. Changes in environment and economics are constantly occurring and therefore, information cannot be guaranteed to be precisely accurate. New campsites may be added. Businesses may suddenly close. Portages deemed "wheelable" could experience severe weather damage resulting in obstacles or rerouting. Even defining the ease of which a portage can be wheeled is subject to quirky conditions or individual interpretation.

Over the years—and since this guidebook was first written—the number of portage options has grown as improvements to the Trail have expanded. This doesn't mean that there are now fewer miles spent on the water—in fact there are even more. Water bodies, such as Spectacle Pond in Vermont and Haley Pond in Maine, were added after the trail's inception. Rather, developing infrastructure continues to address parts of the trail that can be challenging or decidedly dangerous, or simply lacks options. Additional portages have been built to help paddlers around technically-difficult rapids and ledges and some carries have been rerouted away from busy highways. Each year brings new changes as the Trail becomes perfected in its quest to remain the best water trail in North America.

Notices of the most recent changes to the Trail and services are posted on the *NorthernForestCanoeTrail.org* website under *"Trail Updates"* and *"Services Along NFCT"* links.

The Through-Paddler's Companion is intended to be a tool to assist with route decisions as you journey east, but should not be your sole source for navigation. Please exercise all appropriate precautions ensuring your safety, wellbeing and overall enjoyment.

Now get out there and paddle!

------ ◆ ------

PART 1

A Brief Introduction to the
Northern Forest Canoe Trail (NFCT)

Through-Paddling:
Unique Perspectives and Concerns

Practicalities

A Brief Introduction to the
Northern Forest Canoe Trail (NFCT)

HISTORY

The Northern Forest Canoe Trail is a
740-mile inland water trail tracing historic
Native American travel routes through
contiguous rivers, streams, and lakes
through New York, Vermont, Québec,
New Hampshire and Maine. The NFCT is
the longest mapped paddling trail in the
nation, beginning from its western terminus
in Old Forge, New York to its eastern
terminus ending in Fort Kent, Maine.

The Trail flows through developed
areas and backcountry providing both
civilized community and rich wilderness
experiences. Paddlers get to explore the
natural beauty of the Northern Forest
Region's rivers and lakes as well as local
towns through which the NFCT passes.

Donnie Mullen, an Outward Bound
instructor from Northport, Maine,
was the first person to Through-Paddle
the entire route in 2000, taking 55 days
to do so. He paddled a 16' wood-canvas
canoe, which he made himself for the trip.
Within the first decade of the Trail's history,
only an average of half a dozen to a dozen
paddlers annually completed the Trail, but
increased awareness has generated more
interest and participation, even attracting
paddlers from as far away as the United
Kingdom and the Netherlands.

BY THE NUMBERS

23
Rivers and Streams
(Including one designated
National Wild and Scenic River)

62
Lakes and Ponds

77
Carries or Portages
(Totaling about 78 miles)

3
National Wildlife Refuges

49
Communities

FLOW OF THE TRAIL
Downstream and upstream. Water
levels fluctuate due to spring
runoff, drought and dam releases.

LODGING OPTIONS
Overnight options roughly every
15 miles ranging from primitive
campsites, to lovely inns.

LANDSCAPE
Passing through hills and
mountains, forests, farmlands
and village centers.

BORDER CROSSINGS
The Trail crosses the international
border with Canada in two places:
– East Richford, Qué. on the
  Missisquoi River (NFCT Map 5)
  and

– Newport, Vt. via Lake
  Memphremagog (NFCT Map 6)

**The NFCT has been recognized as the preeminent water trail by organization
including the American Canoe Association and publications such as *Canoe and Kayak*
and *Outside* magazine, who honored the Trail as the "Best Canoe Trail"
and a "Best East Coast Adventure."**

The idea for the Northern Forest Canoe Trail was brought to life in the 1990's when Mike Krepner, Ron Canter and Randy Mardres of Native Trails Inc. researched the traditional east-west water routes used by Native Americans and early settlers in the Northern Forest Region, from the Adirondacks to Northern Maine. The organization was incorporated as a nonprofit in 2000 as a way to translate this research into a recreational, community and regional resource.

Through quality management and collaborative community partnerships, the Northern Forest Canoe Trail creates opportunities for outdoor recreation, contributes to the economic resilience of the region, promotes the health of its lands and waters and inspires transformational experiences.

The Trail was officially completed in spring 2006, with 13 mapped contiguous sections offering campsites, portages, trail signs and access points along the entire route. In 2010, NFCT Inc. published its official guidebook. New campsites and/or improved access points and portages are added annually.

THROUGH-PADDLERS AND SECTION-PADDLERS

The Northern Forest Canoe Trail organization recognizes paddlers who document their trip and travel the full trail into two different categories: *Through-Paddlers* and *Section-Paddlers*.

Through-Paddlers complete the Trail by paddling it in one season. Depending on the time of year of the trip and that year's weather conditions, water levels may be too high (2011 spring flooding created dangerous conditions on the Missisquoi River in Vermont for early season paddlers), or too low (the South Branch Dead River between Rangeley and Stratton, Maine, is notorious for being an impassable late-season 19-mile section), and can limit a Through-Paddler's ability to physically paddle every mile.

Section-Paddlers have a better ability to paddle the Trail in segments at the optimal season, and even can avoid any upstream paddling. Section-Paddlers complete the entire trail over a number of different trips and over the course of years.

Both types of paddlers will benefit from experiencing a full range of paddling conditions from lakes to rivers—including flatwater, swiftwater and whitewater. Each stroke of the paddle dips into the cultural and natural heritage of the Northeast as you pass through historic communities, working industrial towns and into the heart of true wilderness.

The NFCT supports and applauds the achievements of all paddlers and maintains a list of Through- and Section-Paddlers on its website. In 2013, categories and requirements were revised as follows:

THOUGH-PADDLERS

Through-Paddlers paddle the entire Trail as one expedition, during a single season. Through-Paddlers are designated into one of the following three categories:

Self-Propelled Paddlers

Paddlers who complete the entire 740 miles in one direction using their own power to paddle, pole and portage. Leaving the Trail via other means of travel for lodging, shopping or other reasons will not count against the self-propelled paddler as long as he or she returns to the same spot to continue the journey on the Trail. Consideration for deviations to this definition will be given to safety, inclement weather and extreme low water.

Integrated Paddlers

These paddlers are those who paddle the Trail as one expedition during a single season in one direction, but may use a shuttle for one or more of the carries, not exceeding 10 percent of the total Trail distance (74 miles).

Integrated "Downstream" Paddlers

In addition to using shuttles, "downstream" paddlers are differentiated for reversing direction in order to descend rather than ascend one or more of the rivers along the route. These paddlers still traverse the Trail as one expedition, during a single season.

SECTION-PADDLERS

Recognition will be conferred upon completion of the entire Trail.

APPLYING FOR RECOGNITION

Applications are reviewed annually and are due each November. Applications and additional information are available online on the NFCT website at *NorthernForestCanoeTrail.org*. Click on the links: *Paddlers > Through & Section Paddler Recognition.*

AVERAGE TRIP LENGTHS AND SPEED RECORDS

Though the average number of days spent on the Trail hovers around 40, Through-Paddlers tend to fall into two categories of travel speed. One group inclines to spend the entire day putting on as many miles as possible and may have few or no zero mileage days. These paddlers complete the Trail in about one month or less. The second group leans toward using towns as natural stopping points and will often take a break as they paddle at a more leisurely pace. They tend to complete the Trail in 50 days or more.

Ages of Through-Paddlers range from teens and young adults in college to seniors in their 70s. The Trail has also attracted more than a few people celebrating 50th birthdays. Even children have experienced the Trail, including a preschooler who accompanied his parents in 2015 and again in 2016.

The average paddle times reflected in this guide are based on solo and tandem paddlers using either a kayak or a canoe. While not absolute, the slower average travel times tend to reflect the pace of a solo kayaker, while the faster averages reflect tandem canoeists.

Averages are only generalized indicators. In May and June 2013, a solo canoeist successfully completed the Trail in less than 30 days, the majority of which were rainy. He averaged 28 miles a day that included ascending up the unseasonably flooded Missisquoi River.

Although the NFCT "List" doesn't note speed records, in 2012, a three-person team paddling a single Wenonah Minnesota III canoe completed the Trail in just 21 days, 3 hours and 45 minutes, the fastest reported time to date. Several kayakers have chased the solo record, with 22 day mark set in 2016.

Best Time to Paddle

Early spring paddlers could find themselves paddling through ice-outs, but will likely find more reliable water levels—and more bugs—than summer paddlers. September and October often provide good paddling weather; better water levels than those found in July and August and fewer bugs. Due to natural and man-made fluctuations in water levels, some sections of the Trail may be too dry to paddle, especially in late summer. See page 10 *"Adapting,"* that details specific water bodies.

Paddlers also will want to be aware of dam releases. Dam releases could flood a shoreline stealth campsite or add unexpected volume and speed to a river. Information from water gauges found across the NFCT can be found on at *AmericanWhitewater.org*. Additional resources can be found on page 238.

So…the best answer to the question of when is the best time to paddle the Trail might very well just be…*whenever your schedule allows.*

Through-Paddling:
Unique Perspectives and Concerns

SKILL SETS

Through-Paddling the Trail is achievable by paddlers of all skill levels. The Trail has been completed by those who were completely new to canoeing and barely knew how to wield a paddle to enthusiasts who built their own canoe as part of their expedition.

Yet Through-Paddling isn't for the faint of heart. It would be foolish to suggest the Trail isn't difficult or at times maddening. Trail markers may not be found where expected. Some days will be monotonous. It might be all you can do to concentrate on propelling yourself forward to the next campsite where you can collapse into an exhausted sleep amid the drone of mosquitoes. But even on the coldest, rainiest and longest days, there are rewards: unexpected kindnesses from strangers, brilliant sunbeams streaming through low-lying clouds, the echoing call of loons, bug-free evenings.

Divorced from the constraints, distractions and demands of "normal" life, the pace becomes determined only by your agenda and physical endurance. Instead of deadlines, weather becomes your most basic concern and subsisting within the confines of 16 feet or so of space will make the world feel both smaller and bigger. You'll see how little "stuff" is really necessary to live well, yet travel far while living a nomadic life.

After paddling hard for hours or even days, you may find yourself appreciating situations and circumstances much more keenly. Something as simple as having a grilled cheese sandwich prepared with slices cut from a wedge of cheddar from a general store's lunch counter can be one of the most exquisite dining experiences you'll ever appreciate. And showers can take on a whole new meaning.

Some sections of the Trail are decidedly dangerous for novice paddlers. And, at times even the most experienced adventurer may misjudge distances and locations in the midst of unfamiliar surroundings. Even with maps and

guidebooks to assist paddlers (including this one), you could find yourself second-guessing your decisions: Am I where I should be? Did I miss the blue and yellow NFCT confidence marker? Should I paddle this section of river or portage around it? Is the carry take-out really this close to the head of the dam?

You'll probably want to take a few test trips with your gear and especially work out any portaging kinks if this isn't something you've done much of previously. Consider adding more walking or hiking, in addition to paddling, as part of your pre-trip training.

The following pages provide an overview of navigating the Trail following its various waterways. It also details some of the more challenging segments.

Your chances of successfully completing the Trail can be due in large part to two things: *adequate planning* and *common sense*.

Adequate planning means you will at least have rough ideas of your options prior to starting out from Old Forge. You will be consulting with local outfitters or area residents about conditions and seeking out current trail advice while on it. You might even have a Plan A and Plan B in mind and will be prepared to adjust your goals if they prove to be too aggressive. The time of year and the conditions under which you travel will almost certainly dictate modifications to even the best laid plans.

Common sense means you'll be paying attention to your circumstances and listening to your gut. You won't paddle on rivers or bodies of water or under conditions that exceed your abilities or the abilities of your travel partner(s).

TRAVEL PARTNERS

If you're reading this book, you likely already know how you intend to experience the Trail—alone in solitude or shared with one or more people.

The majority of NFCT paddlers have completed the route either solo or as part of a tandem pair. There have been only a handful of larger groups paddling the Trail, including three people in 2012, who to date, have been the speediest group to finish it while paddling together in one large canoe.

Regardless, it is important to know your capabilities and take care not to push yourself or your paddling partner(s) beyond them. Tearing a whole in the hull of your boat can prematurely end your trip. Twisted ankles, gear failure or your level of misery may influence how your trip is remembered or whether you are even able to finish it.

Like any outdoor activity, there are inherent risks to the sport and like any major trip, mapping out a plan is an integral component to your overall enjoyment and ultimate success. Know your limits and the limits of your paddling partner(s).

ROUTE PLANNING

While seemingly obvious, it is essential that you obtain the 13 official NFCT maps. Hours should be spent pouring over the maps comparing thin blue lines and the typographic symbols for rapids against Google satellite imagery. Scour blogs of other Through-Paddlers for bits of information and insight.

This process helps you think through the Trail and identify areas where you might expect difficulties. Consider drafting your own proposed itinerary with daily mileage goals and notes about expected water hazards and portages. Plan options about where you might stay each night and when you can utilize trail towns to take advantage of resupplying or resting.

Services located along the Trail are typically signed to be seen by passing motorists from a road. Attempting to locate restaurants and lodging becomes bewildering when seeking them out from the seat of a boat low on the water. It is better to have an idea of where to look for a service prior to needing it. The NFCT kiosks often include information about local businesses and services that are within walking distance once on land.

While the Trail has been successfully navigated without the use of a GPS device, taking one along—and knowing how to use it—will help instill confidence, especially when you are traveling through remote sections. Some cameras offer GPS and you can conserve weight by carrying one that doubles as a navigational device. Many paddlers have carried the SPOT® GPS Satellite Messenger, that in addition to being a GPS device, includes an emergency alert function and off-the-grid messaging. It provides both reassurances to loved ones left at home as well as a source of entertainment for people who are following your trip vicariously online.

NFCT Trail Markers and Registers

The NFCT adheres to a policy of using the least amount of blazes possible for ease of navigation. Nonetheless, the entire route is marked with more than 600 small, metallic blue and yellow, 4"-diamond shaped "confidence" medallions. Unless removed, they are found at designated put-ins and take-outs. Directional arrow markers (of the same size and color as the confidence markers) are also present on some of the carries that follow roadways.

Official NFCT Marker

In addition, a few of the more remote and potentially confusing portage sections of the Trail are marked with 2" x 6" parallel vertical blue and yellow stripes. The painted blazes are intended to stand out enough to reinforce the route without being an eyesore. These supplementary symbols currently appear on tree trunks along:

Directional Arrow Marker

Map 6:	Yale Dale Portage
Map 7:	Androscoggin River Carry
	(after the junction of 110A and 16)
Map 9:	Gull Pond Stream Portage
Map 10:	Spencer Road/Spencer Rips Carry
	(between Fish Pond take-out and Moose River put-in)
Map 10:	Demo Road Portage

Painted Blaze

The NFCT has installed dozens of sign-in boxes with registers. The distinctive canoe bow shaped boxes are scattered throughout the entire route of the Trail beginning in Old Forge, New York. Additional non-NFCT trail registers can also be found throughout the Saranacs and at the Allagash checkpoints. Use them! Registers help organizations keep track of trail usage and issues and can help locate a paddler in the event of an emergency.

About NFCT Portages (or Carries)

The Trail includes 77 established portages totaling about 78 miles. While many are mandatory, others are suggestions. Some, like Lock Dam and the Tramway Carry—both on Chamberlain Lake, offer options. Most portages are short providing safe routes around hazards like dams and rapids. Longer carries connect watersheds and often follow roads. The longest formal portage of the Trail is the 5.7-mile Grand Portage in Québec.

There are, however, additional miles that may be necessary to traverse by land due to exceedingly low water levels or technical whitewater. Notable segments include up to 13.7 miles bypassing the Upper Ammonoosuc River in New Hampshire and up to 20 miles bypassing the South Branch Dead River in Maine.

Throughout the Adirondacks and parts of New England, the term "carry" is always used to describe a portage. Conversely, "portage" (the French pronunciation is PORT-aahj; rhymes with garage) is always used in Québec. Both words describe the same action and in this guide have been used interchangeably.

While some paddlers choose to carry all their gear under their own power or in the historical style of the Voyageurs, many paddlers will use wheels to aid in portaging. It is important to understand that many of the carries are considered not wheelable and gear must, at times, be carried. More information about portage carts or wheels can be found on page 33.

Decision Making
The first 85 miles encompass a good introduction to the Trail within Maps 1 and 2. You'll get to experience small and large lakes, rivers and a decent range of *"wheelable"* and *"not wheelable"* portage trails. You'll develop a feel for locating the blue and yellow metal NFCT confidence markers, your "bread crumbs" leading you all the way to Fort Kent.

Paddling through the picturesque Adirondacks should be pleasant, presenting you with few navigational challenges. In addition, you are never too far from civilization as you work out any kinks or if you would find yourself in trouble.

If all goes well or at least as planned, you are ready to tackle Map 3. Map 3 presents the first real decision-making tests. How technical is this section of the Saranac River today? How high and how fast is the river flowing? Is it too low to feasibly paddle? Can you and your vessel safely run Class III rapids? Can you eddy out quickly between rapids and ledges before a Class IV drop? Can you locate less than obvious take-outs? Will you consider portaging five to eight miles following a rural road in order to avoid whitewater that exceeds your skill set? How tired are you feeling right now? What does the weather portend? Where might the next campsite be found? How far had you planned to travel today?

These are exactly the kinds of daily questions you will continue to weigh throughout your journey.

Adapting

Unlike the linear nature of the Appalachian Trail, the NFCT's eastern land-based cousin, there can be more than one way to traverse a water trail. Wind and weather may require you to tack or ferry across large open bodies of water adding overall distance to your cumulative mileage. You can also choose which shoreline you want to follow getting from Point A to Point B. Lake Champlain, for example, has two different route options following either side of North Hero Island that will lead you from Plattsburgh to the Missisquoi River outlet.

Several river portages offer two take-out options. Early season paddlers or those who find themselves experiencing heavy periods of precipitation will want to use a high water portage option. More experienced or late season paddlers can utilize a low water portage option that may place them closer to a hazard. Always scout first if in doubt.

Seasonal river levels and/or technical whitewater may mean portions of the Trail must be missed or portaged instead of paddled.

For paddlers of all skill levels, two of the most challenging features of the NFCT are the significant portions of continuous upstream paddling and the exposed expanses of sizeable lakes.

The following lists identify potential water condition issues and/or hazards encountered along the route that may affect your ability to paddle every single mile of the Trail. Be prepared to adapt.

Seasonally Affected River Water Levels

Historically, the river sections noted below become rocky or scratchy paddling obstacles—or even dry—in mid to late summer. Local roadways often turn into alternative portage routes for paddlers faced with unnavigable low water levels.

Map 3:	Saranac River between Clayburg, N.Y., and Plattsburgh, N.Y.
Map 5:	The Missisquoi between Richford, Vt., and the Canadian border
Map 6:	The Nulhegan between Wenlock Crossing and Bloomfield, Vt.
Map 7:	The Upper Ammonoosuc River between Groveton, N.H., and Stark, N.H. (or beyond to West Milan, N.H.)
Map 9:	South Branch Dead River
Map 10:	Spencer Stream and Little Spencer Stream
Map 12:	Umbazooksus Stream between Lake Chesuncook and Umbazooksus Lake

Shuttle options are available within some sections, but absent in others. Refer to individual mileage segments for more details and recommendations if faced with water shortages.

Challenging Downstream Class III+ Whitewater Sections

These are the most technically difficult rivers found along the Trail and recommended only for those who possess appropriate paddling skills. Whitewater encountered as an upstream paddler and any mandatory portages around unrunnable whitewater and waterfalls, such as Grand Falls and Allagash Falls, are not included as part of this list. See Appendix 6 on page 239 for the International Scale of River Difficulty definitions.

Map 3:   **Saranac River between Union Falls and Clayburg, N.Y.**
(Class III–IV ledges* and falls)

Map 6:   **Nulhegan River between Wenlock Crossing and Bloomfield, Vt.**
(Class III–IV)

Map 9:   **South Branch Dead River between Lower Dallas Bridge and Stratton, Maine** (Class III–IV)

Map 10: **Moose River between Demo Road and Little Brassua Lake**
(Class III–IV)

* *The ledges after Tefft Falls Pond on the Saranac River have claimed canoes and prematurely altered or ended trips.*

Upstream Sections

As a Through-Paddler, traversing the Trail in its entirety from west to east, you'll be facing five noteworthy sections of upstream paddling. Your first serious trial occurs after crossing Lake Champlain, one of the largest freshwater lakes in the United States, upon entering the Missisquoi River outlet. The Missisquoi River is generally placid, unless you hit spring melt-off and/or periods of heavy rain that will produce stronger currents. Otherwise, expect to encounter intermittent sets of Class I–II rapids while mentally preparing for 74 miles of paddling against a current over the next few days. After the Missisquoi, the next sets of upstream river segments present their own challenges, but are shorter in duration. Adding to the fun, the Upper Ammonoosuc River, Little Spencer Stream and Umbazooksus Stream also are susceptible to seasonal low water levels.

Maps 4/5: **The Missisquoi River in Vermont** (74 miles)

Map 6:   **The Clyde River in Vermont** (30.5 miles including Class II–III rapids around Derby Center)

Map 7:   **The Upper Ammonoosuc in New Hampshire** (19 miles)

Map 7:   **The Androscoggin along the New Hampshire and Maine state borders** (12 class I–II sets of rapids over a 19-mile length)

Map 10: **Spencer Stream and Little Spencer Stream in Maine**
(Boulder fields for six miles)

Stony Creek (Map 2) and Umbazooksus Stream (Map 12) are both short upstream segments and not considered to have taxing currents.

Poling

Poling allows the canoeist to travel upstream and up rapids, a difficult or impossible feat to accomplish using a conventional canoe paddle. A pole can be particularly effective in many of the NFCT sections including ascending the Clyde and Androscoggin Rivers and Little Spencer Stream. Experienced or curious paddlers may wish to make their own pole when needed. However, it may be impractical to pack this 12' or longer piece of additional equipment for the few times it would be useful.

Big Water Crossings

Winds present an additional danger to paddlers, in particular on the larger bodies of water that require passage across open, unprotected expanses. A good rule to follow is to make these water crossings during early morning hours or twilight evenings when winds usually are at their calmest. Paddlers can and should utilize wind shadows created by shorelines and islands. Two lakes along the route offer short ferry crossings if conditions are too rough for open boat paddling.

Map 4:	**Lake Champlain**
	(Vehicle ferry option from Cumberland Point to Gordon's Landing on North Hero Island)
Map 5:	**Lake Memphremagog**
Map 8:	**Lake Umbagog**
Map 8:	**Upper Richardson**
Map 8:	**Mooselookmeguntic Lake**
Map 10:	**Brassua Lake**
Map 11:	**Moosehead Lake**
	(Passenger ferry option from Rockwood, Maine to Mount Kineo)
Map 11	**Chesuncook Lake**
Map 12:	**Chamberlain Lake**

Let your instincts and the rhythm of the paddle guide you and with a little luck, may the wind (mostly) be at your back.

Clean Drain Dry Stations

Aquatic invasives are present in water bodies across the Northern Forest Canoe Trail. Through-Paddlers need to be especially vigilant in helping to prevent the spread of aquatic plant and aquatic animal species as they transition between fresh water habitats. A good practice is to treat *all* waters as though they are infected and follow recommended guidelines.

Clean Drain Dry Stations are located at Louie's Landing on the Missisquoi River and Normandeau Campsite on the Upper Ammonoosuc River and signs are posted across the Trail. Read more about best practices on the NFCT website. Do your part to keep non-native plants and animals from threatening the integrity and quality of these waters.

Practicalities

While life spent on the Trail will be broken down into the most elementary needs—food, water and shelter—there are a few things, like boats, gear lists and how to get home at the end of the journey, that you'll want to think about prior to heading out on the Trail. Once paddling, your biggest daily decision will hang on how far to travel. You'll pay attention to weather, wind and where to spend the night. You'll appreciate knowing what types of services are available as you pass through trail towns and other issues you may face as a Through-Paddler.

The following topics are listed alphabetically and detail needs and common concerns unique to traveling the Trail.

BOATS

You may be limited to using a boat you already own, or you may be looking to build or purchase a new one specifically for this trip. No one craft is perfectly suited for paddling the full range of water conditions that the 740-mile trail traverses. The choice will depend upon personal preference, weight and/or cost. Cedar, canvas and wood, ABS plastic/Royalex®, polyethylene and Kevlar® boats have all been successfully used by NFCT Through-Paddlers. Several paddlers even built the canoe that they used on their trip.

Section-Paddlers have the ability to switch between boats based upon water bodies and conditions.

The capacity to make any repairs on the trail may be another factor in determining what type of boat is best suited for you. It is important to note that even the toughest vessels can take on water, become submerged and pinned to, or wrapped around, boulders. The ledges on the lower Saranac River—between Tefft Falls Pond and Clayburg—are known to have destroyed canoes and altered the plans of through-paddling trips over the years.

Canoes generally have the advantage over kayaks in weight and ease of portaging. Canoes are able to accommodate larger portage packs with useful harness systems. The higher seating position of a canoe provides a better view of the trail ahead and is more convenient to exit when crossing the numerous Trail beaver dams. Canoeists are also able to shift paddling positions throughout the day or as conditions change—switching from sitting to kneeling to even standing while poling.

Shorter kayaks have an advantage of being more maneuverable in whitewater and able to negotiate serpentine rivers. While great on the larger areas of open water, fiberglass sea kayaks (and fiberglass canoes for that matter) are the least desirable through-paddling vessels because of their fragile hulls that will get banged up—and possibly irreversibly damaged—on boulder-strewn rivers.

Kayak cargo areas are best suited to stashing several small dry bags rather than single large ones. Smaller dry bags do not have shoulder straps and suspension systems which means they aren't as easy or convenient to carry on the longer portages.

Both canoes and kayaks should be outfitted with bow and stern ropes (painters) to use when lining or tracking. Installing a kneeling pad in a canoe could be helpful.

Skid Plates

A skid plate is an abrasion-resistant material, such as Kevlar felt, affixed with resin to the bow and/or stern of a canoe. The theory behind preemptively installing skid plates to an undamaged hull is that they will help protect your bow and stern in extreme situations where heavy, sharp impacts or excessive scratching may occur.

Some people feel the need for skid plates is greatly overstated for even moderately careful paddlers. In the first place, you shouldn't be ramming your canoe into the shore or grinding out from it. In the second place, unless your bow is completely threadbare with an exposed core, your hull isn't (yet) in need of repair. The other school of thought is that it is acceptable to add skid plates once serious damage is evident.

Because you may be negotiating a lake canoe, possibly constructed of Kevlar, through rivers full of boulders, even the most conscious and careful paddler will sporadically bang into a submerged rock. Taking an occasional bite out of the bow should not significantly compromise the paddling integrity of your vessel.

The concluding opinion is that skids plates are really more of a repair than a preventative accessory. Wait and see if you need them, if you ever do. However, if it makes you feel better to have that extra layer of protection keeping you from being caught between that rock and a hard place, by all means install them.

COMMUNICATION

Some paddlers (or at least their loved ones) will want to be able to stay in touch. Since the Trail passes through many villages and communities, it isn't hard to phone home from time to time. Mobile devices will work in many, but not all areas. Public phone booths can be found along the Trail including an isolated one on the Forked Lake Carry in the Adirondacks that seems to be in the middle of nowhere. Many towns and businesses offer WiFi hotspots and public libraries provide free computer use and Internet access. If nothing else, a global satellite service such as SPOT®, will allow you to send out "I'm okay" or SOS messages.

Cellular Coverage

Depending upon your provider, cellular phone service is reliable along some parts of the Trail but may be completely absent in others. Poor or zero coverage areas include sections of the Adirondacks, Vermont and most, if not all, of Maine.

When traveling in Canada (and even when traveling near the Canadian border), be aware of international rates that may apply.

Blogging

The proliferation of easy-to-use software makes it convenient to create and maintain a blog even while on the Trail. You can use your phone for real-time posts and tweets or utilize library computers in trail towns for updates. Making your blog public provides extra insight for future paddlers, adding to the volume of trail advice and creating greater overall awareness of the Trail.

Internet Service/Libraries

You will be able to research, reserve, email and update blogs using public library computers with free Internet access all along the Trail from Old Forge, New York to Jackman, Maine. Cellular service is sketchy to non-existent after leaving Jackman until you reach Fort Kent, nearly 200 miles away. If you intend to visit a library, confirm the hours of operation, which vary from town to town. Most are open only certain days of the week or for limited hours. When closed, you still may be able to pick up the free network on your own device by sitting outside the building.

Many motels and restaurants located along the Trail also offer free WiFi.

Assuming you've been taking a lot of photos, consider periodically uploading your photos to an online photo sharing or archiving site. This is always a good idea in case your media card starts filling up in a remote area or if your device would get wet, lost or stolen.

Trail Towns with Libraries and/or Internet Access

Old Forge, N.Y.

Raquette Lake, N.Y.

Long Lake, N.Y.

Saranac Lake, N.Y.

Plattsburgh, N.Y.*

North Hero, N.Y.

Swanton, Vt.

Highgate Center, Vt.*

Enosburg Falls, Vt.

Richford, Vt.

Mansonville, Qué.

Newport, Vt.

Derby, Vt.*

Island Pond, Vt.

Stratford, N.H.*

Groveton, N.H.

Errol, N.H.

Rangeley, Maine

Stratton, Maine

Jackman, Maine

Fort Kent, Maine

*Library is off trail

Satellite Messengers/Personal Locator Beacons

For added piece of mind, some paddlers have included a satellite-based messaging device, like SPOT or Delorme® InReach handheld communicators, with their gear. Using global positioning technology, the device provides a variety of alerts such as live location updates to Google Maps™ that track your progress, notifying family and friends back home of your whereabouts and status and/or alerting rescue officials in the event of an emergency. The device floats and is water resistant. The advantage is that these satellite-based messaging devices will work outside of cellular ranges throughout the Trail. However, they also require a satellite service subscription.

A "last resort" emergency option is a personal locator beacon (PLB) such as the ACR ResQLink® or McMurdo FastFind. PBLs are designed for one purpose only—activating an alert when your life is in peril. This device should be used only in situations of grave and imminent danger, and when all means of self-rescue have been exhausted. It is not intended for use as a recreational tracking device. These devices do not require an additional service subscription.

Keeping Your Devices Charged

Use the opportunity to plug-in and recharge your devices and batteries as you pass through towns, stopping at restaurants or staying at a motel or inn. Even though your mobile device most likely won't receive coverage along many sections of the Trail— especially Maine—you'll still want to make sure everything is powered up for taking photos and traveling the final stretch of the Allagash before your arrival in Fort Kent.

Some paddlers have added solar chargers to their gear list. Solar chargers are helpful, but may not be necessary, especially if you intend to frequent trail towns and businesses.

DRINKING WATER

Most sections of the Trail pass through areas of exceptional water quality. Even so, water drawn from these lakes and rivers should always be filtered, boiled or treated. At times you will pass through public areas or through towns where you are able to refill your water bottles with tap water. In a pinch, don't be afraid to knock on the doors of riverside farms or homes to ask for water.

There are four notable exceptions where planning for your water consumption is imperative. The first is the lower Saranac River where a combination of agricultural runoff and light industry flow into the river between Clayburg and Plattsburgh, N.Y.

The second is the Missisquoi River in Vermont. Due to the number of dairy farm operations located upstream along its banks, it is not recommended that any water be taken or treated from this river. Areas of strong current between East Highgate and the North Sheldon bridge will slow most paddlers and the need for tracking upstream on a hot summer day quickly becomes very thirsty work. Even though towns are not very distant from each other, it may take more than a day to cover eight miles. Traveling up Abbey Rapids between Sheldon Springs and Enosburg Falls is particularly time-consuming.

The risk of microbial infection increases in waters with high concentrations of agricultural runoff. Exposure to microorganisms occurs primarily through ingestion of water, but can also occur when water enters through the ears, eyes, nose and broken skin. Be sure to protect and treat any cuts, scrapes or leech bites as you track up the Missisquoi River. Gastrointestinal disorders, respiratory illness and minor skin, eye, ear, nose and throat infections have been associated with bacterial pollution. The Connecticut River is the third water body where farm fields adversely affect water quality.

A fourth area of concern is the Clyde River. Between Newport Vt. and Derby Center, Vt., tires and garbage can befoul this stretch. Farm fields and cow pastures line some of its banks below Ten Mile Square Road.

Paddlers should plan on carrying a minimum of two quart-water bottles per paddler and a water purification system.

Giardiasis (or Beaver Fever)
Giardiasis is a parasitic disease caused by drinking contaminated and untreated water. It triggers nasty digestive problems. Beavers, dogs, cats, horses, humans, cattle and birds are known carriers of the parasite and spread the disease through fecal matter left in soil and water. Symptoms typically don't begin to appear until one to two weeks after infection and include loss of appetite, diarrhea, upset stomach, stomach cramps and excessive gas. Untreated, the disease may last for six weeks or longer.

EARWORMS (OR HEAD TUNES OR MIXTAPE RADIO STATIONS)

This topic technically doesn't fall under the heading of "Practicalities" as much as the fact that practically all long-distance paddlers will fall victim to them. Earworms are catchy—or some might say annoying—songs, melodies or jingles that get stuck in your head and won't get out. Many times it's just one line repeated over and over again or fragmented bits from songs you love and commercials you hate. Your brain becomes abuzz with a forever play list of its own making. You can't control the selections and you can't pull the plug. It's often best to allow your personal radio station to play on and then turn it into your post-trip sound track.

FIRES

Fire restrictions apply—or permits are required—in some areas along the NFCT. Refer to each of the individual NFCT maps for local regulations if you intend to build camp or cooking fires. Cooking stoves, including denatured alcohol and "twig" stoves, are allowed and may be used anywhere along the Trail as long as no outright fire bans or closures are in effect.

FISHING

Most sections of the NFCT offer excellent fishing opportunities. However, fishing is rarely reported in the blogs of most Through-Paddlers, especially those who are interested in accumulating daily mileage. Only paddlers who reside in one of the Trail's four states—and already possess a license—have been known to fish, and that becomes limited to the state in which they reside. To date, there have been no reported accounts of any Through-Paddler living off the bounty of the water as he or she journeyed across the distance of the Trail.

If you plan to fish, you will be required to purchase a license for each state or province where you drop a line. Fishing license options and fees vary from state to state and between countries. As a nonresident, it is estimated that purchasing a seven-day license per state or province (and a 15-day license for Maine) would cost well over $150. To learn more about regulations and current fees, visit the individual websites of each state or province's natural resource departments or fish and wildlife agencies.

FOOD

With trip durations ranging from under 30 days to more than 50 days, quantity of food and resupplying requirements will vary. Though-Paddlers pack a few days to a week's worth or more of food at a time. Knowing that everything needs to be carried frequently makes traveling light a motivating factor. Hauling a cooler is impractical.

You'll be burning a lot of calories over the course of your trip and its not uncommon to crave fats and proteins after many weeks of paddling. Be sure to consume calorie-rich items to keep your body fueled.

Unlike other managed wilderness destinations, there are no can or bottle bans on any parts of the NFCT, including the Allagash Wilderness Waterway. However, all state areas require that you pack out what you pack in. As a conscientious traveler, you will be practicing "leave no trace" camping ethics and traveling with any garbage you generate. This includes packing out cigarette butts and fruit peels that do not disintegrate.

Always plan on carrying food even though you pass through many villages along the Trail. As early as Map 2, you will find yourself in an area without any services between Long Lake and Saranac Lake, a distance of 42 miles. Your food bag should also include an extra day—or more—of food in the event you become unexpectedly wind bound and unable to make your intended destination. Early season paddlers should confirm store hours. Several general or grocery stores are seasonal and don't open until mid- to late-May.

Typical paddling foods fall into three main categories: Pre-packaged/freeze-dried "backpacking" food, off-the-shelf grocery or convenience food items and make-your-own recipes and portions. As you pass through towns and villages, a fourth option is also available—restaurants and diners—but at no time can you completely rely on restaurants for noshing your way across the entire distance of the Trail.

None of these options alone are the perfect strategy for outfitting the food needs that an expedition requires, but with a little forethought and planning, you should be able to pack ahead and/or purchase food along the Trail that keeps your food bag at a reasonable weight.

Packaged/Freeze-dried Ultralight Backpacking Food

It's very easy to be seduced by rows of shiny freeze-dried gourmet food that requires a minimum amount of preparation. You may want to treat yourself to a few of the more interesting options. But unless money is not an obstacle, you most likely won't fill your food bag solely on freeze-dried omelet, lasagna, beef stroganoff, chicken cashew curry and dessert offerings. Some local outfitters offer these products, but you cannot plan on buying these types of meals throughout the length of the Trail.

Pros and Cons:

- Minimal weight
- Quick and easy to prepare
- Uses less water
- Generally nutritious
- Unusual recipes not typically able to be made on trail
- Most expensive

Off-the-shelf Grocery or Convenience Foods

Many common grocery store items work well in the pack and on the Trail. Purchasing items as you travel through Trail communities support local economies. Instant oatmeal, cereal bars and dried fruit are easy breakfast items. Pepperoni, individually wrapped string cheese and waxed Gouda or Edam cheeses will keep for days without refrigeration, while foil packaged tunas, instant rice pilafs and soups travel well for dinners. Avoid cans and bottles that add weight, take up space and most important, produces burdensome trash that you may find yourself having to carry for days.

Other examples of shelf-stable grocery food items include packaged instant soups and sauces, instant potatoes, pasta side dishes, ethnic (Indian, Asian, Mexican) packaged dinners, hotdogs, flour tortillas, powdered eggs or milk, cheeses, peanut butter, tuna, canned meats, jerky, granola and breakfast bars. These items are readily available throughout the Trail. You can also obtain fresh fruit and vegetables.

Pros and Cons:

- Quick and easy to prepare
- Purchasing food along the Trail contributes to the local economy
- Can be heavier (especially cans or shelf-stable pouches)
- With the exception of fresh fruits and vegetables, many items are less nutritious and full of processed ingredients
- Often bulkier waste/garbage
- Expense varies

Pre-trip Packed Recipes

For some, dehydrating fruits and vegetables and preparing your own recipes are part of the adventure. Homemade beef jerky is less expensive to make than purchased. Canned pineapple chunks, sliced fresh mushrooms, fresh spinach and frozen corn all dehydrate easily. Even spaghetti sauce can be dehydrated into "leather" and reconstituted in camp. Simple soup, rice or pasta dishes and other trail recipes can be found in books or online. You'll need to carry all of your creations and/or utilize one or more mail drops for resupplying.

Pros and Cons:
- Generally most nutritious
- Least expensive
- Typically produce less garbage to pack out
- Recipes may require more water
- Variable weight (flours and grains add weight)
- Some recipes may require longer cooking time (and more fuel)
- More food prep and packing time required prior to trip

Mail Drop Boxes and Restaurants

While you can mail "drop boxes" of food to pick up at U.S. post offices along the way, there are plenty of grocery, general or convenience stores and even some natural food co-ops interspersed along the Trail for resupplying, especially within the first 350 miles. Services become less frequent in Maine and disappear altogether while in the Allagash. A listing of trail town food stores is included as part of the *Towns and Services* section beginning on page 207.

On the other hand, eating out as you travel might be just the carrot you need to reach a certain mileage goal. Some towns offer dining options or pubs that will turn into the destination. Two Rivers Lunch is one such sought-after diner. It is located in Allagash Village after emerging from the Allagash, but make sure to get there for breakfast or lunch. It closes by mid afternoon.

If you utilize mail drops as a means of resupplying, address the package to the post office with the following information:
- Your name
- General Delivery*
- Town, State, ZIP Code

> Be sure to include **"HOLD FOR NFCT PADDLER"** with an expected date of pickup and your return address.

With advance arrangements, you can also ship mail drops to motels or inns using the establishment's address.

* **"General delivery"** *should never be used on packages addressed to any location other than U.S. post offices.*

Shipping Stove Fuel in Mail Drop Boxes

The U.S. Postal Service only allows small canisters of pressurized isobutane/propane stove fuel to be shipped using domestic GROUND mail. The contents must be securely packaged and labeled "Surface Mail Only" and "Consumer Commodity ORM-D." Allow additional time (up to two weeks) for delivery when shipping fuel—even when using Priority Mail. For more information, consult usps.com and search Content Restrictions, Stove Fuel.

GEAR LISTS

With more space available in a canoe, it's easier to bring along extra items that wouldn't fit into a kayak or ever be considered on long-distance hiking trips—but everything still has to be portaged. How much gear you feel like carrying and how much you want to balance comfort with discomfort is a personal choice, although packing a hard-shell cooler is not recommended. The following list represents cumulative data from a variety of gear lists and is intended as a reference. You may pack quite a bit less—or perhaps more.

Paddling Gear
- ☐ Personal flotation device (PFD)
- ☐ Whistle
- ☐ Paddles (including spare)
- ☐ Bow and stern rope (painters)
- ☐ Knee pads or kneeling foam
- ☐ Canoe chairs or seat cushions
- ☐ Portage yoke
- ☐ Pole
- ☐ Bailing bucket or bilge pump
- ☐ Sponge
- ☐ Portage cart (wheels)
- ☐ Straps or tie-downs
- ☐ Spare cart parts (nuts, pins)
- ☐ CO_2 for tire inflation
- ☐ Vessel repair kit (resins, duct tape)
- ☐ Dry suit
- ☐ Spray deck or kayak skirt
- ☐ Paddling helmet
- ☐ Paddling gloves

Navigation
- ☐ Maps
- ☐ Map case
- ☐ Guidebooks
- ☐ Compass
- ☐ GPS
- ☐ Satellite messenger

Camping Equipment
- ☐ Tent with ground cloth or hammock
- ☐ Sleeping bag with waterproof compression or stuff sack
- ☐ Sleeping pad
- ☐ Pillow
- ☐ Tarp
- ☐ Stove
- ☐ Stove fuel
- ☐ Matches
- ☐ Fire starter
- ☐ Knife/Leatherman®
- ☐ Hatchet
- ☐ Collapsible saw
- ☐ Cook set (cook pots, pan, bowls, cups, etc.)
- ☐ Utensil bag (spoons, knives, spatula, knife sharpener, can opener, biodegradable dish detergent, dish cloth, spice jars [salt/pepper, mixed dried herbs, sugar], etc.)
- ☐ Acrylic or polyethylene cutting board

Water
- ☐ Water purification system and/or tablets
- ☐ Water bottles
- ☐ Collapsible jug

Food Storage
- ☐ Dry bag, barrel or canister
- ☐ Rope (with pulley) for hanging at night
- ☐ Food waste bag

Toiletries
- ☐ Sunscreen
- ☐ Mosquito repellent
- ☐ Toothpaste
- ☐ Dr. Bronner's or other soap/shampoo
- ☐ Dental floss
- ☐ Hand sanitizer
- ☐ Aspirin or ibuprofen
- ☐ Hydrocortisone
- ☐ Medications
- ☐ Wet wipes
- ☐ Trowel
- ☐ Toilet paper

Personal
- ☐ Passport
- ☐ Rain gear or splash jacket/pants
- ☐ Sun hat
- ☐ Sunglasses
- ☐ Headnet and/or full body netting bug suit
- ☐ Gloves
- ☐ Watershoes or boots
- ☐ Camp shoes or sandals
- ☐ Clothing
- ☐ Compression sack or stuff bag for clothing
- ☐ Towel
- ☐ Journals
- ☐ Pens/pencils
- ☐ List of important phone numbers and addresses
- ☐ Book
- ☐ Deck of cards/game

First Aid/Emergency
- ☐ First aid kit
- ☐ Survival blanket
- ☐ Sewing or repair kit(s)
- ☐ Flares
- ☐ Personal location beacon
- ☐ Throw bag (rope)

Gadgets
- ☐ Headlamp
- ☐ Flash light
- ☐ Lantern
- ☐ Binoculars
- ☐ Camera
- ☐ Cellphone
- ☐ Tablet or laptop
- ☐ Chargers (electric and/or solar)
- ☐ Watch
- ☐ Alarm clock
- ☐ Waterproof cases or boxes

Miscellaneous
- ☐ Cable lock
- ☐ Duct tape
- ☐ Bandanas or rags
- ☐ Gear ties (bungee cords, Dealee Bobs®, Velcro® straps, carabineers)
- ☐ Extra batteries
- ☐ Candles
- ☐ Ziploc® bags
- ☐ Fishing gear
- ☐ Camp chair
- ☐ Bug (screen) shelter

Dry Bags, Duluth Packs, Barrels, Wannigans, Backpacks and Pack Baskets

As an expedition paddler, you will need to keep your gear organized and waterproof, and carried efficiently. Most paddlers choose waterproof dry bags or plastic barrels, but canvas Duluth packs, pack baskets and Wannigans are other options.

Dry bags are made of high-quality waterproof fabrics such as vinyl and come in various sizes. They include watertight roll-top closures. Packs feature heavy-duty reinforced vinyl bottoms and a shoulder strap. Larger sizes should include a waist belt. While insuring your gear remains dry from external sources of water, they also trap moisture when gear becomes wet and over time, they can start smelling offensive.

Duluth packs are made of canvas or waxed canvas and also are available in a variety of sizes. They are trimmed with leather harnesses and larger styles include the use of a tumpline. Unlike vinyl dry bags, they breathe so moisture will not get trapped inside. They have been prized for their longevity and versatility. A canvas pack is easier to repair than waterproof fabrics. Rivets can be replaced and leather and canvas can be sewn or patched.

Barrels are constructed of rigid polyethylene. A galvanized clamping band that ensures an airtight, watertight and odor-proof seal secures the lid. Not only are they waterproof, they protect your gear better from impacts than a soft dry bag. In addition, they float in the event of a capsize. Make sure to accessorize it with the optional harness system for portaging.

A *wannigan* is a traditional "grub box" and method of carrying gear in a wooden container using a tumpline or pack board. It was used by the voyageurs and has been used on the Trail. Paddlers claim it's easy to pack, keeps everything organized, can be made to fit your canoe perfectly and provides an instant seat or table. Anyone with basic wood working tools can construct one. Modern versions for sale are made of plastic or aluminum.

Internal frame *backpacks* and rucksacks can also be used to transport gear, but the key here is keeping everything inside dry. They are easy to stow, lighter than dry bags or Duluth packs and may be ergonomically more comfortable to carry.

Traditionally used in Maine and the Adirondacks, *pack baskets* are made of woven natural materials like ash or reeds and fit upright in the canoe. These open baskets are outfitted with handles and pack straps. Wood or other solid materials provide a sturdy interior base and runners along the bottom exterior protect the pack from water accumulating in the bottom of the canoe. They can be good for carrying bulky gear but are not watertight. Some paddlers line them with dry bags.

Tumplines, pack boards, shoulder harnesses and hip belts are an important consideration, maybe even crucial, for transporting your gear on the longer portages.

Kayakers will likely need to carry several small dry bags. While these individual packs aren't too heavy, their use likely guarantees the need to double portage. Canoes are able to accommodate larger gear packs typically equipped with harnesses. Large packs may mean heavier loads, but potentially less time spent portaging.

GETTING HOME

One of the biggest dilemmas is how to get yourself and your gear home from Fort Kent, Maine after paddling more than 700 miles away from Old Forge, New York. Most paddlers work with family or friends for the western terminus drop-off and eastern terminus pick-up. There is no single public or private transportation service that will get you back to Old Forge and no car rental, bus or airport services once you arrive in Fort Kent. The nearest daily bus service is located 44 miles away in Caribou, Maine and the nearest commercial airport is almost 200 miles away in Bangor, Maine. Private aviators may operate out of closer municipal general aviation airports and taxis are possible, but both become extremely expensive choices complicated by the presence of a boat. Currently, your only self-service option out of Fort Kent is renting a U-Haul truck.

GPS DEVICES

While smartphones might be used for navigation, a handheld GPS device may be preferred as it is not limited to your cellphone provider's coverage area, runs on replaceable batteries and/or holds a longer charge. It comes equipped with a compass and better weather-tracking services like barometers. The NFCT maps include GPS coordinates allowing you to confirm key trail features and locations while you travel with your device. It also can record a tracklog showing a path of digital bread crumbs and accrued mileage.

Your GPS device should not replace packing the NFCT maps and the need to take along a compass. Dense vegetation can obstruct satellite signals and occasionally, the satellites aren't in an optimal position for accurate calculations. Devices can also run out of batteries and get lost or broken.

INSECTS

Besides facing strong headwinds and paddling through periods of heavy rain, blood-feeding biting flies form the trifecta of trip vexations that are a part of trail life. No one will escape facing more than a few species that will find you and your unprotected skin irresistible. From the no-see-ums nipping at your ankles to the black flies buzzing behind your ears to the ever-present mosquito, it's less about coping than living with the pests. Some days or places are more maddening than others. Consider any barrage of bugs bolstering your character.

Without going into extensive entomology, here's a general overview of the most troublesome insects and parasites you can attempt to escape, and what is the best evasive action.

Bees and Wasps

Bees and wasps are not any more common or aggressive along the NFCT than elsewhere in the United States. Unless you inadvertently agitate a proverbial hornets' nest, or are anaphylactic, a singular sting from a bee or wasp will only deliver localized pain and temporary swelling. For some people, the site will be red and itchy for up to a week. People known to be highly allergic should pack a self-injectable EpiPen (epinephrine) for the treatment of anaphylactic shock.

Black Flies

Painful, biting, blood-drawing barbarians, black flies are the bane of springtime paddling. They find places the repellent missed or where you don't apply it—like under cuffs and hatbands. They fly in your face and are particularly attracted to eyes, ears and the hairline. You don't feel them until they've already drawn blood and left a welt.

Reality: May be present from ice-off to July generally peaking from May to mid-June. They breed in fast, cool flowing water and therefore are more prevalent on the river sections.

Saving Graces: Black flies don't like wind and are active only during the day.

Deer Flies

These parasites are present in wetlands and open areas within forests and are most active during the hottest and sunniest days of summer. Deer flies deliver painful bites.

Reality: Present year round, vigorously breeding in June and July. Not easily distracted by swatting.

Saving Graces: Active during the day only. Attracted to high points on their perceived prey, so deerfly patches—a commercial sticky paper or rolled up duct tape adhered sticky side up to the top of a cap—may effectively capture a good amount buzzing around your head.

TRICK DEER AND HORSE FLIES WHILE PORTAGING WITH YOUR CART AND A PADDLE

Because these flies tend to alight at or near the highest point of their intended victim, try fooling the flies by placing a paddle upright in the bow and pushing the canoe or kayak from the rear on wheelable carries. Some paddlers swear that the flies swarm the paddle and not the person.

Horse Flies

Larger cousin of the deer fly, the horse fly bite produces bigger swellings. Repellents, including those containing DEET, tend to be ineffective.

Mosquitoes

Mosquitoes are present everywhere in various concentrations throughout the paddling season and the Trail.

Reality: Night or day, as long as it's warm enough, mosquitoes can be active. They are carriers of the rare, but serious, West Nile Virus.

Saving Graces: They announce their whiny presence giving you a chance to react before they land and bite. Head nets and repellents are effective defensives.

No-See-Ums, Midges or Moose Flies (Oh My!)

These tiny pests go by different names, but they all pack the same punch—itchy bites that can linger for days. They prefer moist, marshy habitat areas around springs, streams and ponds.

Reality: Present during summer months and hot, humid temperatures. Midges are attracted to light at night and may be able to penetrate netting screens to find you inside your tent.

Saving Graces: They don't like sunlight and are most active in morning and evenings or on cloudy, windless days.

Ticks

The two most common ticks found throughout the Trail are the Deer Tick *(Black-Legged Tick)* and Wood Tick *(American Dog Tick)*. Deer ticks are much smaller than wood ticks. Both are present spring through fall, but most active in spring and early summer. Habitats range from fields to forests at ground level to three feet above the ground.

Reality: Both species can pass several kinds of tick-borne illnesses. Deer ticks are responsible for spreading Lyme disease, a treatable, but potentially debilitating illness if not diagnosed early.

Saving Graces: Tick bites generally don't hurt, although they can leave a mark or bruise, and may induce localized itching when removed. Repellents can be effective. Wearing long pants with the cuffs tucked into socks and conducting a daily tick check are the best protections.

The Bottom Line

Your tolerance to insect bites will dictate the necessity to pack a bug suit, headnet and various formulations of repellents. Deer fly patches and chemical repellents such as Ben's 100 percent DEET or picaridin (active ingredient in Avon® Skin-So-Soft™) are effective, but not always tolerated by the user. DEET is disturbingly caustic enough that it can remove varnish from a paddle. Keeping skin covered with long-sleeved shirts and pants is one of the best defenses.

Carry hydrocortisone, baking soda, witch hazel, and/or Benadryl® to help soothe itches after encounters.

LEECHES

Freshwater leeches are present in lakes, rivers and streams—most notably the Clyde and Missisquoi Rivers—where you will find yourself doing a lot of walking in the water. While they tend to gross you out, leeches cause no real pain or harm, however, the small wound they inflict may momentarily bleed profusely.

Remove any unwanted hitchhikers by sliding your fingernail at the narrow end of the leech (the oral point of contact) and push the sucker sideways while pulling gently, but firmly away from your skin. Likewise, quickly detach the posterior sucker by flicking or prodding.

Is it generally not advisable to attempt removing a leech by applying mosquito repellent, shampoo, or salt; burning with a match or cigarette; or tugging. This can result in the leech regurgitating into the wound and causing infection much worse than the leech bite itself.

Treat leech nibbles with topical antibiotic ointment, such as Neosporin, especially when troubled by the little suckers in any compromised waters such as the Missisquoi River.

MONEY

ATMs are abundant throughout New York and Vermont and at larger towns in New Hampshire and Maine, but availability diminishes after leaving Jackman, Maine. Make sure to bring cash or checks to pay for campsites on the Penobscot River and the Allagash Wilderness Waterway, and for the Churchill Dam shuttle. Credit cards are not accepted. Two Rivers Lunch in Allagash Village, Maine does not accept credit cards either and there is no ATM. Have cash in hand if you plan to eat there.

If you use any services or wish to buy food in Mansonville, Québec, be prepared to carry Canadian currency before entering the country. ATMs are limited and credit cards may not be accepted at some local businesses. Canadian currency is also required for the Lake Memphremagog boat wash permit at Perkins Landing.

PADDLES

Kayakers don't have quite as many options, but for the canoeist, paddles come in a dizzying choice of materials, shapes and weights tailored for different types of paddling conditions.

In addition to a long paddle good for deep lakes, some canoeists carry a shorter paddle specific to whitewater conditions that can stand hard knocks. Blades reinforced with fiberglass resist splitting if they get caught between sharp rocks. Others use the same paddle throughout the duration of the entire trail. Bent-shaft paddles are great for long distances, especially over flat water. They generate powerful strokes with less effort but some paddlers find maneuvering strokes and steering more difficult.

Like boat choices, there is no tidy recommendation about what paddle works best. This is another area dictated by personal preference or skill sets. However, every boat or paddler—whether canoe or kayak—must have a spare paddle on hand in case damage or loss affects the primary one.

PASSPORTS

You will enter Canada from East Richford, Vt., either by walking across the Route 105A bridge or by paddling under it on the Missisquoi River. The Canadian Border Station on the East Richford/Glenn Sutton line is open seven days a week from 8 a.m. to 4 p.m. The office is remote with no running water or nearby services.

American citizens will need to present a passport or a passport card in order to enter Canada. International paddlers will need to present a passport and valid visa (if you are arriving from a country for which one is required). The Canadian government recommends that all travellers carry proof of citizenship such as a birth certificate, a certificate of citizenship or naturalization or a Certificate of Indian Status along with photo identification.

Canadian Regulations

If you are traveling with a dog from the United States, a signed and dated certificate from a veterinarian verifying that it has been vaccinated against rabies within the last three years is required. The certificate must clearly identify the animal. Dog food containing meat by-products, such as beef or sheep, is prohibited.

It is illegal to bring pepper spray or mace into Canada. Travelers should be advised that some knives, even those used for hunting and fishing, could be considered prohibited weapons. Firearms must meet certain requirements and you must declare all weapons at the Canadian (CBSA) port of entry or they will be seized. Seized firearms and weapons are never returned. For more information governing restrictions, visit the Canadian government website at *www.cfc-cafc.gc.ca* prior to entering the country.

Reentering the United States

After paddling Lake Memphremagog from Perkins Landing in Québec to Newport, Vt., paddlers need to report back in with U.S. Customs and Border Security at the Newport Marina using a videophone. Reentering the United States by canoe or kayak has historically created confusion on the part of the customs official. Some paddlers were asked about non-existent registration numbers or even the color of their vessel. With increased participation and trail awareness, current paddlers can hope to expect less hassle regarding their means of arrival than their predecessors. For more information about U.S. Customs rules and regulations visit *www.cbp.gov*.

PERSONAL HYGIENE/BATHROOM ETIQUETTE

Even though most of your time is spent on the water and the ability to get in the water for a refreshing dip is at your whim, a hot shower still can be one of the finest trail rewards sought. It washes away accumulated layers of sunscreen, bug spray, bug guts, dirt and sweat. In cold weather, a hot shower will heat you up.

Experienced backcountry campers know that at no time should you ever take soap or shampoo with you into any water body, even those considered biodegradable. There is no soap that is safe to use in such a way. Biodegradable soap requires soil to breakdown properly and is not biodegradable when it first ends up in a river or lake. If you wouldn't drink it, don't put it in the water.

If you must soap up or want to wash dishes or clothes, do so at least 200' away from rivers and lakes to avoid polluting.

When latrines or public rest rooms are unavailable, 6-8" deep "catholes" must be dug for burying human waste. Choose a place 200' away from any water sources and where others are unlikely to camp or walk. Spots that have organic soil are preferable to sandy soils, which take more time to decompose the waste. Do not bury plastics or any other trash in your cathole, but do add additional soil to cover it up and "naturalize" the area with old leaves and other forest floor detritus leaving no trace of your business.

Under no circumstances should toilet paper ever be left unburied. An even better practice is to pack it out. There is nothing more disturbing or disgusting than setting up camp in a beautiful spot only to find a minefield of toilet paper puffs scattered in the woods or field behind your site. Toilet paper does not immediately disintegrate and exposed human waste contains pathogens that can contaminate ground and surface water.

These are NOT wild flowers!

Women also have a responsibility to properly dispose of personal care items. Carry out all plastic or cotton feminine hygiene products. Do not bury them. A menstrual cup is another option, if you already know how to use one, and eliminates the need to carry or dispose of tampons or pads altogether. Disposable wipes are made from nonbiodegradable materials that also must be carried out rather than buried, burned or left in privies.

A "pee pad," long favored by female expedition backpackers, is also a good alternative to toilet paper. This is a soft piece of cloth used for "blotting." An old bandana or a microfiber washcloth works well. Either can be hung from the outside of a pack and sanitized by the ultraviolet rays of the sun, or kept in a Ziploc bag, washed out and reused.

POISONOUS PLANTS

The Northeast is home to several noxious plants that can cause problems for those with skin sensitivities or allergies. Poison ivy and wild parsnip are found along the edges of portage trails and roadways and should be watched for when carving out a riverside stealth campsite. Other pernicious plants include stinging nettles and poison sumac.

Camp first aid treatments include soaking the affected area in cool water to remove urushiol oils or embedded plant hairs, applying calamine lotion or hydrocortisone cream to soothe itching and refraining from scratching.

Poison Ivy

Poison ivy grows along sandy riverbanks, open fields and the edges of roads and can be found throughout the NFCT. Poison ivy is easily identified by its alternating clusters of three almond-shaped, smooth leaves that become shiny with maturity. The edges may or may not be ridged. It is most often found

[Toxicodendron radicans]

as a trailing vine or groundcover, but also takes form as a climbing vine or shrub. Brushing up against the plant results in reactions ranging from mild rashes and itching to severely blistered skin. Symptoms last one to two weeks. Hospitalization could be required in extreme cases. Attempt to refrain from itching and keep the affected area clean to avoid infection.

Wild Parsnip

Wild parsnip likes to grow along sunny roadsides and field edges and in pastures or natural areas. The portage trails from Ore Bed Road to the lower Saranac River near Redford, N.Y. and the put-in above Sheldon Springs Hydroelectric Project along the Missisquoi River are known habitats.

[Pastinaca sativa L.]

The stalk is hollow and grooved and the plant grows two to five feet tall. It has saw-toothed leaves resembling those of celery. Brushing against the plant results in skin reddening, rash development—and in severe cases—blisters and a burning or scalding type pain. Exposure to sunlight can intensify the symptoms. Wild parsnip burns often appear as elongated spots or streaks. Dark red or brownish skin discoloration develops where the burn or blisters first appeared and can last for several months.

Stinging Nettle

Stinging nettle is a broadleaf weed that often exists in colonies in moist soils. The plants can grow to be two to four feet tall. Stinging nettle leaves are serrated round ovals and both the leaves and stems are covered with long, fine to bristly hairs that can irritate skin when handled. Reddish patches or blisters, accompanied by itching and burning, appear quickly after exposure, but typically last for only a few hours. A prolonged tingling sensation may persist on the affected skin for more than 12 hours, even after visible symptoms have faded.

[Urtica dioica]

Poison Sumac

Although its rarity reduces the incidence of human exposure, the plant is far more virulent than poison ivy. Poison sumac is found exclusively in wet soils, typically in peat bogs and swamps of the eastern United States and Canada. Itchy rashes and blisters develop soon after exposure.

Poison sumac grows as a shrub or small tree. Unlike poison ivy, poison sumac leaves come in long, paired rows with an additional leaf at the end. The leaves may have black spots made up of urushiol oil, which turns dark upon exposure to air. The fruits are semi-spherical, small and white, while non-poisonous sumac berries are red.

[Toxicodendron vernix]

PORTAGE CARTS OR WHEELS

Choosing to tackle the Trail without the use of portage carts or wheels is certainly possible for those possessing the strength and stamina. Others won't be able to imagine doing the Trail without them and will want to know what has been used successfully. This section is written for paddlers who are planning on bringing and using wheels. Keep in mind that you will be adding seven to seventeen pounds of weight to your gear load when they need to be carried on unwheelable portages.

It is important to note that regardless of the style of wheel used, many Through-Paddlers have experienced equipment malfunctions or a breakdown at some point during their journey. The trails are rough and the many portages are hard on carts. Only one canoeing team reportedly made it all the way to Fort Kent without a problem using a PaddleCart® *(www.paddlecart.com)*.

Styles

There are two main styles of portage wheels favored by Through-Paddlers:
1) a twin "bicycle tire" type cart with wheels that are skinnier and provide a higher clearance under the canoe; or

2) a lower profile cart with wider 4" wheels intended for kayaks, but also works well for canoes.

Both are designed to allow the canoe or kayak to be centrally balanced, distributing more of the overall weight. Either system should be able to support a minimum of 200 lbs., be foldable and lightweight enough to carry on unwheelable portages.

There are advantages and disadvantages to both systems. Both use straps to secure the cart to the boat.

1" Wide "Bicycle" Tire Cart Style
Pros and Cons:

1" Wide "Bicycle" Tire Cart Style

- Wheel height and ground clearance is as much as twice that of other carts
- Wheeling over rocks and other obstacles is less demanding
- Enables the canoe to be easily pushed as well as pulled
- 16"–20" pneumatic tires may be more easily prone to puncturing
- Rims are easier to damage
- Not practical for kayaks (both use and storage)
- Weight: 15–17 lbs.

4" Wide Lower Profile Cart
Pros and Cons:

4" Wide Lower Profile Cart Style

- 10" x 4" (pneumatic or hard plastic) tires less prone to rim problems or puncturing
- Takes up less space when folded
- Lower clearance may mean needing to lift vessel out of ruts or over rocky areas
- Vessel requires pulling
- Bushings may heat up and damage (melt) plastic wheel parts on long hauls
- Weight: 7–9 lbs.

PaddleCart®

The choice comes down to paddler preference and ability to handle any repairs on the Trail. You will want to carry extra replacement nuts and pins as these frequently loosen and fall off or break over rough terrain. Consider applying Loctite® to the nuts or placing tape over them to help prevent against total loss. Loctite protects threads from rust and corrosion and prevents loosening from shock and vibration.

As you pass through trail towns, check the pressure of your tires and keep them inflated. Some paddlers have carried CO_2 for filling tires as not all service station air lines easily match valve stems. Adding a sealant such as SLIME® to wheels that use tube tires creates an additional layer of protection, repairing punctures as they occur. Sealants aren't effective, however, in tubes losing pressure from sidewall punctures, bead leaks, damaged rims or faulty valves.

The one model to completely avoid is a stern cart. Stern carts are designed primarily to assist getting a boat from a vehicle to the water's edge and perform best on flat surfaces. The frame of this cart style cannot support

Stern Cart Style

the weight of your vessel and gear over rugged terrain. It places all of the pressure on one end of your boat and is not only hard on the cart frame, but also on your body since you are required to pull it from the bow. These models are known to have failed early on for previous Through-Paddlers. There is no way this model will survive the entire trail.

The Trail is also not the place to test a Do-It-Yourself cart constructed of PVC pipe or other low-cost materials. These likely will not make it all the way to Fort Kent.

With 22 of the 77 portages occurring within the first 100 miles in New York, you will surely be tempted to wheel over some of the rougher portage trails. The question becomes whether it is preferable to work the wheels over a slightly rugged 1.3-mile trail in New York when you will really want them to perform over the 5.7-mile Grand Portage at mile 258 and along the remote Spencer Rips logging roads in Maine. If water levels are low on the Upper Ammonoosuc or the South Branch Dead River, you may find yourself relying on those wheels even more.

One of the keys to successful wheeling is how much weight is left in the boat and where it is placed. Experiment with centering the weight over the wheels or placing it to be slightly bow or stern heavy. Almost any vessel can be pushed or pulled with determination, but you may find yourself fighting the Trail and your paddling partner with effort and consternation if you leave too much gear in it. It is much easier to maneuver around rocks and over roots when each paddler shoulders a pack. In addition, you aren't putting unnecessary pressure on the wheel bearings, frame or tires helping to ensure the wheels will last to the end of the trip. You wouldn't place yourself in a canoe on dry land, so why would you load your boat like a cart with the same weight's worth of gear balanced on your pneumatic lifeline?

If you intend to use wheels, plan on obtaining a quality piece of equipment that can take abuse and still be maintained along the journey. Treating your portage cart with care and regularly inspecting it for damage will increase the odds it will last to the end.

Bring Your Cartop Carrier Straps Along

Web load straps with quick release buckles work well for attaching the portage cart firmly to your canoe. The straps also come in handy if you decide to accept a ride. Instead of lamenting: "If only you had a way to secure your boat..." you can yank out the strap, strap your boat to the roof rack and be good to go. Of course, you can always say, no thank you and continue down the road, pulling your perfectly balanced vessel to the put-in while you swat away at the deer flies.

USE YOUR BOWLINE AS A HARNESS

If you are using low profile wheels, a good way to gear up for a long haul over portages that follow a road is to use your bowline to harness yourself to the front of your boat. After balancing and securing your canoe or kayak on the wheels, let out the bowline for 8–10'. If you are using barrels to keep your food or gear dry, you can thread the rope through the hard plastic handles and back again to the bow. This can also work with soft dry bags, but take care not to put excessive strain on any straps. This hands-free method allows you to pull the vessel like the draft horse you are becoming.

Forked Lake — Raquette River Carry

SAFETY

Paddling the Trail is not without inherent risks. This guidebook is not a substitute for outdoor skills or good personal judgment. Know your limitations, pay attention to your surroundings, know how to self-rescue and practice good common sense.

Personal Flotation Devices (PFDs)

The waters of the Northern Forest Canoe Trail are as varied as the landscapes the Trail crosses. Always exercise caution and wear a life jacket. Nationally, 85 percent of all canoeing and 48 percent of all kayaking fatalities were because victims were not wearing a life jacket.* Life jackets not only provide additional flotation in case of capsize or an unexpected swim, but they also provide an essential layer of warmth in cold water. Some states dictate the use of a PFD.

Source: U.S. Coast Guard Office of Auxiliary and Boating Safety

Cold Water Safety

According to the American Canoe Association, a cold water situation occurs anytime the water temperature drops below 60°F (16°C) or when the combined air and water temperature is less than 120°F (49°C). Heat is lost much more quickly in water than in air. A water temperature of 50°F (10°C) can lead to death in as little as one hour and hypothermia can kill in as little as fifteen minutes when water temperatures are near freezing.

Physical incapacitation occurs within five–fifteen minutes in cold water. Your body reacts by decreasing blood flow to the extremities in an effort to preserve heat in the core in order to protect vital organs. This means you will lose meaningful movement in your hands and feet, followed by your arms and legs. If you are not wearing a flotation device, you will be unable to stay afloat and will drown.

Early spring or late fall paddlers should consider including a dry suit as part of their gear.

Motorized Boats

Most parts of the Trail are open to motorized watercraft. Take care paddling busy lakes where inattentive speedboats may not expect to see slower moving canoes and kayaks. The Fulton Chain and Lower Saranac Lake in New York can experience periods of heavy motorized traffic that require defensive paddling. Crossing Lake Champlain is another waterway where self-propelled canoes and kayaks are less common. Only one 8.2-mile "Natural Section" of the Connecticut River in New Hampshire has a full motor ban. Where motors are allowed within the Allagash Wilderness Waterway, they are restricted to under 10 horsepower.

Personal Safety and Theft

Although the NFCT is statistically safer than most places—and certainly should not be considered any more dangerous than any other trail or town you might visit as a non-paddler—there is still no guarantee that you or your unprotected gear will be completely safe from theft everywhere along the Trail. The majority of paddlers neither experience nor harbor any personal safety concerns. Unfortunately, there have been a few reports of theft or attempted theft when gear has been left unsupervised. Safety awareness is one of your best lines of defense.

- Always carry your most important valuables on you—including your passport, money/credit cards, camera gear and devices.
- Be especially vigilant in remote areas where portaging a canoe along a state highway attracts attention and suggests vulnerability. Would-be thieves have access to a quick getaway that you do not.
- Attempt to conceal any unprotected gear as much as possible, especially near any populated areas or along highways.
- Keep your gear in view when stopped at restaurants or stores.
- Consider carrying a cable lock for securing your vessel when you must leave it unattended.
- Use Trail sign-in boxes and registers. Sign in, leave notes and/or report suspicious activities.

- Never tell strangers about your plans. Be friendly, but cautious. Trust your instincts and avoid people who act suspiciously or make you feel uncomfortable.
- Leave an itinerary with family or friends and don't post any real-time messages to your online blogs, journals or social media feeds about your upcoming plans.

Many of the official campsites are located in remote and unseen areas, but there may be times when you may find yourself carving out a campsite for a night near an urban area and wish not to be noticed. The color of your tent may be a determining factor in how noticeable you are. On one hand, a brightly colored tent can be more obviously spotted when stealth camping while a camouflaged color will allow you to blend in with the landscape and escape attention. On the other hand, a brightly colored tent may help locate your whereabouts in the event of an emergency.

Wildlife
Black bears are common, although not commonly seen, and can be found anywhere along the Trail. While attacks on humans are rare, a startled bear or a female with cubs may react aggressively. If you encounter a bear while portaging, make noise and give it time to move away. Once in camp, the best preventive defense is preparing and storing food properly. Conventional wisdom suggests hanging your food bag along with any scented items like toothpaste, suspended 10' from the ground and 6' away from the tree, well away from your campsite.

While bears are to be respected, there are other wildlife "threats" you will want to be mindful of as you travel.

Rodents
Mice, chipmunks, squirrels and their ilk present the greater threat to your food stores, especially from those who have become acclimated to visitors. They can be a nuisance at popular campsites. Expect your site to be cased by pint-sized critters along the Penobscot and Allagash waterways. They seem to know when food bags are left ignored on the ground and will eat their way through tents to reach that forgotten granola bar. You are more likely hanging food to keep the rodents from getting to it than protection from bears. Rigid plastic dry barrels further discourage cheeky rodents from filching your food.

Moose
Moose attacks are actually more common than bear attacks and can be just as dangerous. More than 30,000 moose live in Maine. At least 4,000 can be found in New Hampshire, averaging about one per square mile in the White Mountains. Smaller populations exist in New York and Vermont.*

Any moose, at any time of year, may respond aggressively and charge you if provoked by your presence, though the chances of a confrontation increase during certain times of year. Cows with calves are particularly protective, especially in early summer when their young are most vulnerable. In the fall, bull moose often act more aggressively as they compete with other males for females. Regardless of the season, the best defense is to keep your distance and avoid a confrontation in the first place.

As of 2013, moose populations across swaths of the United States are declining at an unprecedented rate.

Hunting Season

Spring and late-season paddlers will want to educate themselves on local hunting seasons. Wild turkey season runs in April and May throughout several areas of the NFCT and state migratory waterfowl dates can begin as early as late August in some places. In the Allagash, moose hunting begins around the third week in September.

SHOES

Paddling

Many paddlers prefer Keen® or Teva® brand water shoes when paddling. These sandals hold up well to abuse, dry out quickly and the enclosed toe style is helpful when tracking up or wading along cobbled riverbeds. Other paddlers like neoprene or rubber boots that keep their feet warmer and dry. In all cases, beware of hitchhiking invasive aquatic species that may lurk within your laces and damp shoes.* Crocs® are also a popular option and are especially nice to wear around camp. The problem with most of these paddling shoes is that they don't double well for long distance or rugged portaging.

The use of felt soled wading boots are banned in Vermont and strongly discouraged elsewhere because they contribute to the spread of invasives including "rock snot."

Portaging

Even though you are spending the majority of time on the water, the number and length of significant portages should cause you to consider comfortable hiking footwear. While the longest official carry is the 5.7-mile long Grand Portage in Québec, the reality is that you may find yourself doing many more miles of walking due to low river water levels. There are times when your trip might feel more like a backpacking expedition than a paddle trip. Think about what type of shoe you can comfortably wear covering unexpected long distances by foot. Your water shoes may or may not work.

SHUTTLE SERVICES

Shuttles are not available along all parts of the Trail. Where services do exist, they tend to be associated with local recreational segments and may provide an option for you in the event of impassable paddling sections. There is no shuttle service, however, that will get you back to your starting point in Old Forge after completing your journey.

Refer to *Towns and Services* beginning on page 207 for contact information about available shuttle services by town. To date, the communities with businesses or organizations offering shuttle services include:

- Old Forge, N.Y.
- Long Lake, N.Y.
- Saranac Lake, N.Y. (Lower Saranac River)
- Montgomery, Vt. (off trail/serves Vermont section of the Missisquoi River)
- Glen Sutton, Qué. (Grand Portage)
- Newport, Vt. (Clyde River)
- West Charleston, Vt. (Clyde River, Nulhegan River)
- The Fen (Clyde River, Nulhegan River)
- West Milan (Upper Ammonoosuc River, Androscoggin River)
- Errol, N.H. (Androscoggin River)
- Rangeley, Maine (South Branch Dead River)
- Northeast Carry
- Churchill Dam, Maine
- Saint Francis, Maine
- Allagash, Maine

SLEEPING

The uncertainty about where you'll find yourself and what you'll find at the end of each day can be nerve-racking at first. An unfamiliar town is crisscrossed with unknown streets. A silent forest is full of heart pounding rustlings. Getting a good night's sleep equates with getting in a good paddle the next day.

The NFCT is loaded with picturesque campsites and most trail towns offer options for a roof over your head. Sometimes your camp will be carved out of necessity. Most days it will be the destination.

LODGING

If you are seeking a roof over your head and a real bed, the communities through which you pass offer family-owned, non-franchised motels, B&Bs, hostels or cabins. Many can be found trailside. Plattsburgh, N.Y. is the largest city on the NFCT and while it offers many services, there are remarkably few lodging options easily accessible to paddlers.

Towns offering trail-friendly and most-likely-to-be-available, same day, single night* accommodations include:

- Old Forge, N.Y. (motels)
- Long Lake, N.Y. (inn, motel)
- Saranac, N.Y. (B&Bs, motels)
- Plattsburgh, N.Y. (motels)
- North Hero Island, Vt. (inns, motels, cabins)
- Swanton, Vt.** (motel)
- Enosburg Falls, Vt. (B&B, inns)
- Richford, Vt. (B&B)
- Newport, Vt.** (B&Bs, motel)
- Island Pond, Vt. (motels)
- Stark, N.H. (B&B)
- Errol, N.H.** (motel)
- Rangeley, Maine (B&B, motels, hostel)
- Stratton, Maine (B&B, inn, motels, hostel)
- Maine Huts & Trails (lodge)
- Jackman, Maine (motels, cabins)
- Rockwood, Maine (cabins)
- Fort Kent, Maine (motel)

Refer to *Towns and Services* in Part III beginning on page 207.

Internet-based CouchSurfing.com or AirBnB.com may offer additional options along the trail.

* *Availability is more likely on weekdays vs. weekends. It is a good idea to confirm ahead, if possible, to avoid disappointment.*

** *Motels in these communities are located away from the water, about one mile from take-out.*

CAMPING

For the most part, campsites are found at regular intervals along the entire route of the NFCT. Many sections of the Trail provide numerous possibilities insuring you'll have a place to pitch your tent or hang your hammock. Other sections have fewer options—or are placed distantly apart from each other. You'll need to hit mileage goals in order to reach these designated sites.

Camping locations indicated on the NFCT maps include public lands, state campgrounds, private campgrounds and NFCT-developed sites. Mind weekend travel, especially around the Fourth of July holiday, when competition for any of these campsites may be fiercer. The NFCT endeavors to add new sites across the Trail. Check the website for the latest updates.

Regardless where you camp, always practice leave no trace camping principles.

Public Lands

Camping is permitted on most public lands, but rules vary from state to state. Typically, there are limited or no facilities, and no fees. Fires may or may not be permitted. Refer to "Local Regulations," for more detailed information listed on each individual NFCT map regarding specific areas and any fire restrictions.

State Campgrounds

State parks or state-managed campgrounds have numbered or labeled sites with picnic tables and outhouses or rest rooms. Some, but not all, may have potable water available. Fees and reservations are associated with usage. On busy summer weekends, state campgrounds may be full.

Map 8 features some of the finest campsites, but all are fee-based, and only two (off trail) are available on a first-come basis. The majority of these campsites are posted and require reservations. Rangers have been known to force campers to move out of unregistered sites within this section. At more than 400 miles into the trip, it will be difficult to predict where you'll end up on Map 8 in order to make reservations. Mileage Segment 22 includes more details and advice about how to plan for this unique trail situation.

Private Campgrounds

There are several privately owned campgrounds that can be welcome havens found along the Trail. Although usually the most expensive camping option, some offer hot showers and other services. Bakers Acres, located between Union Falls and Plattsburgh, N.Y., is ideally situated on the Saranac River where no other camping options exist. It features hot showers and a swimming pool. Pelletier's located on the St. John River near Saint Francis, Maine, offers an economical last night trail campsite with access to a convenience store, but it does not have showers.

NFCT Camp Sites

Where the Trail traverses private land, the NFCT has worked with landowners carving out trailside campsites. Notable examples of these partnerships include Lussier and Doe on the Missisquoi River and Samuel Benton on the Connecticut River. Additional locations are occasionally being developed.

All NFCT managed sites are considered primitive with moldering or no toilets and no running water. A picnic table may or may not be present. Some sites are known only to NFCT members and are indicated solely on NFCT maps. All sites are free and most available on first-come basis. A few landowners (like the Cemetery Watch lean-to located northeast of Saranac Lake, N.Y.) request advance notice and are noted as such on NFCT maps.

"Unofficial" Campsites

This guidebook points out several campsite options that have been described as unofficial. These sites are not endorsed by the NFCT or the author, but have been used by other Through-Paddlers and included as options for the paddler who may be in desperate need to stop. Some locations, such as Perkins Landing on Lake Memphremagog or property near the Middle Dam caretaker's house on Lower Richardson Lake, have historically allowed Through-Paddlers to camp with permission. Other sites, such as the sandy riverside clearing adjacent to Separator Rapids along the Saranac River and clearly a "party" site or the private land signed as "Dickie's Camping Site" situated before reaching the Sheldon Springs Hydroelectric Project on the Missisquoi, have been created through local usage and may or may not be desirable stopping places.

Stealth/Renegade/Bush/Wild Camping

Whether you call it stealth camping, renegade camping, bush camping, rough camping, wild camping, off grid camping or just sleeping under the stars, camping of this nature refers to setting up your camp outside of an established campsite. Ideally it means removing yourself quietly in the morning without being detected or disturbing your surroundings and leaving no trace. Though it would commonly be seen to be illegal, stealth camping does not have to break the law, as long as you take care to stay off private land and don't trespass in areas that are clearly signed.

Circumstances may dictate that you (insert your preferred terminology here— camp) at least once during your trip.

There are a few basic common sense rules:

- You should be undetectable. Brightly colored tents do not lend themselves well to stealth camping. If you have any camouflage mosquito netting or tarp, consider draping it over your tent.
- Choose non-sensitive areas with a durable surface and leave the site in the exact condition as you found it.
- Bury human waste in cat holes, 200' from any water sources. Remove all litter including any toilet paper.

STOVES AND STOVE FUEL

All types of stoves and stove fuels are permitted along the NFCT, including the use of twig stoves. However, the ability to purchase replacement pressurized fuel canisters or liquid fuels, such as white gas or denatured alcohol, is limited. If your stove relies on specific brands or types of fuel, it is recommended that you contact local outfitters, hardware or general stores in the towns located along the Trail prior to departure to confirm availability. Another option is to ship fuel ahead of you in mail drops. Be aware that ONLY non-liquid fuel and propane or isobutane pressurized canisters can be shipped to mail drops via domestic ground mail and this can add one to two weeks to your delivery, even when using Priority Mail. Address the package to the post office with the your name in care of "General Delivery" with the town, state and ZIP code. Packages must be marked "Consumer Commodity ORM-D." A final option is to pack enough fuel to last the entire trip.

TAKE-OUTS AND PUT-INS

Unless stolen or otherwise noted, all officially mapped take-outs and put-ins are marked with a small blue and yellow diamond-shaped NFCT confidence medallion. There are some parts of the Trail, however, where taking out or putting in is at the discretion of the paddler. There may only be descriptions suggesting the whereabouts of suitable locations—and even then, suggestions could be dependent upon water levels.

For example, there is no established portage trail around the Samsonville Dam ruins between Enosburg Falls and East Berkshire on the Missisquoi River, yet a farming tractor trail parallels the river on river left. You decide when or if you will take out and where to put back in, potentially bushwhacking through thigh-high grasses and riverside muck. Or you continue to track upstream to quieter water.

The Bottom Line
Look for marked take-out and put-in locations, but expect to exercise common sense and adapt as you navigate your way across the Trail.

TRAIL ANGELS AND MAGIC

Like elsewhere, there truly are more good people than bad. Most paddlers will find that all the towns and villages through which they pass are warm and welcoming. People are interested in and supportive of your journey. Paddlers often encounter "trail angels," random strangers who provide an unexpected kindness. It might be someone who offers you a ride or a cold beverage, or generously pays for a meal. They might even give you a place to stay for the night. You shouldn't count on it, but trail magic does have a knack of occurring when a person's spirits are very low.

PART 2

Mileage Segments

Maps

Mileage Segments

Mileage Segments

OVERVIEW

The Northern Forest Canoe Trail Through-Paddler's Companion has broken the Trail down into 35 mileage segments reflecting many common stopping points. It is unlikely that the Trail can be (or should be) paddled exactly as specified within these segments. Weather conditions, stamina or interest will dictate your own mileage goals. Use each segment description as a tool to assist with route decisions as you journey east.

Each of the 35 segments include the following details:

NFCT Map:	The official NFCT map(s) being referenced
Total Miles:	The number of miles covered within the segment description
Milepost:	Cumulative trail mileage reached by the end of the segment
Portages:	The number of portages detailed within the segment
Type of Watercourse(s):	The number and kind(s) of water bodies each segment traverses

Information about each portage, including designations regarding how "wheelable" each may be, follow a segment overview. Points of interest, a generalized list of services found in any nearby trail towns and overnight options are included as part of every segment chapter.

Mileage distances noted for overnight options between segments have been rounded to the nearest tenth or at times, half mile. All other mileages and portage distances correlate with the official NFCT guidebook and each of the 13 NFCT maps.

Individual services including address information and distances from take-outs can be found in *Towns and Services* beginning on page 207, following this section.

WHAT CONSTITUTES A "WHEELABLE" PORTAGE?

Definitions

For purposes of this guide, portages have been designated into four categories: *Carry, Wheelable, Not Wheelable* and *Not Easily Wheelable.*

Portages noted as **"Carry"** are short and only require you to get around obstacles. There is no need to take the time to put on wheels, even if the area would be level enough for wheeling. A few of the dams encountered along the river sections will fall into this category.

A portage will be considered completely **"Wheelable"** only if it is paved or maintained in such a way that most, if not all of it, is smooth. This includes trails in which rocks or roots have been removed or minimized or if a portage follows a road.

Portages designated **"Not Wheelable"** are ones in which the terrain is uneven, boulder-ridden, swampy, muddy, and/or so full of obstacles that it is impossible to use wheels for any sustainable distance.

Many portages will fall into the **"Not Easily Wheeled"** category. The portage may be a combination of rugged trails with parts that level out. While technically possible to wheel, these portages will require more effort, maneuvering your canoe or kayak over bumps and around obstacles in order to take advantage of the sections that are smooth.

Exceptions to these definitions could change on a seasonal basis, such as a severe storm that results in downed trees creating obstacles on a defined "Wheelable" carry. Sustained periods of precipitation may temporarily transform a "Not Easily Wheelable" portage into an "Unwheelable" one.

It is important for the paddler bringing wheels to understand that you will NOT be able to use wheels on every portage. You will get a taste of this early on in the Trail when you get to Buttermilk Falls at milepost 37.5. Characterized by large boulders, uneven ground, roots and stepped areas, this portage is impractical to wheel.

Expect to carry your gear and plan for a means of doing so as efficiently and comfortably as possible. Canoes and kayaks can be fitted with yokes. Being able to transport a kayak on a long, unwheelable portage is essential.

With a minimum of 55 miles of portages, you will want your cart to last. Trying to wheel questionable portages will place unnecessary strain on this key piece of equipment.

New York Overview

NFCT Maps 1, 2 and 3

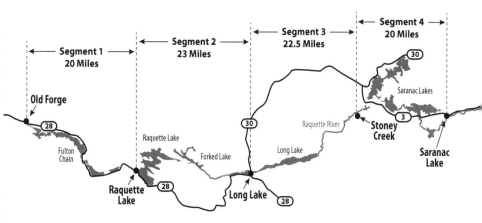

The first three maps provide a great introduction to the variety of waterways you'll encounter throughout the Trail. You will also find yourself quickly perfecting portaging skills because one third of all the NFCT carries occur within New York.

Communities and services alternating with remote areas make the breakdown of Maps 1 and 2 fairly predictable for the Through-Paddler. Paddling from village to village, inn to inn or even having the opportunity to eat at restaurants, combined with getting a taste of isolated rivers as you tick through the first 85 miles, makes the journey rather civilized.

True wilderness is mostly absent here, but the scenery is spectacular. The Fulton Chain can be abuzz with motorized watercraft and more than one summer paddler has commented they were glad to be off those busy lakes. The Saranac Lakes are jewels strung together between the Raquette and Saranac Rivers.

From Old Forge, you'll pass through the larger tourist towns of Long Lake and Saranac Lake. Heading on to Plattsburgh, you paddle past smaller villages with full-time residents, but offering few or no services.

Goal distances become less predictable following the downstream flow of the Saranac River after leaving Saranac Lake. Depending on your skill level, the next few days will be peppered with portages around dams and rapids as you make your way to Lake Champlain. Some paddlers may find themselves doing a lot more walking and/or possibly needing to get shuttled if river levels

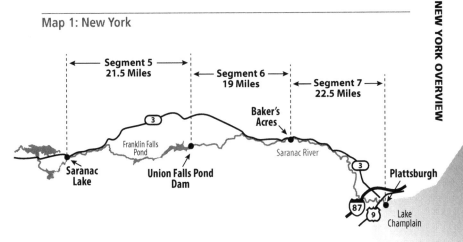

are low or rapids aren't run. Others, especially if paddling a river kayak or whitewater canoe—and with good water levels—will enjoy this challenging section. From Saranac Lake to Plattsburgh, paddlers face rapids rated from Class I to Class IV between long stretches of quieter water.

Assuming you are already familiar with using your equipment, much of this first week or two on the Trail is spent getting into the rhythm of hours consumed by paddling, learning to match the maps to the portage signage and working out any portaging issues.

Many paddlers take their first down day or break in Saranac Lake after finishing Map 2. Plattsburgh is another logical stopping point after finishing the Saranac River and before heading across the big water of Lake Champlain.

Camping is permitted on all Department of Environmental Conservation (DEC) lands unless marked with a "Do Not Camp Here" marker.

AVERAGE PADDLE TIMES

Old Forge, N.Y., to Saranac Lake, N.Y.	As little as 3 days/as many as 9 Average 4.5
Saranac Lake, N.Y., to Plattsburgh, N.Y.*	As little as 2 days/as many as 6 Average 3.5

* *Variables include portaging or taking a shuttle around the Class IV–V Tefft Pond Falls area along the Saranac River between Union Falls Pond and Clayburg and/or missing the Saranac River between Clayburg and Plattsburgh, if water levels are too low.*

Old Forge, N.Y., to Raquette Lake, N.Y.

NFCT Map: 1
Total Miles: 20
Milepost: 20
Portages: 3
Type of Watercourse(s): 8 lakes, 1 downstream creek

While most paddlers will likely tackle the first day of the Trail less aggressively, it is possible to travel 20 or more miles in one day, especially if you start early in the morning and the wind is in your favor. The most popular stopping points for commemorating the end to your first day tend to be the primitive lean-to sites on Seventh Lake or Eighth Lake, or the Eighth Lake State Campground. Once you leave Eighth Lake, you are committed to continuing on to Raquette Lake or paddling one mile off the route in order to camp at the Brown Tract Pond State Campground on Lower Pond.

Shoal Point Lighthouse
Fourth Lake

The last two portages detailed within this segment create desirable ending points—you can either tackle them first thing in the morning or "get them over with" before stopping.

Depending on the day of the week and the time of the year, expect to find yourself among motorized boats and Jet Skis. The shorelines here are dotted with docks, vintage camps and lakeside cottages throughout this section. Development thins out in Seventh Lake and several beautiful lean-to and camping sites are located along the north shore and on the island near the Seventh Lake take-out.

Overnight accommodations are available in Inlet and Raquette Lake, but may require advance reservations. Most of the state-managed campsites of Alger Island and Eighth Lake State Campground are by reservation only and may not have openings on busy summer weekends. Alger Island's registration and permit station is located at the boat landing off South Shore Road along Fourth Lake and the park office for Eighth Lake State Campground, located by the Route 28 entrance, is a good hike away from the carry take-out and shoreline sites.

PORTAGE DETAILS

#1) Fifth Lake Carry
.4 miles: Wheelable

Route 28 crossing to Sixth Lake

After weaving your way through the channel
behind Inlet businesses off of Fourth Lake, you
emerge into the very tiny Fifth Lake. The portage
trailhead is located past a private lean-to on the
far southeastern shore. Although the distance through the woods is short,
this is a good first test to see how the wheels work on a less-than-level
surface and is a taste of some of the portages ahead—many of which
will be rougher and longer. After emerging from the woods, follow the
sidewalk up the hill along Route 28. Your calf muscles may start to feel
the first burn of the trip. The portage is well marked to Sixth Lake. Take
care crossing busy Route 28.

#2) Eighth Lake Campground Carry
1 mile: Wheelable

Follow the well-marked gravel campground road from the Seventh
Lake dock to the boat launch on Eighth Lake. Take advantage of the
opportunity to fill up water bottles here from the campground's water
spigots as you pass by them.

#3) Brown Tract Carry
1.3 miles: Not Easily Wheeled/Wheelable

From the north end of Eighth lake, the portage passes the set back lean-to
and follows a rough, not easily wheeled trail through the woods. The first
half of the trail is uneven and there are roots. Route 28 is occasionally
visible on your right. The second half of the carry tends to be wheelable as
is smooths out after passing the DEC registration box. The portage ends
with a boardwalk and small pier into lily-covered Brown Tract.

POINTS OF INTEREST
* ✯ Photo op/sign-in: western terminus NFCT kiosk in Old Forge
* ✯ Historic dams at Fulton and Sixth Lakes
* ✯ Shoal Point Lighthouse on the southwest shore of Fourth Lake
* ✯ Brown Tract

Brown Tract Carry

SERVICES

Old Forge, N.Y. (page 211)
Grocery Store, Convenience Store, Outfitter, Shuttle, Restaurants, Lodging, Camping, Library, Post Office, Bank, ATM, Hardware Store, NFCT Kiosk

Inlet, N.Y. (page 212)
Grocery Store (seasonal), Restaurants, Lodging, Library, Laundromat, Post Office, ATM, Hardware Store

Raquette Lake, N.Y. (page 213)
General Store, Restaurant, Lodging, Library, Post Office, NFCT Kiosk

OVERNIGHT OPTIONS AND DISTANCES FROM OLD FORGE, N.Y.

Fourth Lake..5.5 miles
Alger Island state campground, lean-tos (fee)

Inlet, N.Y. ....10.5 miles
B&Bs, motel(s)

Seventh Lake ....13.5–15.5 miles
Lean-tos and campsites

Eighth Lake...16 miles
Eighth Lake state campground (fee)

Eighth Lake...17.5 miles
Lean-tos

Lower Pond*...20 miles
Brown Tract Pond state campground (fee)

Raquette Lake Village..20 miles
Inn

Raquette Lake ....22.5 miles
Big Island campsites

* Brown Tract Pond State Park on Lower Pond is off the Trail

Raquette Lake, N.Y., to Long Lake, N.Y.

NFCT Map: 1
Total Miles: 23
Milepost: 43
Portages: 4
Type of Watercourse(s): 3 lakes, 1 downstream river

During the summer, revelry and taps may greet the paddler who spends the night on Raquette Lake. The Raquette Lake Camps for Boys & Girls have continuously operated on this lake since 1916. Motorboat "taxis" can be seen transporting campers and staff from the Raquette Lake hamlet and between the two camps. The tourist boat, the *W. Durant*, offers seasonal nightly cruises. The town has a general store, a taproom and a library with Internet access. It is a busy hub for vacationers.

Raquette Lake is your first big lake with open stretches of bays where wind conditions can be unpredictable, but there are also several islands and coves where you can seek refuge. Forked Lake is less developed than the lakes through which you've traveled thus far and will seem far wilder.

Two state-run campgrounds along the route, several lean-tos and public DEC land offer many camping options all the way to Long Lake. Both Forked Lake and Tioga Point State Campgrounds have fee collection stations and the ability to register for an open campsite or lean-to on the same day. Forked Lake has potable water. Tioga Point does not.

The Village of Long Lake has restaurants, lodging, a general store and a library. Pontoon planes use the lake for their runways, which are both a novelty and a nuisance.

Four portages will make this a long, 23-mile day. Two portages can be considered completely wheelable, but be prepared to carry your gear around Buttermilk Falls and the portage around the rapids in the Raquette River.

Overnight accommodations in addition to camping are available within this section.

Raquette Lake/Outlet Bay take-out

PORTAGE DETAILS

#1) Forked Lake Carry
.5 miles: Wheelable

The well-marked take-out is adjacent to a summer camp off of Outlet Bay on Raquette Lake. The carry follows a gravel road to the put-in at the boat landing on Forked Lake. Strap on those wheels and go. At the intersection of North Point Road, you'll see one of the more unusual signs of civilization seemingly in the middle of nowhere, a public phone. While Map 1 makes it appear as though Outlet Bay connects directly to Forked Lake, the waterway is boulder-strewn and bony with typically low water and is considered impassable by boat.

Portage "point of interest"

#2) Forked Lake Campground Carry
1.5 miles: Wheelable

Follow Forked Lake Road, a maintained gravel road, from the boat landing out of the campground to the marked turn-off around a gate at a bend in the road. The uneven trail leads to the river. Put in by the riverside lean-to/camping area. This camping site is popular and can be crowded. If you are using wheels, this road provides an opportunity to try experimenting harnessing yourself to your boat with the bowline to pull it behind you. Don't forget to fill up your water bottles by the Forked Lake Ranger Station before heading out.

#3) Buttermilk Falls
.1 mile: Carry

This is a short, unwheelable carry around the scenic Class IV waterfall following a well-worn, uneven trail over boulders.

#4) Deerland Carry
.6 miles: Not Wheelable

Parts of this trail can be wet and soft, and the occasional boardwalk and large stepping-stones make wheeling questionable over this rocky and rooty trail.

POINTS OF INTEREST
✶ Freestanding phone booth on Forked Lake Carry
✶ Long Lake NFCT kiosk

SERVICES

Long Lake, N.Y. (page 213)
General Store, Convenience Store, Outfitter, Shuttle, Restaurants, Lodging, Library, Post Office, Bank, ATM, Hardware Store, NFCT Kiosk

OVERNIGHT OPTIONS AND DISTANCES FROM RAQUETTE LAKE, N.Y.

Raquette Lake ....2.5 miles
Big Island campsites

Lonesome Bay ....4.5 miles
Campsite/lean-tos

Tioga Point ....5 miles
State campground (fee)

Outlet Bay..8.5–9.5 miles
Lean-tos

Forked Lake ....12.5 miles
DEC lean-to, at the edge of the state campground boundary (unnumbered)

Forked Lake ....14 miles
State campground with numbered lakeside sites (fee)

Raquette River ....15.5 miles
Portage lean-to

Long Lake ....18.5 miles
Deerland lean-to

Long Lake ....21 miles
DEC public lands opposite Moose Island

Long Lake ....23 miles
Hotels, motels, cabins

NFCT
MILEPOST

65.5

Long Lake, N.Y., to Stony Creek

NFCT Map: 2
Total Miles: 22.5
Milepost: 65.5
Portages: 1 or 2
Type of Watercourse(s): 1 lake, 1 downstream river

Long Lake stretches for another 9.5 miles after leaving the village of Long Lake. Wind conditions can affect your ability to put on miles, but there are many lean-tos and beautiful campsite options along the east and north shores for breaks. The Raquette River picks up again as a gentle, meandering river from the north end of Long Lake for the first five miles before your only portage within this section. If the wind is at your back and with the river's current, you should be able to easily paddle all 22 miles, and possibly more, in one day.

Keep to the left of the long narrow island as you enter the river through the deepest channel near the northeast shore of Long Lake. The first 1.5 miles includes two lean-tos on river left and the confluence of the Cold River on river right, discernible by its upstream current from the Raquette River's downstream flow. Smallmouth bass can be found lurking in the mingling waters.

Warning signs indicate the mandatory portage trail around the falls and rapids. The Raquette Falls lean-tos and campsites, situated under towering pine trees near the old Mother Johnson's homestead, is a popular stopping point for some groups—as is the put-in for swimming after the long carry. Look for additional campsites dispersed throughout the forest near the rapids if the Mother Johnson area is crowded. The river continues on for another 6.5 miles passing several more lean-tos before the marked turn-off to Stony Creek.

Raquette Falls take-out

There are no services within this section once you depart the village of Long Lake. Plan on camping.

Raquette Falls Carry

PORTAGE DETAILS

#1) Raquette Falls Carry

1.3 miles: Not Easily Wheeled

The canoe landing take-out can be a tight fit for a large number of canoes and gear, and depending on the day or time of summer, could be a busy area. Wheels are not going to be useful, at least for the first half of what is essentially a hiking trail. The initial incline is steep and stepped. Rocks and roots just upset the wheels. As you near the end, particularly around the camping and lean-to areas, the trail is level and wheeling is more viable.

The put-in is past the camping area and lean-to beyond the lower falls. A nice beach makes this an appealing swimming hole after a sweaty portage.

#2) Stony Creek/Stony Pond Area Bridges

Carry (Seasonal)

Two low clearance bridges may require portaging in spring or during periods of heavy precipitation. In low water, you can paddle under them.

POINTS OF INTEREST

* ⭐ Fishing hole at the confluence of the Cold River
* ⭐ Photo op by the broken canoe carry sign
* ⭐ Enjoying some down time in the Raquette Falls area after the portage

SERVICES

None

OVERNIGHT OPTIONS AND DISTANCES FROM LONG LAKE, N.Y.

Long Lake ....<9.5 miles
Lean-tos and campsites are located at regular intervals all along the east shore and north end of Long Lake

Raquette River ....11 miles
Deep Hole lean-to

Raquette River ....15.5 miles
Lower Falls/lean-tos and camping area

Raquette River ....16 miles
Raquette River lean-tos

Raquette River ....22.5 miles
Stony Creek lean-to and campsite

Two additional lean-tos are located between the Raquette River lean-tos and Stony Creek on river right.

Stony Creek to Saranac Lake, N.Y.

NFCT Map: 2
Total Miles: 20
Milepost: 85.5
Portages: 2
Type of Watercourse(s): 1 upstream creek, 3 ponds, 5 lakes,
1 downstream river

The beauty of all three Saranac Lakes is the highlight of this predominantly flat-water portion of the NFCT. A rich landscape of charming boathouses, Adirondack architecture and the unique upper and lower locks on the Saranac River make for a memorable paddle.

A large part of the land surrounding Upper Saranac Lake and Oseetah Lake to the town of Saranac Lake is privately owned and populated. Expect to see summer camps and motorboats. Middle and Lower Saranac Lake offer state camping options, but require reservations or registration at the Lower Saranac Lake ranger station, located around milepost 78.

The entrance to Stony Creek is marked with a sign, but can be confusing to pick upstream through to the Stony Creek Ponds. Springtime flooding may make the area broader than summer and fall levels when the stream is narrower and shallow. The map reflects the total wetland footprint and not the specific channel you need to follow. To assist your bearing, keep your eyes on the underwater plants that undulate in the direction of the strongest current. When in doubt, stay left.

The marked entrance to Stony (Stoney) Creek (in low water)

After making quite a few "S" turns that may make you question whether you are headed in the right direction, the forest opens up as the first of the two Stony Creek Ponds become apparent. Pass under a second bridge into the northern pond where there are campsites and access to the Indian Carry portage.

You won't be spending much time on Upper Saranac Lake as you round Indian Point and continue east into Huckleberry Bay to the Bartlett Carry. From the Bartlett Carry put-in, paddle northeast to the mouth of the Saranac River flowing out of Middle Saranac Lake. A large stand of rushes obscures the river until you near the entrance, which is marked with red and green navigational channel buoys.

The Saranac River sections before and after Lower Saranac Lake feature hand-operated locks. If no one is around, you'll be operating the locks on your own following the instructions posted on a large sign (or portaging around the locks.) If you've never been in a lock before, don't miss this opportunity to experience the rather sedate, but historically significant engineering feat of taming wild rivers.

Experienced whitewater paddlers may be able to avoid the first lock by running the Class II drop, river right. Scout first before attempting. A large boulder is inconveniently positioned near the base of the rapids.

After exiting the lower locks, channel markers indicate the obstacle-free route through Oseetah Lake as it flows into Lake Flower and to the village of Saranac Lake. The carry take-out is to the left of the bridge and dam warning sign where there is a NFCT kiosk. A second take-out option is located just before reaching Saranac Lake on the far eastern shore of Lake Flower at Baldwin Park (identifiable by its tennis courts). This take-out, left of the Route 86 bridge, provides closer access to some additional services but is .5 miles away from the portage route.

Camping without reservations is tricky within this section. There are several beautiful fee-free DEC sites on Stony Creek Pond near the Indian Carry take-out, three sites after the carry on Upper Saranac Lake before Indian Point and one primitive NFCT site in Huckleberry Bay. All of the numbered shoreline campsites on Middle Saranac Lake and Lower Saranac Lake are state-managed and fee-based. Non-fee sites aren't available again until you reenter the Saranac River after Lower Saranac Lake.

The Saranac Lake Islands State Campground headquarters is located east of the Route 3 bridge at the State Bridge boat launch and collects fees for both Middle and Lower Saranac Lake campsites. Like Forked Lake, if a site is open, you can register and pay the same day. The headquarters is close enough to the sites on Lower Saranac Lake to make this somewhat feasible, however, it is impractical to paddle to the campground headquarters and back to the sites on Middle Saranac. Call the local number and have a credit card handy if you wish to stay in an open site on Middle Saranac Lake. Phone numbers and reservation information for these sites can be found on page 211. Overnight lodging is available once you reach the town of Saranac Lake.

Indian Carry trail near Stony Pond take-out

PORTAGE DETAILS

#1) Indian Carry

1.1 miles: Not Easily Wheeled/Wheelable

This ancient portage route enters deep woods with large moss-covered boulders before crossing the Olympic Scenic Byway/Route 3. The carry should be considered in two phases. The first half is a trail that ascends from Stony Creek Pond. It is rooty and rocky. Wheeling will be challenging but not impossible. The second .6-mile section follows a gravel road after crossing Route 3 and is completely wheelable.

Indian Carry sign on Route 3

#2) Bartlett Carry

.4 miles: Wheelable

This carry follows a road for the majority of the portage. From the road, a trail leads to an outlet on Middle Saranac Lake. The take-out is located at a hand-carry boat access, east of a small island, only a short distance into the north (left) arm of Huckleberry Bay. The portage is completely wheelable on the road, although parts are hilly. An interesting photo op appears at the top of one hill by a curve— two large mirrors help drivers see around the blind curves— and allow you to take pictures of yourself and gear.

Bartlett Carry

You are very close to the put-in when you leave the gravel road and head into the woods following the marked trail. Like other challenging portage trails, this one too, is rocky, but the distance is short.

....

POINTS OF INTEREST
- ✵ Photo op by the roadside mirrors
- ✵ Pulpit rock
- ✵ Saranac River locks
- ✵ Camping at one of the Saranac Lake Islands State Campground water access-only sites

Middle Saranac Lake

SERVICES

Saranac Lake, N.Y. (page 214)
Grocery Store, Natural Food (Co-op), Convenience Store, Outfitter, Shuttle, Restaurants, Lodging, Library, Laundromats, Post Office, Bank, ATM, Hardware Store, Medical Facility, NFCT Kiosk

OVERNIGHT OPTIONS AND DISTANCES FROM STONY CREEK

Stony Creek Ponds ....3 miles
Several campsites along far north shore

Upper Saranac Lake ....4 miles
Indian Point (DEC) campsite

Huckleberry Bay Campsite ....5 mile
NFCT primitive site

Middle Saranac Lake ....9 miles
Saranac Lakes Islands State Campground (fee)
(Headquarters at state bridge boat launch 4 miles ahead)

Lower Saranac Lake ....13 miles
Saranac Lakes Islands State Campground (fee)
(Headquarters at state bridge boat launch)

Saranac River ....14.5 miles
Lean-to and campsite near Lower Lock

Saranac Lake ....20 miles
Motels, B&Bs, some accessible from water

Note: Lean-tos on Middle Saranac Lake are part of the state campground (sites #63 and #81) and subject to reservations and fees. Norway Point on Lower Saranac Lake, site #45, also has a lean-to.

Saranac Lake, N.Y., to Union Falls Pond Dam

NFCT Map: 3
Total Miles: 21.5
Milepost: 107
Portages: 3 or 4
Type of Watercourse(s): 1 downstream river, 2 ponds (lakes)

The put-in for the Saranac River is a few hundred yards past the dam beyond the Saranac Lake Police Station following the river walk. St. Regis Outfitters is located along the Trail, river left on Dorsey Street, a very short paddle from the put-in. Besides offering shuttle services, gear, safe boat storage and showers, they provide advice on the upcoming section of the Saranac River's water levels and conditions—especially important if you are a late summer paddler or have questions about the technically difficult rapids between Union Falls Pond and Clayburg. You'll be traveling (or missing) this section of the river for all of Map 3 over the next couple days. Conditions range from flatwater to Class IV rapids and ledges and flows over seven dams requiring portaging. Franklin Falls and Union Falls Ponds offer a break from river paddling on its descent from the Adirondacks to Lake Champlain.

As you leave the village of Saranac Lake, pass under the Pine Street bridge and its short Class I rapids (barely discernible in high water). The river follows Route 3, gently weaving in and out of lowlands and forested ridges. Cemetery Watch lean-to, available to NFCT members, is located just before the low McCasland (aka La Duke) bridge. Depending on your pace, Class II–III Permanent Rapids appears after a two to four hour paddle from Saranac Lake.

Paddlers with the appropriate skill set and craft may be able to avoid portaging and instead run Permanent Rapids. If your palms start getting sweaty with just the thought of committing to a mile of unknown rapids this early in the trip, you can take out and portage along River Road. There are two obvious clearings to the road that are easily discernible from the river. Trail markers, though, often disappear from this area. A high water take-out featuring a stone stairway appears first, just past a roadside guardrail. A low water take-out option is located a few hundred yards farther, past a primitive DEC campsite,

Union Falls Dam in low water

NFCT MAP #

① ② ③ ④ ⑤ ⑥ ⑦ ⑧ ⑨ ⑩ ⑪ ⑫ ⑬

(river left) at the next cleared bank where the road is also easily accessed. The first sign of the rapids appears downriver at this point. Follow River Road to a track and stone stairway leading to a popular camping area and the put-in on Franklin Falls Pond. Paddling the length of the picturesque pond will take you to the portage around the first dam in this segment, at Franklin Falls.

Although River Road parallels the Saranac River, it isn't easily accessible if you change your mind once you pass the take-outs and start running the rapids. There is only one opportunity where the road becomes accessible again—between the second and third series of rapids. You'll need to be on your game looking for the indiscernible take-out as the river bends north, back toward the road, river left.

Like Franklin Falls Pond, Union Falls Pond is a reservoir created by the dammed Saranac river. At low water, submerged trunks show where the former forest once stood. The Union Falls Dam is blocked by a floating barrier.

A well-worn trail can be seen as you approach the point to the right of the dam, but you can paddle closer to the booms where the official take-out exists. This take-out is 40–50' from the dam's falls, where the cable comes ashore, and is initially hard to spot. If paddling in fall, be sure to check out the apple trees before portaging onward.

Several nice camping spots are present on both ponds and adjacent to Union Falls Dam by the take-out. There are no accommodations within this section. Plan on camping.

PORTAGE DETAILS

#1) Saranac Lake, N.Y.
.1 miles: Wheelable

The take-out is left of the bridge/dam on Lake Flower in the village of Saranac Lake. A NFCT kiosk is located on the corner. Cross the street and proceed behind the village police department following the river walk to the put-in just beyond the Route 3 overpass.

#2) McCasland Carry (La Duke Bridge)
Carry (seasonal)

This is a low bridge and in high water, you will need to portage left carrying your boat and gear over and around it. In low water, you can paddle under it.

#3) Permanent Rapids Carry
1–1.2 miles: Wheelable (until trail and stairway leading to river)

The carry follows River Road. The road is level until reaching the dirt track leading to a camping area near the river's outlet to Franklin Falls Pond. The high water take-out, with a stone stairway, appears first. The low water take-out appears a few hundred yards farther downstream the second time the road comes clearly into view—and past a DEC primitive campsite, river left. It is easily accessible above the first set of rips in low water. A weathered wooden cross, nailed to a tree, marks this second take-out.

#4) Franklin Falls Dam Carry
.3 miles: Wheelable

Take out on the left and head over the bridge. (The dam is under a bridge and protected by a barrier.) There are sharp turns in the road leading to the put-in. Keep your eyes and ears open for cars that won't expect to see a boat on the side of the road. Several trails lead from the road well before the guardrail begins, back down to the river.

POINTS OF INTEREST
- ✶ Saranac Lake NFCT kiosk
- ✶ Permanent Rapids
- ✶ View of Whiteface Mountain
- ✶ Bald eagles

N

BOAT
LAUNCH

PUT-IN
(and Campsite)

Franklin Falls
Pond

River Rd

Dinsmore Rd

Access point
to road

LOW WATER
TAKE-OUT

HIGH WATER
TAKE-OUT

Permanent
Rapids

River Rd

Saranac River

Franklin Falls Dam take-out

SERVICES
None

OVERNIGHT OPTIONS AND DISTANCES FROM SARANAC LAKE, N.Y.

Moose Creek Campsite ....**3.5 miles**
  DEC primitive site

Cemetery Watch Lean-to ....**6.2 miles**
  Note: Available to NFCT Members only from Mother's Day to
  Columbus Day by reservation only

River Road Campsites..**9–11 miles**
  Primitive campsite above Permanent Rapids on river left and one DEC
  campsite along River Road (just before reaching the Dinsmore private road),
  accessible only when portaging along the road

Franklin Falls Pond...**12.5–13.5 miles**
  Primitive campsites; several at the end of the Permanent Rapids Carry,
  another on an island and two on the west shore

Union Falls Pond ....**18.5 miles**
  Two primitive campsites on east shore (Bear Point)

Union Falls Pond ....**21.5 miles**
  DEC primitive sites adjacent to take-out by dam

Union Falls Pond Dam to
Bakers Acres, Picketts Corners

NFCT Map: 3
Total Miles: 19
Milepost: 126
Portages: 4*
Type of Watercourse(s): 1 downstream river

* Your paddling skills and ability will determine how many and which portages you'll be doing within this section.

Depending on your love of whitewater, the day will either be potentially thrilling or rather tedious. This section of the Saranac River can be rocky and water levels fluctuate with dam releases and seasonal rainfall. After portaging back to the river from Union Falls Pond, and with ample water, you'll be riding five miles of Class II rapids until you reach and bushwhack around a Class IV–V drop at Tefft Pond Falls. A series of complex Class II–III ledges, drops and hydraulics will demand expert paddling and lining skills from Silver Lake Road bridge to Clayburg. *It is highly recommended that you carefully research the Tefft Pond Falls area. Canoes have swamped, then wrapped around boulders below the falls, prematurely ending trips.* Refer to the NFCT official guidebook, website and forum for more details and consult one of the outfitters in Saranac Lake for seasonal advice.

Because of the degree of difficulty and for safety reasons, many paddlers end up walking along Casey and Silver Lake Roads for most, if not all of this section of the Saranac River. There are only a few places where you can access the road from the river after leaving Union Falls Pond. Many paddlers do feel comfortable paddling the 2.5 mile distance to the Casey Road Access, a signed trail tucked between a set of Class II rapids. However, the access trail hasn't always been easy to locate from the river. And, once you pass the Casey Road Access, there is not another official take-out option until after Class V Tefft Pond Falls.

Even though there is a bridge crossing the Saranac River before entering the Class V Tefft Pond Falls area, property at all four corners of the Silver Lake Road bridge is steep and posted and at present, is not considered to be an access point on the NFCT. The Casey Road Access is one of your

last opportunities to take-out before committing to intermittent whitewater the rest of the way to Clayburg.

Casey Road markers by Union Falls Dam

From Clayburg, the river broadens out for almost two miles until Separator Rapids, a pair of short Class III rapids with a ledge that experienced paddlers may chose to run. Scouting is recommended. The first set appears within sight of the carry take-out and ends by the beach area and road access. The second set of rapids flows under the bridge. After running or portaging, the river again broadens and becomes deeper the rest of the way to Picketts Corners with one break to portage around High Falls Dam and the High Falls Gorge.

Increased signs of industry and agriculture make purifying water from the river questionable. Carry enough water or fill water bottles from local taps from here to Plattsburgh.

A gas station/convenience store is located along Route 3 in Redford, downstream of Separator Rapids, between the Ore Bed Road and Pup Hill Road bridges. It is the only service found within this section until reaching Bakers Acres in Picketts Corners. Union Falls, Clayburg, Moffitsville, Saranac, Elsinore, Cadyville and Morrisonville are hamlets that do not have additional services.

Most of the adjacent land through which the Trail now passes is privately owned and currently no official camping spots exist until you reach Bakers Acres Campground another .8 miles past Picketts Corners. However, three campsite options can be encountered before reaching Bakers Acres. The first is at Trail Rapids by the Casey Road Access take-out on DEC lands where public camping is permitted. Paddlers have reported camping at the point on the upside of the river left cove as well as at the top of the rocky outcrop on the downside of the cove. A second, but typically trashy "party" site, is located where the portage trail emerges from the woods near a beach area and road access by Separator Rapids. A third unofficial site can be found river left, adjacent to the booms by High Falls Dam, before paddling to the carry take-out.

Privately owned Bakers Acres Campground has a swimming pool and showers (and a golf driving range) and welcomes Through-Paddlers. Watch for a small sign, river left, near a mowed path that leads up to the campground area. The Saranac Country Store in Picketts Corners is within walking distance from Bakers Acres.

There are no accommodations within this section. Plan on camping.

AVOIDING THE CLASS III–V TEFFT POND FALLS AREA

There are almost nine miles of discontinuous, and at times, extremely technical whitewater paddling between Union Falls Pond and Clayburg. If you are uncomfortable with these conditions you must either use Casey and Silver Lake Roads for portaging or arrange for a shuttle.

PORTAGE OPTION(S)

Casey and Silver Lake Roads parallel the Saranac River and can be used as a portaging alternative to reach Clayburg. However, there are limited access points and only two options for accessing the road before reaching Tefft Pond Falls.

7.9 miles: Wheelable

Don't put back in on the river after portaging around Union Falls Dam. Instead continue following Casey Road and walk all the way to Clayburg, a distance of just over eight miles. Casey Road joins Silver Lake Road and leads to a hand-carry access back on the Saranac River at the bridge by Route 3.

4.9 miles: Wheelable

Or—paddle for 2.5 miles after putting in below Union Falls Dam, until reaching the Casey Road Access (see portage detail #2a, right) and walk the remaining 4.9 miles of road to the Clayburg put-in.

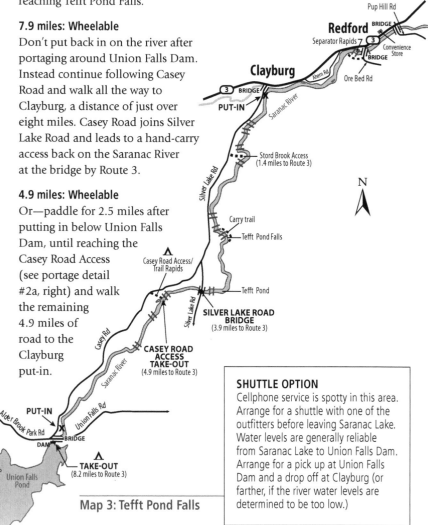

Map 3: Tefft Pond Falls

Pup Hill Rd

Redford BRIDGE

Separator Rapids 7 (3) Convenience Store

BRIDGE

Clayburg Ahern Rd Ore Bed Rd

(3) BRIDGE

PUT-IN Saranac River

Stord Brook Access
(1.4 miles to Route 3)

N

Silver Lake Rd

Carry trail

Tefft Pond Falls

Casey Road Access/
Trail Rapids

Tefft Pond

Silver Lake Rd

**SILVER LAKE ROAD
BRIDGE**
(3.9 miles to Route 3)

Casey Rd

**CASEY ROAD
ACCESS
TAKE-OUT**
(4.9 miles to Route 3)

Saranac River

PUT-IN

Alder Brook Park Rd Union Falls Rd

BRIDGE

DAM

TAKE-OUT
(8.2 miles to Route 3)

Union Falls
Pond

SHUTTLE OPTION

Cellphone service is spotty in this area. Arrange for a shuttle with one of the outfitters before leaving Saranac Lake. Water levels are generally reliable from Saranac Lake to Union Falls Dam. Arrange for a pick up at Union Falls Dam and a drop off at Clayburg (or farther, if the river water levels are determined to be too low.)

PORTAGE DETAILS

#1) Union Falls Dam Carry
.4 miles: Wheelable

Take out to the right of the dam and boom. Several car-accessible primitive DEC campsites are located here. Head toward Union Falls Road, turn left crossing over the bridge. Turn right on Casey Road, and right again past the surge tower to a parking area. Put in upstream of the chain link fence and paddle on river right to stay away from the hydro facility current.

#2a) Casey Road Access/Trail Rapids Portage
4.9 miles: Wheelable (after trail from river to road)

Avoid the technically more difficult water at Tefft Pond Falls and beyond by taking out here, well before reaching the Silver Lake Road bridge. The river left DEC trail/access to Casey Road appears very quickly between the second and just above the third set of Class II rapids. (The distinction between these sets of rapids may not always be clear.) Keep a sharp eye out for the take-out. Camping is permitted on this DEC slice of land.

Two helpful landmarks to watch for include:

Casey Road Access/Trail Rapids take-out (looking upstream)

1) An obvious small cove or bay, river left, below the second rapid *as if* another river is entering; and

2) A noticeable height of rock referenced as a scenic rock "gate." The outcrop juts up from the river at the downstream side of the mouth of the cove.

You can slip into this cove to scout the take-out that appears less than 100 feet after passing it and the rock "gate." Remain river left along the quickwater and eddy out when the carry take-out comes suddenly into view.

After carrying your gear through the .25 mile woods path to the road, turn right, following Casey Road to Silver Lake Road, and put back in on the river below the bridge that connects to Route 3 at Clayburg. The Casey Road Access can be buggy in spring and early summer.

#2b) Tefft Pond Falls
300 – 500 feet: Carry

This is an unmaintained trail and difficult to spot from the river. It is located about 1.5 miles downstream from the Silver Lake Road bridge, river right, at the top of the falls/Class V drop. Portage right, around the falls, and put in just below it. Immediately ferry over to river left and line to avoid running the Class III–IV ledge staircase that quickly follows a Class II rapid. This is a tricky area where canoes have been trapped and destroyed.

Optional Portage: Stord Brook Access
1.4 miles: Wheelable (after trail)

If you've paddled to and around the Tefft Pond Falls, there is still one more option to either avoid a section of the Class III–IV ledges or to use as an exit for a self-rescue. Access an unsigned fishing trail above Stord Brook, river left, from a set of rapids. From the rough trail, follow Silver Lake Road to the put-in at the bridge at Clayburg.

#3) Separator Rapids Carry
.8 miles: Wheelable (after trail)

The bridge over the second set of Separator Rapids in high water

A fishing trail parallels the rapids on river right. Portage signage often disappears from this area. To ensure a shorter and easier carry during low water, avoid taking out at the first indication of a trail, instead continue carefully advancing closer to the head of the rapids watching for the well-used take-out opposite a small island. The low water take-out is within sight of the rocks or white line of water signaling the start of the first drop. In high water, you may want to access the fishing trail sooner. The narrow trail, uneven terrain and any downed trees will make this section impractical to wheel until you emerge from the woods. The rapids are close to a road and you may see people fishing or swimming within the eddies. A "party site" can be found here.

From the rapids, the dirt trail connects to a dirt road and is easily wheelable. Turn left, following it for a short distance where it merges onto Ore Bed Road and crosses over the bridge. After crossing the bridge, lift over the guardrail and head down to the put-in, river left, within a quiet pool downstream of the bridge. Watch out for wild parsnip growing along the faint path in the unmowed hillside. It will burn unprotected skin.

The Redford convenience store can be accessed by water, taking out at a river left grassy lawn .35 miles from the Ore Bed bridge put-in. By foot, continue over the Ore Bed Road bridge and turn right on Route 3, portaging for another .5 miles.

#4) High Falls Carry
1 or 1.4 miles: Wheelable

Paddle beyond the warning buoys and take out at the signed point of land lying between the dam (river left) and overflow power house bay (river right), threading between the two sets of protective barriers in front of each hazard. The banks can be quite muddy when the water is drawn down. Wheel along the hilly

View of "unofficial" campsite from High Falls take-out

and sometimes buggy gravel road. Take time to look at the High Falls Gorge (bushwhack for viewing) before crossing Soper/Pup Hill Road back to one of the two put-in options on the river. The high water option is one mile from the take-out just below the Soper Road bridge, where you will enter Class II rapids beyond the hydro plant. Turn left on Soper/Pup Hill Road to access the high water option. The second, calmer low water option is another .4 miles farther downstream following this same road to the NYSEG public access.

POINTS OF INTEREST
★ Union Falls Dam and steel bridge
★ Surge tower by Union Falls Dam
★ High Falls gorge

SERVICES

Redford, N.Y. (page 215)
Convenience Store

Picketts Corners, N.Y. (page 215)
Convenience Store, Camping

Bakers Acres Campground

OVERNIGHT OPTIONS AND DISTANCES FROM UNION FALLS POND DAM

Casey Road Access/Trail Rapids .... **2.5 miles**
DEC land on either side of the cove preceding the take-out

Separator Rapids .... **10.5 miles**
Unofficial "party" site are located near the take-out, adjacent to the first set of rapids

High Falls Dam .... **14.5 miles**
Unofficial campsite, river left (left of the dam), before reaching the take-out

Bakers Acres Campground .... **19 miles**
Private campground (fee)

NFCT
MILEPOST
148.5

Bakers Acres, Picketts Corners to Plattsburgh, N.Y.

NFCT Map: 3
Total Miles: 22.5
Milepost: 148.5
Portages: 3 to 5
Type of Watercourse(s): 1 downstream river

This diverse section of the lower Saranac River begins in rural New York and includes flatwater, whitewater, wildlife and industry as it finishes the descent out of the Adirondacks to its outlet on Lake Champlain.

Four (or possibly five) portages will make this one very long day ending on a frothy ride through downtown Plattsburgh on continuous Class I–II rapids. Proficient Class II whitewater skills are a must. Great Blue Herons often accompany paddlers between Morrisonville and the Clinton Airfield.

From Bakers Acres, the first seven miles of the Saranac River are deeper and flat. A freshwater spring decants into the river on the left just after the Duquette Road bridge. After portaging around the Cadyville Dam and Kent Falls, the river picks up steam again with six miles of continuous Class I–II rapids that will demand your attention. From mid-summer, low water levels can make for a scratchy, bumpy or impassable paddle. Finally, there are three more portages around dams on the outskirts of the city, before paddling through downtown Plattsburgh to the Plattsburgh boat launch and the NFCT kiosk. (Note: The first edition 2005 map shows the last two dams—Indian Rapids Dam and Imperial Mills Dam—outside of Plattsburgh in the wrong location. Subsequent map updates have corrected this error. The NFCT website's *Trail Updates* link also includes the amended information.)

Neither Indian Rapids Dam nor Imperial Mills Dam have historically had barriers or posted warning signs. Pay close attention to the hazards when paddling this segment. In high water, fast and treacherous Class II+ rapids are present from the put-in at the Treadwell Mills Carry (Fredenburgh Falls) to the Indian Rapids Dam Carry take-out. Indian Rapids Dam is an unprotected breached dam with dangerous hydraulics. The urban section of the river following Imperial Mills Dam also contains debris, tires and concrete rubble.

Due to intermittent construction projects and river remediation work between Saranac Street and Broad or Bridge Street, a fifth portage may be in effect after Imperial Mills Dam, closer to Plattsburgh's downtown. Be prepared to take out when warned and follow any mandatory portage instructions. Check the NFCT website's *Trail Updates* link for the latest information.

There are a few camping opportunities within this section. The first is a primitive NFCT site marked with a 4″ x 4″ post that states "La Pierre Property" and appears a short distance past the Route 22B steel bridge, river left. It has level tent sites and a picnic table, but no other facilities. This campsite is located well before reaching the closed Clinton County Airport area. Another campsite was added in 2015 along the rerouted Treadwell Mills Dam carry. It has a grill, picnic table, sign-in box and privy, and overlooks the Saranac River on the hydropower's property. It can be accessed from a side trail soon after beginning the portage. A third option may be found at Cumberland Bay State Park, three miles northeast of Plattsburgh on Lake Champlain. The state park is accessible from the water after leaving the Saranac River. Campsites are subject to availability without a reservation. Call ahead to inquire before your arrival.

Food and supplies are available in Plattsburgh, most within walking distance from the Broad Street or Bridge Street bridges, although there is no secure place to stash your boat and gear. The Samuel de Champlain Memorial is found river left after passing under the arched stone Bridge Street bridge. An NFCT kiosk is just a little further downstream, river right, at the Green Street boat launch and parking area, after passing under the last (pedestrian) bridge and before reaching the mouth of the river. Lodging can best be accessed from the northern shores of Cumberland Bay.

PORTAGE DETAILS

#1) Cadyville Dam/Kent Falls Carry
2 miles: Wheelable (with a short paddle break in the middle)

Paddle beyond the Cadyville beach and boat landing toward the "Danger Dam" sign (almost to the buoys). Take-out and follow the marked portage and map directions through the village streets to the condemned and closed bridge. Reload, put-in upstream of the bridge, paddle under the condemned graffiti-embellished bridge and immediately take-out again where you pick up the road. Continue to the angler's public access area and the beginning of the 6-mile stretch of Class I–II rapids. This interesting portage includes following a huge green penstock pipe as you descend back down to the river. If you wish to view Kent Falls, paddle upstream .5 miles from the bridge before continuing the second half of the portage. The waterfall is within sight of the base of the Cadyville Dam.

#2) Treadwell Mills Dam/Fredenburgh Falls
.8 mile: Wheelable

In 2015, the former portage following Military Turnpike Road and Carbide Road was rerouted. The safer, improved portage now follows a hydro facility access road on the north side of the hydropower canal. From the hand-carry boat access take-out, located on the far right of the bridge span(s) at the end of a guardrail, cross over Route 190/Military Turnpike Road and turn left. The chain link, fenced-in gravel access road is located within eyesight of the take-out on hydro facility property. A side trail leading to the Treadwell Mills Campsite will be found soon after entering the property and crossing over the water. The portage follows the access road to the put-in upstream of the I-87 bridge within some rapids. In high water, swift current may push the rapids beyond Class II. This access road also continues toward Indian Rapids Dam, where that put-in can be accessed by foot using a connecting road. (See Google Earth.)

#3) Indian Rapids Dam
.1 miles: Not Easily Wheeled/Carry

This portage comes up shortly after the Treadwell Mills Dam portage—as quickly as five minutes if the water is fast and the paddling furious. At lower water levels, it's still only a short fifteen minutes or so of paddling. ***This is a dangerous area.*** Watch for crumbling concrete walls that extend out from both sides of the river. There are no warning signs or booms blocking the breached dam. Do not attempt running. Hazardous hydraulics exist. The portage is currently an unmaintained trail. It will be easier to carry than try to work with the wheels for the short distance on this rough terrain. (Easier, in this instance, is a relative word.) Take out river right following the overgrown trail, up over a steep berm and back down to the river at the base of the dam.

#4) Imperial Mills Dam
.2 miles: Not Easily Wheelable

There are no warning signs or booms signaling the dam, but the industrial red-bricked mill is apparent on your right as you approach and the horizon line disappears. Upon entering the marshy bay, you may see a clearing and trail ahead and on your left before heading east toward the dam. This fishing or party spot may provide you with an unofficial camping option. A trail from the site will also lead you to the put-in, but it makes for a longer portage than from the official take-out. There is another gravel road in the area, so be sure to scout back to the chain-link fence if you do take out earlier.

The official take-out is adjacent to the dam's berm on river left. Take-out and follow the underused trail along the chain-link fence. Make a U-turn around it and head back to the river following a dirt track to the put-in under the utility lines at the base of the dam. If the river is running too fast, continue following the track to a public fishing access area located a short distance farther downstream.

#5) Plattsburgh River Remediation Work
1 mile: Wheelable

As of 2017, a "temporary" but mandatory portage was still in effect within the City of Plattsburgh requiring another departure from the river during remediation work. *Heed posted warning signs.* Construction-related concrete barriers and riverwide cables have been part of the project and create true paddling hazards. A take-out is present on a bend, river left, .5 miles beyond the Catherine Street/Route 22 bridge. A small landing area with steps leads up to the Saranac River Bike Trail and Pine Street. The portage route takes you past a police station and middle school following Pine Street to Broad Street. Turn right, crossing over the Broad Street bridge. Turn left (north) on Peru Street/Highway 9 to Bridge Street. Cross Bridge Street to Green Street. Green Street is slightly right of the Peru and Bridge Street intersection. The road lies between two red brick buildings and leads to the NFCT kiosk and Green Street boat landing.

Additional river remediation work farther downstream is anticipated to be undertaken from 2019 to 2021 and the mandatory portage area would be re-established. Check the NFCT website's *Trail Updates* section and Google Earth for additional information and be prepared to adapt as necessary.

POINTS OF INTEREST
- ✯ Spring entering the Saranac River past Duquette Road
- ✯ Kent Falls (short paddle back upstream after portage to view falls)
- ✯ Giant green penstock along second half of the Kent Falls Carry
- ✯ Great Blue Herons and other wildlife
- ✯ Surfing wave under the Broad Street bridge in downtown Plattsburgh
- ✯ Samuel de Champlain Memorial (river left)
- ✯ NFCT kiosk at the Green Street landing (river right)

SERVICES
Plattsburgh, N.Y. (page 215)
Grocery Store, Natural Food (Co-op), Convenience Store, Restaurants, Lodging, Camping, Library, Laundromat, Post Office, Bank, ATM, Medical Facility, NFCT Kiosk

OVERNIGHT OPTIONS AND DISTANCES FROM BAKERS ACRES
La Pierre Property...**11.25 miles**
NFCT primitive site

Treadwell Mills Campsite ....**15 miles**
NFCT primitive site

Plattsburgh..**22.5–25 miles**
Hotels, motels, B&Bs

Cumberland Bay State Park..**24.5 miles**
State campground (fee)

Vermont and Québec Overview

NFCT Maps 4, 5 and 6

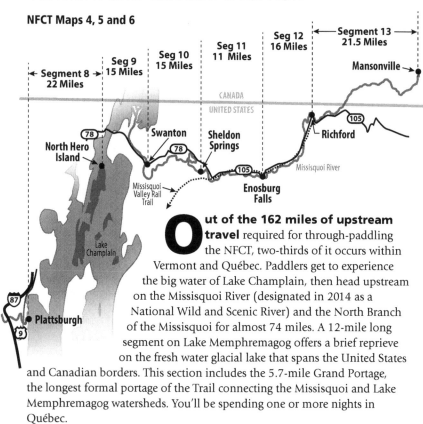

Out of the 162 miles of upstream travel required for through-paddling the NFCT, two-thirds of it occurs within Vermont and Québec. Paddlers get to experience the big water of Lake Champlain, then head upstream on the Missisquoi River (designated in 2014 as a National Wild and Scenic River) and the North Branch of the Missisquoi for almost 74 miles. A 12-mile long segment on Lake Memphremagog offers a brief reprieve on the fresh water glacial lake that spans the United States and Canadian borders. This section includes the 5.7-mile Grand Portage, the longest formal portage of the Trail connecting the Missisquoi and Lake Memphremagog watersheds. You'll be spending one or more nights in Québec.

After checking in at U.S. Customs using the video phone at the Newport Marina, and possibly taking a well-deserved break exploring the town, it's back to paddling upstream for another 30.5 miles on the Clyde River to Island Pond, Vt. The six-mile segment between Newport and Derby Center is considered by many Through-Paddlers to be one of the most challenging parts of the entire trail if paddling and not portaging around the continuous string of Class II–III rapids through which you will need to pole or track.

You'll get a break paddling across Pensioner Pond, before meandering through agricultural pastures and forested lands and a rare natural bog known as an intermediate fen. For the upstream paddler, this area will be a little trickier to negotiate as there are several channels entering and exiting the wetland. It's another five miles to Island Pond where the river flows under an historic hotel, ending at its source at Island Pond.

Island Pond offers many services including some great restaurants. Beyond Island Pond, the Trail resumes downstream on the narrow, twisted and beaver

Map 4: Vermont and Québec

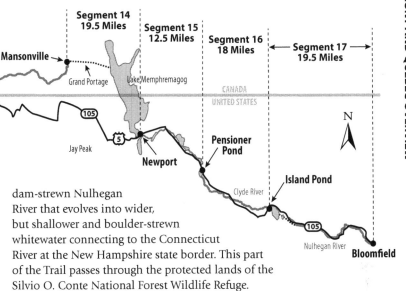

dam-strewn Nulhegan River that evolves into wider, but shallower and boulder-strewn whitewater connecting to the Connecticut River at the New Hampshire state border. This part of the Trail passes through the protected lands of the Silvio O. Conte National Forest Wildlife Refuge.

From the put-in at Nulhegan Pond, the Nulhegan River typically has enough water for seasonal paddling to Wenlock Crossing, but as the river drops in elevation and boulder fields and rapids appear, low water levels will make paddling difficult if not impossible. When water levels are high enough for paddling, the section beyond Wenlock Crossing is challenging and requires a high level of skill. Class III–IV rapids and technical ledges lie within the Upper Gorge and around the Old Stone Dam.

If paddling the Nulhegan is questionable, past Through-Paddlers have either had to walk more of Route 105 or have been able to successfully find rides from locals by asking around. A recreational kayaking tour service operates out of West Charleston on the Clyde River and prefers to shuttle no farther than Island Pond. The Clyde River House, located near Ten Mile Square Road, offers shuttling services upon request. The NFCT organization is constantly partnering with local services and updating its trail directory. Check the website to see if other options become available.

AVERAGE PADDLE TIMES*

Plattsburgh, N.Y., to Enosburg Falls, Vt.	As little as 3 days/as many as 8 Average 4
Enosburg Falls, Vt., to Island Pond, Vt.	As little as 3 days/as many as 7 Average 5.5

* Variables include taking the ferry across Lake Champlain or portaging past sections of the Missisquoi River using the adjacent Missisquoi Valley Rail Trail (MVRT) or roadways.

NFCT
MILEPOST

170.5

Plattsburgh, N.Y., to
Stephenson Point, North Hero Island

NFCT Map: 4
Total Miles: 22
Milepost: 170.5
Portages: 0 or 1
Type of Watercourse(s): 1 lake

From Plattsburgh continue east or northeast through Cumberland Bay, staying within the wind shadow of Cumberland Head and keeping an eye on any heavy boat traffic. Only experienced paddlers should attempt crossing Lake Champlain as dangerous conditions can develop quickly. Check local forecasts before proceeding and consider an early morning or evening crossing when winds diminish. The Grand Isle Ferry is available if conditions are too dangerous for paddling. The ferry departs regularly from Cumberland Head to Gordon Landing on South Hero Island. If paddling, stay well away from the path of the ferry.

After crossing the lake, enter "The Gut" and paddle under the U.S. Highway 2 bridge. As a last resort, Through-Paddlers are permitted to camp at Campmeeting Point at Knight Point State Park. Otherwise continue heading north hugging the east shoreline of North Hero Island. There are several cabins or resorts where accommodations are available between The Gut and Stephenson Point on both sides of the North Hero if you know where to look for them. Although they are slightly off course, island camping is available through the state parks and as part of the Lake Champlain Paddlers' Trail east of North Hero Island.

A stop over at the City Bay Marina on North Hero Island is a nice break where you'll find the NFCT kiosk at the visitor center, a general store with a bakery and a nearby restaurant/inn.

Once you reach the Carrying Place, another mile beyond City Bay, you have two route choices, both of which will get you north to Stephenson Point, the tip of North Hero Island and the location of North Hero State Park. The park is now operated as a day use area, but does allow paddlers to camp in the old campsites.

Hibbard Point north of City Bay, Lake Champlain

INNER PASSAGE

Portage over U.S. Highway 2 or pull yourself through the narrow culvert that joins Alburg Passage. Paddle north through this inner passage to Stony Point/Stephenson Point and North Hero Island State Park. The paddler campsites are accessible from this side of the island.

OUTER PASSAGE

Continue north following the eastern shore of North Hero Island to Stephenson Point. Round the point to reach Stony Point and the North Hero Island State Park.

Access to the paddler-only campsites in the state park is located between Bull Rush and Stony Point on the island's west shore. Look for a LCPT (Lake Champlain Paddling Trail) sign affixed to a tree. A trail leads through the woods to the old campground loops. The sites have picnic tables and fire rings, but are not maintained and offer no other services, including potable water. The sites are notoriously buggy—even in daytime and late summer. After North Hero State Park, there are no other official NFCT camping options along the Trail until Highgate Falls dam, well up the Missisquoi River. There are, however, two private RV resort-type campgrounds located on either end of Hog Island. Campbell's Bay Campground on Donaldson Point offers tent sites.

The motels, lakeside cabins, B&Bs and historic hotels located along the shores of either side of North Hero Island are not always obvious from the water. Plan on camping or lodging.

* * * * * *

Lake Champlain is subject to seasonal blue-green algae blooms. Keep dogs from drinking from the lake and avoid swimming when algae blooms are present. The bright green pea soup looking scum can kill pets and cause severe stomach problems in people. Humans can also develop a rash or other skin irritation from coming into contact with the compromised water.

PORTAGE DETAILS

#1) The Carrying Place
Carry (Optional)

Lift over the guardrails and cross U.S. Highway 2 or pull yourself through the culvert under the highway only if using the inner Alburg Passage north.

POINTS OF INTEREST
★ Grand Isle Ferry
★ City Bay/North Hero NFCT kiosk
★ The Carrying Place

SERVICES

North Hero, Vt. (page 217)
General Store, Restaurants, Lodging, Camping, Library, Post Office, NFCT Kiosk

OVERNIGHT OPTIONS AND DISTANCES FROM PLATTSBURGH, N.Y.

Cumberland State Park..2.5 miles
State campground (fee)

Gordon's Landing ....4.5 miles
Camping permitted at the discretion of the ferry company (very open/public)

Knight Point State Park ....11 miles
Camping with permission of the park manager at Campmeeting Point

North Hero/City Bay ....12–14 miles
Lodging: lakeside resorts south and north of City Bay

Knight Island State Park...15.5 miles
13 sites (fee)

Alburg Passage ....19.5 miles
Lodging

North Hero State Park ....22 miles
Day use park with paddler-only site

Lakewood Campground ....23.5 miles
Private RV campground on Clark Point (fee)

Campbell Resort...28 miles
Cabins and private RV campground with tent sites on Donaldson Point (fee)
Accessible from water/beach area or boat landing

Stephenson Point, North Hero Island to Swanton, Vt.

NFCT Map: 4
Total Miles: 15
Milepost: 185.5
Portages: 1
Type of Watercourse(s): 1 lake, 1 upstream river

The one-mile crossing from Stephenson Point on North Hero Island to Clark Point on Hog Island is short enough, but subject to high waves on this unprotected open stretch of water. If possible, leave early in the morning or paddle later in the evening, or else take care to watch the wind directions at other times of the day.

The NFCT route follows the eastern shore of Lake Champlain around Hog Island and enters the Missisquoi River through the national wildlife refuge at Shad Island, home to hundreds of herons, egrets, cormorants, ducks and geese. Look for colonies of impressively large Great Blue Heron twig nests weighing down tall trees and listen for their loud Jurassic-sounding squabbling and squawking. Once you locate the river, you should have little trouble paddling it upstream. This section of the Missisquoi is flat and broad all the way to Swanton, where you will encounter your first dam.

At present, no official NFCT campsites exist between North Hero Island and the Highgate Falls dam. Private properties line the shoreline from Clark Point all the way to Missisquoi National Wildlife Refuge. However, two private campgrounds are located on Hog Island before entering the Missisquoi. Both are geared toward the full-time camper where space is rented for an entire season and many trailers are permanent fixtures. Campbell's Bay Campground welcomes Through-Paddlers and does offer a tenting area and hot showers for the overnight traveler. Their boat landing and dock is located near shoreline rental cabins on the far northeast end of Donaldson Point.

Camping is not permitted within the refuge, and you will be hard pressed to find any firm ground until you reach Mac's Bend, one of the refuge's boat access and parking areas.

Louie's Landing Clean Drain Dry Station

There are 50 known non-native and invasive species present in Lake Champlain. It is especially important for Through-Paddlers to follow recommended Clean Drain Dry protocols before proceeding upriver.

A signed Clean Drain Dry station with instructions is located at Louie's Landing near Route 78.

Swanton offers some services including restaurants, and a Laundromat close to the portage route. It is also home to the Swanton Motel, located off the river, and about a one-mile walk through town. The motel offers discounts to NFCT members. Reservations may need to be made in advance, especially if you arrive in Swanton on a weekend. Some paddlers have stealth camped at the town park or along a riverside gravel bar. The next official campsite is another 6.5 miles upstream—a two- to three-hour paddle—at the Highgate Falls Dam Carry.

LAKE CHAMPLAIN PORTAGE OPTIONS TO SWANTON

The Missisquoi National Wildlife Refuge is an interesting and worthwhile section of the NFCT not to be missed. Shad Island is home to Vermont's largest Great Blue Heron Rookery. But if conditions on Lake Champlain prove hostile on the day of your passage there are two alternatives for accessing the Missisquoi River sooner by foot.

Route 78 to Louie's Landing

1.1 or 2.6 miles: Wheelable (following roads)

When wind conditions on Lake Champlain are treacherous, some paddlers have taken out at either the boat launch by the Route 78/ Missisquoi Bay bridge or at the hand-carry access point located deep within the protected cove south (Charcoal Bay/Charcoal Creek), around Donaldson Point, that also accesses the highway from Campbell Bay Road. Follow Route 78 to the boat landing at Louie's Landing. Route 78 is a busy highway with little shoulder space and some paddlers might consider portaging along Route 78 to be more dangerous that staying on the water. The distance from the Route 78 boat landing on Lake Champlain to Louie's Landing is 2.6 miles. From the hand-carry access take-out at the end of Campbell Bay Road where it joins Route 78, the distance is 1.1 miles.

Maquam Bay/Route 36 to Swanton

1.8 miles: Wheelable (following roads)

Another alternative to reaching Swanton, if lake conditions warrant safety, is to head directly east from North Hero Island, paddling along the shoreline of Maquam Bay. Swanton Beach, a small lakeside park with a covered picnic area, toilets and boat landing, is located along the upper eastern shore of the bay. The park easily accesses the less busy Route 36 (Maquam Shore Road). Follow Route 36 east (Maquam Shore Road/ Lake Street) for 1.6 miles to S. River Street. Turn left on River Street for one block, then right on Depot Street, crossing over the bridge to put in above the dam beyond the NFCT kiosk.

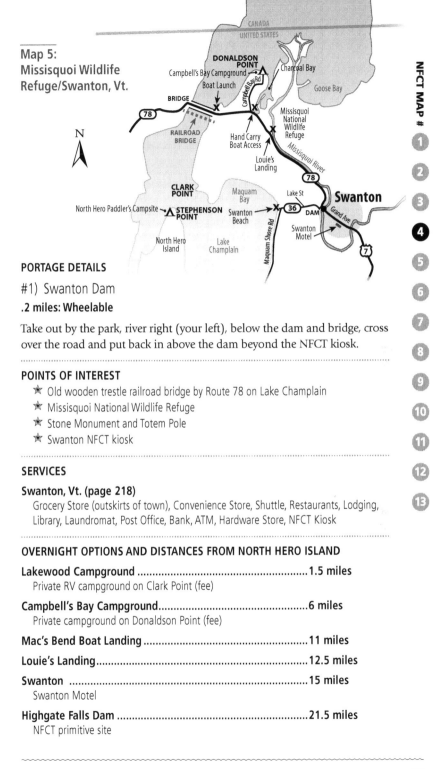

Map 5:
Missisquoi Wildlife
Refuge/Swanton, Vt.

PORTAGE DETAILS

#1) Swanton Dam

.2 miles: Wheelable

Take out by the park, river right (your left), below the dam and bridge, cross over the road and put back in above the dam beyond the NFCT kiosk.

POINTS OF INTEREST

- ☆ Old wooden trestle railroad bridge by Route 78 on Lake Champlain
- ☆ Missisquoi National Wildlife Refuge
- ☆ Stone Monument and Totem Pole
- ☆ Swanton NFCT kiosk

SERVICES

Swanton, Vt. (page 218)

Grocery Store (outskirts of town), Convenience Store, Shuttle, Restaurants, Lodging, Library, Laundromat, Post Office, Bank, ATM, Hardware Store, NFCT Kiosk

OVERNIGHT OPTIONS AND DISTANCES FROM NORTH HERO ISLAND

Lakewood Campground ....1.5 miles
Private RV campground on Clark Point (fee)

Campbell's Bay Campground..6 miles
Private campground on Donaldson Point (fee)

Mac's Bend Boat Landing ....11 miles

Louie's Landing..12.5 miles

Swanton ....15 miles
Swanton Motel

Highgate Falls Dam ....21.5 miles
NFCT primitive site

Swanton, Vt., to Sheldon Springs Hydroelectric Project

NFCT Map: 4
Total Miles: 15
Milepost: 200.5
Portages: 3
Type of Watercourse(s): 1 upstream river

This section marks the beginning of several days of serious upstream paddling. While large segments of the Missisquoi River are flat and deep and the current presents fewer problems under normal to low water conditions, you'll still be finding yourself working hard, poling or needing to get out of the boat to track over occasional gravel bars and through several sets of boulder gardens. Leeches are present in this river. Springtime paddlers will likely experience higher water with stronger currents.

The Missisquoi traverses farmlands and suffers from agricultural runoff. *You absolutely cannot draw or treat any water from this source.* Paddling upstream will be thirsty work. You MUST carry or find municipal water sources. Plan on buying an additional gallon or more of water that can last for the next two to three days. This is imperative—particularly in summer or any duration of oppressive heat.

After returning back to the river from Swanton, paddle 6.5 miles of easy flat-water to the Highgate Falls dam. A small, secluded NFCT campsite (single tent pad and composting toilet) is located a short distance up along the hillside portage trail in the woods. The stone stairway take-out is on your left (river right) adjacent to a small beach area (present during low water).

Back on the river, you will now encounter intermittent boulder fields, gravel bars and/or rapids that will require you to get out and do more tracking or poling and portaging. The last half-mile of river prior to reaching the Sheldon Springs Hydroelectric Project is full of rocks and a swift current.

A private landowner has a fire pit and picturesque campsite carved out along the bank on river right (your left) where the boulder fields begin. "Dickie's Camping Site" is accessible by the ATV trails that line this side of the river bank. Do not be fooled by these trails. They do NOT lead to the portage. Although not an official NFCT campsite, Through-Paddlers have stopped to camp at Dickie's.

Missisquoi River take-out (below East Highgate dam ruins) in mid-summer

While there are two Sheldon Springs portage options, when water levels are adequate to low, Through-Paddlers using a portage cart will want to take the river right (your left) fully wheelable road originating from the Sheldon Springs Hydroelectric Project overflow channel to Shawville Road. This northern take-out is located between the penstock/powerhouse and at the base of an area of rapids extending downstream from the dam. The carry follows a steep 1.2-mile uphill paved road through a solar collection field before heading back down to the river via a soggy meadow path.

In high water or under flood conditions, the northern river right portage becomes inaccessible. When water is released, turbulence makes the low water take-out extremely difficult and dangerous, if not impossible, to reach when approached from downstream. The high water take-out is across the river from the low water take-out. A dark trail enters the woods that connects to an ATV trail and follows the utility line corridor up a steep hill. This slightly shorter, but less wheelable portage option will join roads south of the dam and bridge.

Do not attempt putting in where the Shawville Road bridge crosses the river above the dam. The current can be dangerously swift.

Camping is permitted anywhere on the power facility property as long as you stay well away from equipment and operations. There is also space to stealth camp in the woods near the high water take-out. The next official site, Lussier, is another 5 miles upstream after battling the rapids and the Sheldon Springs Hydroelectric Project portage.

Plan on camping within this section, but be mindful of the potential of rapidly rising water as you near Sheldon Springs. The dam can release water without notice. Camp on high ground well away from the river.

Two convenience stores are located beyond the hydro plant, off trail, along Route 105 east of Sheldon Springs. See the next segment for details.

PORTAGE DETAILS

#1) Highgate Falls Dam
.7 miles: Not Wheelable/Wheelable

From the take-out, ascend the trail, passing by the designated camping spot on your right. This first section is a footpath and not wheelable. Continue up the wooded hill, through a meadow under the power lines where the trail joins a sandy, uneven dirt road leading to a blocked parking area. From the parking area, cross over Route 207 and follow the rocky and potentially washed out trail, crossing Mill Hill Road down to the river and put-in just above the inflatable rubberized dam and the historic iron bridge. This is a rough portage and wheeling may only be an option toward the end of it.

#2) East Highgate Ledges and Old Dam Site
.6 miles or more: Wheelable

Route 78 parallels the river on your left and it's a matter of how far you can easily ascend the river's obstacles and where to best take-out along the river right bank. Cautiously wheel along Route 78. There is one blind curve as you approach the houses that make up East Highgate and very little shoulder. Continue straight for a few hundred yards on Pine Plains

Ledges, exposed during low-water, at the put-in above the Machia Road bridge

Road past the intersection where Route 78 turns east. A marked path beyond private land indicates the put-in above the Machia Road bridge. Paddlers are permitted to access the river even though the land is posted. Track upstream to resume paddling in the flatwater above the ledges, boulder field and cobbles.

#3) Sheldon Springs Hydroelectric Project
LOW WATER (NORTH) OPTION
1.4 miles: Wheelable

The rocky low water take-out is located river right (your left) between the powerhouse/overflow channel and the river. The portage follows a road from the powerhouse and is steep, but paved and easy to follow. The first edition of the official NFCT guidebook and maps state this is .75 miles long. It is not and is instead 1.2 miles to Shawville Road. When you emerge from the hydro project road and arrive at Shawville Road, turn left (north/northeast). Walk another 250 yards east on Shawville Road watching for a field on your right with the path leading back to the river. This path is marked with signage facing the opposite direction that favors portaging downstream paddlers.

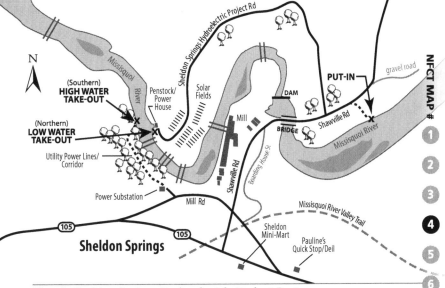

Sheldon Springs

Map 6: Sheldon Springs Hydroelectric Project Portages

HIGH WATER (SOUTH) OPTION
1.25 miles: Not Wheelable/Wheelable

When high water conditions make reaching the low water portage option dangerous or impossible, a second portage (not wheelable until reaching the road) is located on river left, (your right) opposite the low water take-out. In low water, a sandy beach is present and there are several clearings where camping (and partying) is possible. After passing through the woods, ATV trails follow the corridor of a utility line field before reaching Mill Street. While slightly shorter, this portage has historically been unsigned, wetter, less used and more overgrown. Follow the utility lines south-southeast ascending a steep hill to the power substation where a driveway joins Mill Street. Take a left on Mill Street (east) to Shawville Road and turn left (north) at the intersection. Stay on Shawville Road for .5 miles passing a mill before crossing over the steel bridge and river and continue walking farther up the road.

View from the Sheldon Springs low water take-out; looking at the high water take-out

View from Sheldon Springs high water take-out during high water

High water portage following the utility line corridor/ off-road ATV trail connecting to Mill Street

River access at the bridge is not recommended. Banks are steep, mucky and overgrown upstream of the bridge and the dam is located downstream of it. Both the dam and protective barrier can be seen from either side of the bridge.

Follow Shawville Road for several hundred yards farther, passing by the Sheldon Hydroelectric Project signed road leading down to the penstock/powerhouse where the low water take-out option is located. Look for the marked path from the road on your right that leads through the field back to the river.

The put-in area back on the Missisquoi River—after carrying around the Sheldon Springs Hydroelectric Project via Shawville Road

POINTS OF INTEREST
★ Highgate inflatable rubber dam
★ Highgate historic iron bridge

SERVICES
Highgate Center, Vt. (page 218)
General Store, Bakery/Restaurant, Library, Post Office, Hardware Store

OVERNIGHT OPTIONS AND DISTANCES FROM SWANTON, VT.

Highgate Falls Dam Campsite..6.5 miles
NFCT primitive site

"Dickie's Camping Site" ....14.5 miles
Private property with campsite sign

Sheldon Springs Hydroelectric Project...................................15 miles
Unofficial camping anywhere along the low water portage route (grassy area near take-out, in the woods along the road, etc., but away from any equipment or operations)
Unofficial camping on the beach or woodsy areas by high water take-out

Lussier Campsite ....20 miles
NFCT primitive site

Sheldon Springs Hydroelectric Project to Enosburg Falls, Vt.

NFCT Map: 4
Total Miles: 11
Milepost: 211.5
Portages: 1 (or 2, if using the rail trail*)
Type of Watercourse(s): 1 upstream river

The Missisquoi River continues with more upstream paddling, ascending rapids and/or portaging. Enosburg Falls offers restaurants, a coffeeshop with WiFi and a coin-op laundry.

From the put-in well above the Sheldon Springs bridge, the river is relatively flat and deep until you reach Abbey Rapids. Depending on water levels, ascending and tracking up the Class II–III Abbey Rapids will be challenging. An alternative option to paddling is to utilize the adjacent Missisquoi Valley Rail Trail (MVRT) and walk or wheel along this packed dirt and crushed gravel pathway all the way to the North Sheldon bridge (or even all the way to Richford). While the Missisquoi Valley Rail Trail closely parallels the river from Sheldon Junction to the North Sheldon bridge, at times it moves farther away and higher up from the river. If you miss the easiest access to the trail, you'll find yourself climbing up a steep hill and possibly having to get yourself and your gear over a four-foot high wire fence.

It can take several hours to ascend the mile of rapids in low water. You will likely run out of drinking water on a sweltering, muggy day and there are few houses along the banks to ask to have your water bottles refilled if in need. Sheldon Springs has some services, but the closest mini-mart is located on Route 105, a half mile to one mile away in the opposite direction of the Trail (depending upon your take-out location).

The first convenient option for water and food is located two miles upstream of the hydroelectric project along the Missisquoi in Sheldon Junction. As of 2016, a pizzeria and creemee stand (formerly managed under the names of Chur-Chillin's and Devyn's) was located close to the Route 105 bridge. You won't immediately see the business from the water. The Missisquoi Valley Rail Trail can also be easily accessed from the business. Take out at the steep banks by the Route 105 bridge. (See "Alternative Portage Option," below, for more details.)

The second option is found at The Abbey Restaurant, located along the rail trail, another two miles past Sheldon Junction. It also can be accessed from the restaurant's riverside picnic area, but only after completing your grueling ascension of Abbey Rapids. The Abbey maintains a mowed path from the river to the restaurant. If you stop here for food or drink while following the recreational trail, this could be an alternative put-in to North Sheldon bridge, which is another .75 miles farther along the MVRT by foot.

From the North Sheldon bridge, the six remaining paddling miles to Enosburg Falls are smoother with only the occasional need to punch through some current or get out and walk if the water is low. There are ledges just below the Enosburg Falls dam that can be tricky to ascend, especially in high water, but a high water take-out option is available near St. Albans Street before reaching the ledges and dam. The high water carry transports you though village streets passing by or close to the services this larger town offers, but you will miss seeing the scenic gorge just below the Bridge of Flowers and Light.

Three official camping options are present within this section. Lussier is an NFCT site located just before ascending Abbey Rapids, river left (your right). You will bypass it if you are portaging along the rail trail on the opposite bank. The NFCT Brownway campsite was added in 2016. It is located about .75 miles upstream of Lawyers Landing, river right (your left) within a Vermont Land Trust conservancy area. A trail leads to the site from a stone ramp. Camping is also permitted at the privately owned, but more exposed, Lawyers Landing put-in area.

Enosburg Falls offers many services including restaurants, an outfitter, lodging, a Laundromat and a quaint little library.

PORTAGE DETAILS
#1) Enosburg Falls Carry
HIGH WATER OPTION
.5 miles: Wheelable

This first take-out option is located well below the ledges and the dam. Take out river right (your left) downstream of Enosburg Falls where a small red brick utility building can be seen from the river. The hand-carry boat launch accesses St. Albans Street. Follow St. Albans Street and cross the river on West Enosburg Road/Route 108. The Lawyers Landing put-in is located on your left off West Enosburg Road, above the dam and the Bridge of Flowers and Light (where the NFCT kiosk is located.) Many services can be accessed north from the intersection of St. Albans Street and Route 105/108 prior to crossing the bridge.

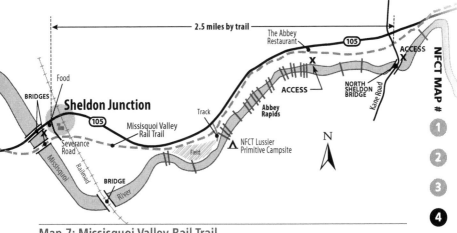

NFCT MAP #
① ② ③ ❹ ⑤ ⑥ ⑦ ⑧ ⑨ ⑩ ⑪ ⑫ ⑬

Map 7: Missisquoi Valley Rail Trail

LOW WATER OPTION
.2 miles: Wheelable

Continue ascending the river, tracking over Class I–II ledges, rapids and strong current. Take out river left (your right) at the stone shoreline and staircase to access Duffy Hill Road. Follow Duffy Hill Road north, passing by the Bridge of Flowers and Light to West Enosburg Road (Route 108), turn right to access Lawyers Landing across the street on the left.

---

*ALTERNATIVE PORTAGE OPTION
#2) Missisquoi Valley Rail Trail (MVRT)
From Route 105/Severance Road intersection: 2.5 miles to Kane Road (and 7.5 miles to Enosburg Falls, Vt. or 17 miles to Richford, Vt.) Wheelable

The best opportunity to access this recreational trail prior to ascending the Abbey Rapids is located at Sheldon Junction. Take out, river right (your left) on the upside of the first of two bridges. (The first bridge is Route 105. The second bridge is an old railroad bridge now part of the Missisquoi Valley Rail Trail.) The banks by these bridges are very steep and unimproved. A slice of land leads up from the river at the Route 105 bridge to a pizzeria (as of 2016). The business located here was formerly run as Chur-Chillin's and Devyn's. Ask permission to walk through the private backyard en route to the Route 105 and Severance Road intersection. The Missisquoi Valley Rail Trail is accessible a few blocks from the intersection following Severance Road, east, behind the feed mill.

The next closest access to the rail trail after the Route 105 bridge is present beyond the third bridge (an operational railroad), after the river bends and before the first set of larger rapids. Past paddlers have bushwhacked through riverside brush to a farm field visible from the river. Follow the riverside edge of the field, eastward to a track that intersects the rail trail at the top of a hill. Note that this land is posted, from the road, as private.

If you continue onward and beyond the second set of rapids (which at first seem similar in comparison to the rapids you ascended near Dickie's Camping Site before reaching Sheldon Springs), you will now be in Abbey Rapids with the sounds of Route 105 and the elusive rail trail continuing to move farther away from you atop the increasingly steep hillside.

After by-passing Abbey Rapids by trail, return to the river either at The Abbey Restaurant's riverside picnic area or by turning right where the MVRT intersects Kane Road .75 miles ahead. Head south toward the North Sheldon bridge. The river can be accessed on upside of the bridge, river right (your left). Cross over the guardrail and put in at the shoreline ledges. In high water, however, these ledges may be underwater making access and launching difficult.

The Missisquoi Valley Rail Trail continues through Enosburg Falls and ends in Richford.

Enosburg Falls Dam in low water

POINTS OF INTEREST
* Iron railroad bridges
* Enosburg Falls library
* Enosburg Falls dam
* Bridge of Flowers and Light
* Enosburg Falls NFCT kiosk

SERVICES

Sheldon Springs, Vt. (page 219)
Convenience Stores, Lunch Counter (off trail)

Sheldon Junction, Vt. (page 219)
Pizza/Ice Cream Stand; Access to the rail trail

Enosburg Falls Dam in high water

Enosburg Falls, Vt. (page 219)
Grocery Store, Convenience Store, Outfitter, Shuttle, Restaurants, Lodging, Camping, Library, Laundromat, Post Office, Bank, ATM, Hardware Store, NFCT Kiosk

OVERNIGHT OPTIONS AND DISTANCES FROM SHELDON SPRINGS

Lussier Campsite ....5 miles
NFCT primitive site

Enosburg Falls ....11 miles
Lawyer's Landing camping permitted at field near put-in
Lodging

Brownway Campsite..11.75 miles
NFCT primitive site (Nature trail, picnic table, privy. Limit 10 people/night. No fires.)

NFCT
MILEPOST

227.5

Enosburg Falls, Vt., to Richford, Vt.

NFCT Map: 5
Total Miles: 16
Milepost: 227.5
Portages: 1 to 2
Type of Watercourse(s): 1 upstream river

The goal of this segment is the town of Richford, Vt., still paddling upstream on the Missisquoi; still needing to get in and out of your vessel as conditions dictate. If you haven't already experienced "the smell of money," you will within this section. Fertilizing fields with manure is a common agricultural practice and you'll see, hear and smell several of Vermont's more than 1,400 dairy farms.

If water levels are low, the river may be scratchy in route to Richford, but there are none of the continuous boulder fields or rapids to track through compared to Abbey Rapids. The Samsonville Dam ruins (a quarter mile plus series of gravel bars, ledges, rock gardens and ruins) and Magoon Ledge breaks up an otherwise flat section of river. There are no established portage trails around either of these obstacles.

Under normal water conditions, the first seven pastorally scenic miles from Enosburg Falls can be paddled fairly quickly. Route 105 and the Missisquoi Valley Rail Trail continues to accompany you on your left as Jay Peak rises ahead on your right.

The NFCT Doe campsite, a pretty site located on a hill overlooking the river, about a mile away from East Berkshire, is on your right (river left) if you need a place to stop before reaching Richford. Another NFCT campsite ("Believe It or Not") was added to the Trail in 2013 a short distance south of Richford. It is located on the eastern shore of the overflow canal, downstream of Davis Park. As you paddle closer to Richford, watch for a narrow point marking the beginning of the large island south of the town. Turn right on a channel (river left) that ends up skirting the eastern side of this island. This is the overflow canal. The campsite is located a short distance from the turn-off on your right (river left bank.) If you stay at this campsite, return to the main channel back on the Missisquoi in order to pick up the Trail and find the take-out at Davis Park. Do not continue north on this overflow channel. It ends up above Davis Park and is obstructed by a concrete barrier.

Take out at the stone stairs leading up to Davis Park, where camping is also permitted. The park has a small covered gazebo, picnic tables and port-a-potty. Or, you could get a room at the Grey Gables Mansion B&B just across the street from the park. The proprietors welcome Through-Paddlers and offer a discounted rate. The breakfasts are awesome.

PORTAGE DETAILS

#1) Samsonville Dam
A few hundred yards or more:
Not Easily Wheeled

Track the vessel through the dam remains or pull out along the bank, river left (your right). A dirt tractor trail parallels the river along the edge of a farm field. You'll likely

Tractor trail adjacent to the ruins of the Samsonville Dam

need to bushwhack through riverside grasses and slippery banks to gain access from—and back to—the river. A riverside residence is located above a bend in the river, about halfway through the ruins where the largest drop occurs. You may want to request permission to access the not easily accessible trail. Follow the trail and put back in above the dam remains and ledges.

#2) Magoon Ledges
Carry (Optional)
If low water makes tracking difficult, unload and carry over the exposed ledges.

POINTS OF INTEREST
* ✯ Enosburg Falls ice deflectors
* ✯ Samsonville Butterchurn Factory ruins
* ✯ Magoon Ledge
* ✯ NFCT kiosk at Davis Park

SERVICES

Richford, Vt. (page 220)
Grocery Store,Convenience Store, Restaurants, Lodging, Camping, Library, Post Office, Bank, ATM, NFCT Kiosk

OVERNIGHT OPTIONS AND DISTANCES FROM ENOSBURG FALLS, VT.
Doe Campsite ....**10.3 miles**
NFCT primitive site
Richford "Believe It or Not" Campsite ....**15.5 miles**
NFCT primitive site
Richford, Vt. ....**16 miles**
Primitive camping at Davis Park
Grey Gables Mansion B&B

NFCT
MILEPOST

249

Richford, Vt., to Mansonville, Qué.

NFCT Map: 5
Total Miles: 21.5
Milepost: 249
Portages: 2
Type of Watercourse(s): 1 upstream river, 1 upstream stream

① ② ③ ④ **⑤** ⑥ ⑦ ⑧ ⑨ ⑩ ⑪ ⑫ ⑬

Although this section covers 21.5 miles, you are likely to divide up this mileage—and the following section—more leisurely. The 5.7-mile Grand Portage lies ahead and where you stay over the next night or two will dictate how and when you tackle it. Québec offers the chance to savor a little French Canadian culture along the Trail. Mansonville is a larger town with an excellent bakery and other services that may tempt you to linger a bit longer.

The first seven miles between Richford and the border will also prove challenging for upstream paddlers. It is not uncommon for summer and fall Through-Paddlers to end up portaging along Route 105/105A due to exceedingly low water levels. There are no carry options, no established shuttle services and no easy way to get around the most troublesome areas. Route 105 and Route 105A (Glen Sutton Road) is not easily accessible once you leave Richford and commit to the river.

An almost two mile section of braided islands prior to reaching the Stevens Mills area creates continuous Class 1 rips at high water or exposed gravel fields at low water. If it is getting late in the day, the Coons family welcomes paddlers to camp on their riverside property located river left (your right) after the islands. The NFCT has established a campsite here in partnership with these trail enthusiasts.

After passing by the cement wall remnant of the old mill, river left (your right), there is one last set of the largest rapids to ascend within this area. However, an exposed cobbled shoreline provides a route to carry around it. You'll need to cross clear-running Stanhope and Mountain Brooks before putting back in above the head of the rapids. You can now return to paddling—mostly fast-running flatwater—up to the border. Lucas Brook joins the river just before reaching the U.S. Border Patrol take-out, creating a final set of up to Class II rapids.

Have your passport ready as you enter Canada. Until a formalized trail is established leading from the river to the Canadian customs office, the easiest way to enter the country is by taking out river left (your right), at the signed trail that appears just before the green steel international bridge on the U.S side. If you feel comfortable doing so, leave your gear here and follow the trail leading up to the U.S. customs office. (Check in with the U.S. customs office to let them know what you are doing.) Cross over the bridge by foot and present yourself to the Canadian Border Service Agency office, which is open 8 a.m. to 4 p.m., seven days a week to check in. Return to the river on the U.S. side and continue paddling upstream passing under the international bridge. Although entering the country without a vehicle is no longer the rarity that it once was during the Trail's infancy, the U.S. Border Patrol may still question Through-Paddlers.

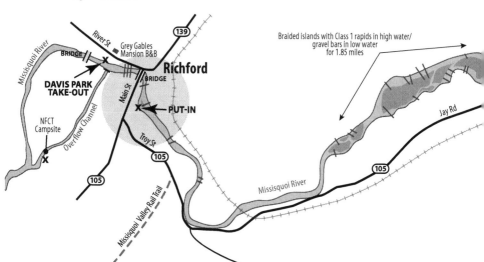

The Missisquoi River is decidedly deeper and less challenging to paddle once you cross the U.S./Canadian border and you may be able to put on more miles in one day than you've been able to do over the past few days. There are still the occasional low spots or areas of stronger current to punch through, just less of them.

After passing under a bridge that leads to the hamlet of Glen Sutton (as of 2016, no services were available) another hour of paddling will bring you to the shore of Canoe & Co., an outfitter and shuttle business on your right (river left). Francois (Frank) and his family are big trail supporters and offer camping on their property. You can also arrange a shuttle with him for the 5.7-mile Grand Portage.

The Missisquoi continues lazily northeastward, flowing by the occasional sandbar and offering up some current or exposed boulders at the site of the ruins of an old bridge by Ruiter Brook.

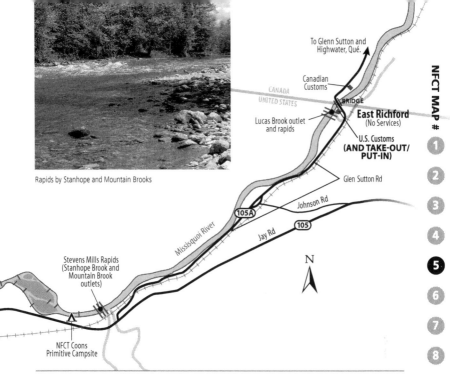

Rapids by Stanhope and Mountain Brooks

To Glenn Sutton and Highwater, Qué.

Canadian Customs

CANADA
UNITED STATES

BRIDGE

East Richford
(No Services)

Lucas Brook outlet and rapids

U.S. Customs
(AND TAKE-OUT/PUT-IN)

Glen Sutton Rd

Johnson Rd

105A

Jay Rd   105

Missisquoi River

N

Stevens Mills Rapids
(Stanhope Brook and Mountain Brook outlets)

NFCT Coons
Primitive Campsite

Map 8: Stevens Mills Islands and Rapids

Another two miles will bring you to Camping Nature Plein air (formerly Camping Carrefour) on river right. The private campground is divided into two sections. As a Through-Paddler, you'll pass by the "rustic" section first, which appears as a mowed, park-like area with 30 riverside campsites and picnic tables. This area extends around a bend in the river for a quarter mile. You cannot easily access these sites from the water because the banks are very steep and the poison ivy abundant. Paddle an additional quarter mile to the small floating dock that also serves as the arrival point for their recreational kayak service, O'kataventures. This take-out provides the closest access to the camp office. The office is located away from the water, at the top of a hill in a house by the road. (Canadian) coin-operated hot showers are available and the office/camp store offers treats and basic camping supplies for sale.

Another mile beyond Camping Nature Plein air, you'll turn left (north), heading upstream on the North Branch Missisquoi River. The confluence is opposite a two-story house before reaching the Route 243 bridge. This twisting and possibly tree-strewn stream leads to Mansonville. In spring, the stream may overflow its banks creating lakes out of surrounding fields, but in summer, the stream becomes so narrow you may question whether you are following the right water way. Eventually the take-out for Mansonville comes into view after two to three hours of paddling, four miles from the bridge north of Highwater. Don't be enticed to take out too early to reach the road. At least two paths look like they may be portage trails, but hang tight until you get to the well-marked landing that leads up to the informational kiosk and the Mansonville welcome sign. If you miss this take-out, you will find yourself within steep banks approaching the waterfall and surrounded by private property.

Mansonville has many services including a grocery store, convenience stores, restaurants and Boulangerie Owl's Bread bakery (days and hours of operation vary). Check ahead to confirm if lodging is available. Former inns have closed, but new ones may have opened. Air BnB's may also be an option.

Portage through town to Secteur Nautique, the small riverside park where a dock provides access back to the river.

Plan on camping. In addition to Canoe & Co. or Camping Nature Plein air, past paddlers have camped in the centrally located, but very exposed Mansonville town's square or at the more secluded Secteur Nautique put-in. The unofficial campsite near the put-in can be located by following the path around a gate just beyond a sign. There is room for one tent by a picnic table. Beavers frequent the pool by this picnic area. It is not advisable to draw water from beaver-infested waters as they are known carriers of giardia, a particularly nasty intestinal parasite.

PORTAGE DETAILS

#1) Richford Carry
.5 miles: Wheelable (along roads)

After passing under a bridge, look for the stone steps that lead up from the river to Davis Park, river right (your left). From Davis Park, turn right and follow River Street to Main Street, crossing over the Missisquoi River/Route 105 bridge for .4 miles. Head toward the riverside gas station located within one block of the bridge and use an old stairway to the right of it that accesses the grassy field behind some buildings. Go past the power substation and descend toward the river. Depending on water levels this access area at the riverbank could be steep and slippery.

The portage route will also pass a grocery store located just over the bridge on your right.

#2) Mansonville Carry
.7 miles: Wheelable

Take out at the steps and well-used trail leading to a welcome sign and NFCT kiosk. The portage begins from the shoulder of Route 243 on the outskirts of the village before sidewalks appear. Take care portaging around a blind curve, then ascend the hill toward Mansonville. It feels steep at the end of a long day, but not nearly as steep as the Sheldon Springs Hydroelectric Project portage. The climb ends at the town's square. Continue through the village passing by the bakery and proceeding downhill to the signed entrance and put-in at Secteur Nautique. The park is adjacent to a grocery store where a pay phone also is conveniently located. If you haven't made shuttle arrangements with Frank at Canoe & Co, and have changed your mind about walking the Grand Portage, you still have an opportunity to give him a call. (Local call with Canadian coins.) International calling rates may apply if you use a mobile phone.

POINTS OF INTEREST
- ✶ International bridge at East Richford
- ✶ Canoe & Co.
- ✶ Beach areas along the Missisquoi for swimming
- ✶ Bridge ruins by Ruiter Brook
- ✶ Mansonville falls
- ✶ Mansonville town park and historical walk
- ✶ Boulangerie Owl's Bread (bakery)
- ✶ Secteur Nautique

U.S. border take-out trail (looking downstream toward Lucas Brook rapids)

SERVICES
Glen Sutton, Qué. (page 221)
Shuttle, Camping

Highwater, Qué. (page 221)
Camping

Mansonville, Qué. (page 221)
Grocery Store, Convenience Store, Restaurants, Bakery, Lodging (confirm), Library, Post Office, Hardware Store, NFCT Kiosk

OVERNIGHT OPTIONS AND DISTANCES FROM RICHFORD, VT.

Coons Campsite...**4 miles**
NFCT primitive site (knock on front door of house for permission)

Canoe & Co....**12 miles**
Private campsite (fee)

Camping Nature Plein air ....**16 miles**
Private campsite (fee)

Mansonville ....**21.5 miles**
Lodging (confirm with NFCT website or by researching)
Town Square (unofficial campsite)
Secteur Nautique picnic area (unofficial campsite)

Mansonville, Qué., to Newport, Vt.

NFCT Maps: 5 and 6
Total Miles: 19.5
Milepost: 268.5
Portages: 1
Type of Watercourse(s): 1 upstream stream, 1 lake

If you've arranged for a shuttle from Canoe & Co., you'll likely will be getting picked up at Secteur Nautique and taken to Perkins Landing leaving you with only the twelve mile section of Lake Memphremagog to paddle.

Otherwise, from Secteur Nautique, paddle a few more miles meandering upstream on the North Branch of the Missisquoi to the unmarked Chemin Peabody bridge take-out that accesses the Grand Portage. The portage follows the steep road of Chemin Peabody before descending to Perkins Landing on Lake Memphremagog. Be sure to have your water bottles filled and perhaps purchase additional water at the convenience store before heading out. Portaging paddlers will pass the Jewett General Store near the end of the carry, a welcome reward. In addition to cool drinks and groceries, the store offers sandwiches, ice cream and Boulangerie Owl's Bread bakery items.

Having arrived from different inland waters that could contain aquatic invasive species, expect to have your boat washed at the Perkins Landing boat washing station. A valid washing certificate (fee—Canadian dollars) is required for travel on Lake Memphremagog. Camping is also permitted at the Perkins Landing picnic area at the discretion of the park's manager.

You'll be paddling several hours before checking in with U.S. customs via a videophone at the Newport Marina. It is a good idea to obtain a weather forecast before starting out. Lake Memphremagog's open expanses mean waves can kick up with little warning. Steep cliffs border much of the western Canadian side of the lake and the shoreline is privately owned. Boathouses provide the only option for seeking safe refuge if in peril.

An NFCT campsite, constructed in 2013, is located within a small, sandy cove near Eagle Point, just south of the border on the east shore of the lake. Camping is also available at Prouty Beach, a city-owned, fee-based campground in Newport, Vt. The campground has hot showers and coin-op laundry facilities. Tent sites are near the beach area. Check in at the park's

The Grand Portage

entrance booth upon arrival to avoid confusion or setting up in a site reserved for someone else. Reservations are helpful, but only necessary during holiday or tournament weekends.

Newport is a small city with lodging options, stores, a natural food co-op, restaurants and other services. The NFCT kiosk is located away from the marina and U.S. customs videophone—at the east end of the waterfront boardwalk and downtown area. More services are located between Newport and Derby Center, at the I-91 interchange.

PORTAGE DETAILS
#1) Grand Portage
5.7 miles: Wheelable

The approved (but less-than-ideal) take-out is upstream of the bridge on the northwest side at Chemin Peabody. The landowner has granted permission for accessing the portage route here from the river. All four corners of the bridge are steep and undeveloped. Follow the quiet road passing rolling pastures, pretty houses and leafy forests over the St. Francis/Missisquoi watershed divide. The portage begins with a long, uphill climb that rises almost 600' in elevation over the first 3.5 miles. An open vista, bordered by manually placed boulders on the south side of the road, marks the apex of the carry's ascension. Look closely at the rocks and you will see signs of prehistoric "Stonehenge" etched petroglyphs. From here the portage descends 780' in elevation to Perkins Landing. At the end of Chem Peabody, turn right onto the busier Chemin Du Lac road, for .5 miles. Turn left on the dirt road past the Jewett General Store and follow this steep road .7 miles to the put-in at Perkins Landing.

Chemin Peabody petroglyphs

Newport marina and location of U.S. customs

POINTS OF INTEREST

⭐ "Stonehenge," faint petroglyphs on roadside stones, adjacent to a farm field, after cresting the hilltop plateau

⭐ Mont Owl's Head rising on your right

⭐ Jewett General Store near the end of the Grand Portage

⭐ Newport Marina/U.S. customs video phone

⭐ Interpretive boardwalk along Newport's waterfront

SERVICES

Perkins Landing, Qué. (page 221)
General Store, Camping (with permission of the park manager)

Newport, Vt. (page 221)
Natural Food Co-op, Convenience Store, Outfitter, Shuttle, Restaurants, Lodging, Camping, Library, Laundromat, Post Office, Bank, ATM, Hardware Store, Medical Facility, NFCT Kiosk

OVERNIGHT OPTIONS AND DISTANCES FROM MANSONVILLE, QUÉ.

Perkins Landing, Qué. ....7.5 miles
Unofficial camping

Eagle Point, Lake Memphremagog..14 miles
NFCT primitive campsites on east shore, just south of the Canadian border

Newport, Vt. ....19.5 miles
Prouty Beach camping (fee)
Lodging

NFCT
MILEPOST

281

Newport, Vt., to Pensioner Pond

NFCT Map: 6
Total Miles: 12.5
Milepost: 281
Portages: 3 or more
Type of Watercourse(s): 1 upstream river, 1 lake, 4 ponds

The NFCT traverses the entire length of the Clyde River—upstream from its outlet on Lake Memphremagog to its source at Island Pond—and is detailed over the next two chapters. Luke O' Brien, of the NorthWoods Stewardship Center, has written an excellent overview of the entire river in his publication: *Clyde River Paddling and Fishing Guide.* Although written from the perspective of the downstream paddler, he further breaks down the Clyde into ten mapped sections. The 56-page pamphlet can be ordered through the center's website at *www.northwoodscenter.org.*

While the first section of the Clyde River from Newport to Salem Lake constitutes only a few miles of the NFCT, it is arguably one of the toughest sections of the Trail for Through-Paddlers. Steep banks with overhanging trees and strainers flank the narrow, swift-flowing river making tracking extremely difficult amidst boulder fields. In places, discarded tires litter the river bed. It is not recommended that any water be drawn or treated from this section of the Trail. Be sure to fill up your water bottles at a tap or buy bottled water prior to leaving Newport.

The NFCT established a portage in 2015 that helps paddlers avoid the most difficult section of continuous rapids near Derby Center. The Yale Dale portage allows paddlers to take out upstream of the Interstate 91 bridge following a marked trail through the adjacent farm to a road. The portage also includes a campsite with a lean-to.

Your ability or desire to fight continuous sets of challenging rapids or low water while ascending the Clyde River will determine the number or length of portages you do within this stretch. Some paddlers have opted to portage five miles from Newport to Derby Center or even on to Salem Lake following Route 5. Be aware that Route 5 is a very busy highway and Route 105/5A leading to Salem Lake lacks a substantial shoulder. Another option is to extend the distance of the Clyde Street bridge carry following the less busy back roads around Clyde Pond. These alternative routes pass many services near the Interstate 91 intersection and in Derby Center including an ice cream/creemee stand by the North Country Union Junior High.

Shuttle services are available if you wish to avoid all of the rapids or roads. The Great Outdoors in Newport can provide a ride, subject to availability. The service is only possible if a vehicle and driver are around at the time of your arrival. Clyde River Recreation is a rental outfitter operating from West Charleston that offers shuttle services along the Clyde River.

The ascent of the Clyde River begins by paddling from Newport, out of Lake Memphremagog toward, but not into, South Bay. Pass under the Route 5 and railroad bridges and immediately head north (turn left). The river parallels Route 105/5 for a short distance before veering east.

Haul through and/or portage around Class II–III+ rapids, the remains of an old dam and the hydro facility to placid Clyde Pond, a nonmotorized scenic reservoir with an undeveloped shoreline and two campsite options. You now face the option of portaging three additional miles of roadways or sticking to the river. Keep an eye out for informal riverside bushwhacking paths and the official Yale Dale portage to help you maneuver around the more difficult spots. From the Bridge Street boat access near Derby Center there is still a series of Class II–III rapids awaiting you—wedged within the undeveloped but picturesque tree-lined valley—as you make your way to Salem Lake.

The Clyde River quietly resumes out of Little Salem Pond meandering between fields and cedars for 2.3 miles before reaching the Fontaine Road bridge near West Charleston and the start of two sets of boulder gardens and ledges. The NFCT guidebook describes the section between the bridge and the powerhouse as a run of Class II+ ledges that only expert paddlers should attempt. For the upstream Through-Paddler, this means reaching the powerhouse involves tracking up these same obstacles. Most paddlers will likely wish to consider taking out by the Fontaine Road bridge and carry once again along Route 105. The upside of taking out here is that you will be portaging through the village of West Charleston and passing Scampy's Country Store and Deli. Many Through-Paddlers like to stop here to eat. The downside is that your portage follows the busy highway, but only for a short distance this time.

Some paddlers have chosen to continue portaging along Route 105 ascending to the bridge put-in after Great Falls, bypassing tiny, but scenic Charleston Pond. This adds an additional mile of portaging along the steep and narrow highway, but eliminates the Great Falls portage.

There are many overnight opportunities between Newport and Salem Lake. Two primitive camping options (no facilities) exist on Clyde Pond. Hidden Leaf, the eastern shoreline site, is accessible only by boat. Pond View, on the northwest shore, includes a portage option connecting to Crawford Road. Hotels are located near the I-91 interchange and a lean-to can be found along the Yale Dale portage.

Coutt's Campsite was added to the Trail in 2014. It is located on the northeast shore of Salem Lake and has a picnic table and sign-in box. Public restrooms are available at the adjacent Lake Salem Beach House Park. You could also reach the campsite following Route 111 for another two miles by foot, if portaging an alternative route via West Street or Derby Center. (See page 109/110).

Privately owned Char-Bo Campground (hot showers and laundry facilities) is located between Salem Lake and Little Salem Pond. Char-Bo Campground can be accessed by paddling to the Vermont Department of Fish and Wildlife David H. Wood Memorial Access Area (located on the southeast end of Salem Lake) and portaging across Hayward Road uphill to the campground entrance.

After paddling beyond Little Salem Pond, your camping options are limited to an NFCT campsite established on the south end of Charleston Pond near the take-out. The campsite is also accessible by road and irresponsible visitors sometimes leave this site trashed. The adjacent land is posted. Your next reliable opportunity to camp isn't until Ten Mile Square Road, more than another nine miles upstream.

Restaurants, stores and lodging can be found near the I-91 interchange, and in Derby Center.

PORTAGE DETAILS

#1) Clyde Street /Upper Clyde Street to Clyde Pond

If you do decide to commit to upstream travel, there are four opportunities to leave the river before reaching Clyde Pond ascending Clyde Street and upper Clyde Street. Upper Clyde Street parallels the river to the north.

PORTAGE OPTIONS

1.2 miles from Western Avenue Bridge

The take-out is river left (your right) immediately after passing under the Western Avenue bridge where a boat access is located by a field. This is the earliest and easiest take-out point. This is also the longest portage option. Turn left and portage up Clyde Street, crossing over the Clyde Street bridge and the Clyde River, then turn right on upper Clyde Street. When upper Clyde Street ends at the "T" intersection, turn right on Crawford Street, heading .1 miles toward the Clyde Pond dam. The put-in is located from a marked path north of the dam.

1 mile from Clyde Street Bridge

After passing under the Western Avenue bridge and paddling another .2 miles through flatwater with increasing current, take out by the fishing trails, river left (your right), near or at the next (Clyde Street) bridge.

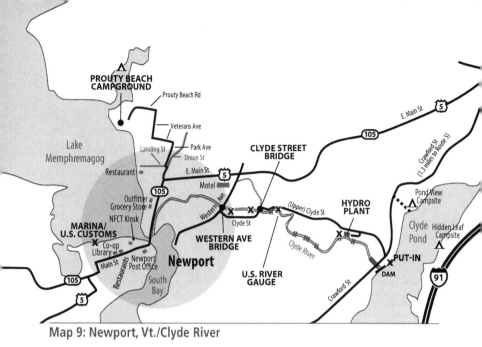

Map 9: Newport, Vt./Clyde River

Some small rapids begin to appear upstream of the bridge before turning into Class II–IV. Turn right on upper Clyde Street. From here the road continues to steeply ascend all the way to the put-in on Clyde Pond.

.8 miles from Upper Clyde Street Access
A USGS river gauge adjacent to a clearing and fishing access provides another opportunity to reach upper Clyde Street after ascending through boulder fields.

.4 miles from Hydro Plant Mandatory Carry
If you've made it up this far, you now will leave the river and portage around the hydro plant to the put-in on Clyde Pond. From the take-out, ascend the hydro plant's driveway for .1 mile to upper Clyde Street. Turn right and pick up the portage route following the steepest hill of the portage on upper Clyde Street, then right on Crawford Street to Clyde Pond.

* * * * *

OPTIONAL CRAWFORD STREET/WEST STREET PORTAGE
CLYDE POND TO DERBY CENTER

3 miles: Wheelable
An alternative route that gets you to Derby Center and provides access to many services while minimizing your contact with busy Route 5, is to extend your portage from Clyde Pond. You can choose to either return to the water paddling for a short distance on Clyde Pond and taking out by the boat

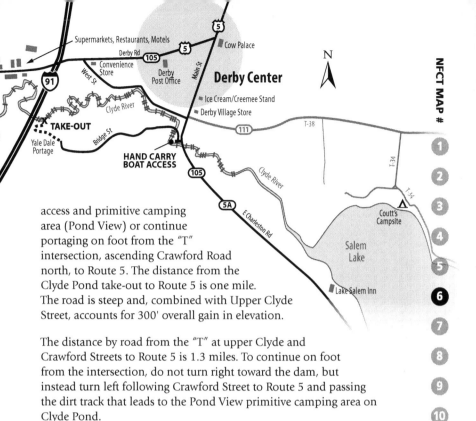

access and primitive camping area (Pond View) or continue portaging on foot from the "T" intersection, ascending Crawford Road north, to Route 5. The distance from the Clyde Pond take-out to Route 5 is one mile. The road is steep and, combined with Upper Clyde Street, accounts for 300' overall gain in elevation.

The distance by road from the "T" at upper Clyde and Crawford Streets to Route 5 is 1.3 miles. To continue on foot from the intersection, do not turn right toward the dam, but instead turn left following Crawford Street to Route 5 and passing the dirt track that leads to the Pond View primitive camping area on Clyde Pond.

Upon reaching Route 5 (E. Main Street/Derby Road), turn right following it for .8 miles to West Street, the first street beyond the I-91 overpass. Turn right on West Street for .8 miles to Route 105/5A. Turn right and follow Main Street through Derby Center for .1 mile.

The put-in back on the Clyde River is another .1 mile down the road off of Bridge Street at the hand-carry access and parking area. There are several more difficult sets of Class II–III rapids to ascend before reaching Salem Lake. Or, you can choose to continue following 105/5A (Charleston Road) to Salem Lake. Lakeside residents have allowed paddler access to the lake from their property with permission.

#2) Yale Dale Portage

1.2 miles: Wheelable (after trail)

This portage avoids Route 105. Take out, river left (your right), after the I-91 bridge and follow the quarter-mile trail through the woods to the farm located at the end of Bridge Street. Follow Bridge Street, east, for one mile to the put-in at the riverside access. Or, do pick up Route 105 from Bridge Street and follow it for an additional 1.25 miles to Salem Lake, accessing the lake with permission of the private landowners.

#3) West Charleston Pond Dam
HIGH WATER OPTION
.5 miles: Wheelable (on roads)

Take out downstream of the Fontaine Road bridge before reaching West Charleston. A rusting car skeleton identifies the take-out. In summer, the riverside banks are brushy and stinging nettles are present. Houses with riverside yards, river left (your right) present the easiest take-out option, but ask permission first. Otherwise, bushwhack to the road from the take-out. Turn right on Fontaine Road for .1 mile, then left on Route 105 passing by local businesses in the small village. Take the first left on (unmarked) Durgin Road, crossing a bridge back over the river. (Citizen's Utility Road joins Durgin Road just after the bridge on your left.) Turn right on Gratton Hill Road and take the second driveway, right, to the trail that leads to the put-in above the dam. Put back in above the warning buoys.

LOW WATER OPTION
.4 miles: Wheelable (until trail)

If the current isn't overpowering or if you choose to stay on the river a bit longer until the mandatory carry begins, track under the Fontaine Road bridge and continue ascending through two short, but impressive, Class II ledges and rapids. Take out river right (your left) by the powerhouse after the river's bend. Follow Citizen's Utility Road from the powerhouse and turn left on Durgin Road, picking up the portage route information listed above that leads you to Charleston Pond.

#4) Great Falls Carry
.3 miles: Wheelable (after trail)

Take out at the far south end and left channel of Charleston Pond where camping is permitted. Follow the trail that leads up past the Barton Electric powerhouse to Great Falls Road and Route 105. Turn right crossing the Route 105 bridge and put in, river left, above it.

The Clyde River is wider and slower from here to Pensioner Pond. Clyde River Recreation is located along Route 105 just before reaching Pensioner Pond via water or road.

....

POINTS OF INTEREST
- ✯ Class II–IV rapids (depending upon water levels)
- ✯ Clyde River hydro dam
- ✯ Ice cream/creemee stand near Derby Center
- ✯ Great Falls gorge

SERVICES

I-91 Interchange (page 222)
Grocery Store, Convenience Stores, Restaurants, Lodging, ATM, Hardware Store

Derby Center, Vt. (page 223)
Grocery Store, Convenience Store, Restaurant, Ice-Cream/Creemee Stand, Library, Post Office

West Charleston, Vt. (page 223)
General Store and Deli, Shuttle, Post Office

Surge tower and penstock
near the Clyde Pond dam

OVERNIGHT OPTIONS AND DISTANCES FROM NEWPORT, VT.

Clyde Pond..2 miles
Primitive campsites on eastern (Pond View) and northwest (Hidden Leaf) shorelines

Yale Dale Portage Lean-to.......................................3.5 miles

Salem Lake/Little Salem Pond...............................5-6 miles
NFCT Coutt's campsite on Salem Lake
Private Char-Bo Campground (fee) between Salem Lake and Little Salem Pond

Charleston Pond..10 miles
NFCT Great Falls campsite

Pensioner Pond...12.5 miles
Unofficial, campsite on east shore (corporate property with a beach, picnic tables and an outhouse)

Great Falls Carry take-out on Charleston Pond looking west from campsite (in high water)

Pensioner Pond to Island Pond, Vt.

NFCT Map: 6
Total Miles: 18
Milepost: 299
Portages: 0 to 3
Type of Watercourse(s): 1 pond, 1 upstream river

Paddle through Pensioner Pond and reenter the Clyde River. After a short time, you'll pass by another photo opportunity—a large sculptural turtle—on your left. Continue meandering up the Clyde through forests and farmlands. At times it will seem as though you are making 180-degree turns, and in essence, you are.

Despite the number of trees blanketing the banks and lying in the water, the river between Pensioner Pond and Ten Mile Square Road is maintained and kept open for recreational day use. This section of the Clyde is quiet and the current is generally mild. Beaver dams and blown-down trees can be more frequent after the fen, between Five Mile Square Road and Island Pond.

The navigationally challenging fen lies between Ten Mile and Five Mile Square Roads. In high water or when the leafed-out alluvial thickets block your view, a GPS may be helpful for determining the main channel. For more details and advice, see page 116.

Although some paddlers have elected to portage the 2.5 miles along Route 105 from Five Mile Square Road to Island Pond, the next section of the Clyde River passes through cedars and undeveloped shorelines and is very beautiful. There are only two sections of fastwater within this segment that occur a mile or so after leaving Five Mile Square Road and "the Tubes." Remnants of a logging-era dam and a boulder garden will likely require you to carry around these two obstacles. There are no established portages. Bushwhack along the banks through the forest or track, if possible.

The river will continue to narrow as you paddle amid cattails and over beaver dams the closer you get to Island Pond. Arrive at the village by paddling *under* an historic hotel and onto the lake; the source of the Clyde River.

The Clyde near Cross Road

NFCT MAP #

The village of Island Pond has many services including lodging, some restaurants and a grocery store. Camping is available at the private Lakeside Camping on the far east-southeast shore or at Brighton State Park located on Spectacle Pond. The state park can be accessed en route to the Nulhegan Pond Carry. See page 118 for details.

Lodging is also available at the Clyde River House located along the north side of the fen. The owners, Bill Manning and Pat Moyer, are trail supporters who also operate a seasonal farm stand adjacent to the Ten Mile Square Road boat launch. They are happy to dispense fen paddling advice as well as offer camping and shuttle services.

The most photographed turtle on the NFCT

If you don't reach Island Pond, you likely will need to consider camping at the Five Mile Square Road boat launch adjacent to Route 105, or stealth camp. In low water, there are sand bars and some forested areas along the river where a tent could fit, but none on public lands. There is also a long ignored picnic area-like clearing a few twists of the river beyond Five Mile Square Road. An old track accesses Route 105, but this unofficial site is more secluded than either of the boat launches.

Lakeside Camping, on Island Pond, has showers and a coin-op laundry and is open mid-May through Labor Day. Brighton State Park, on Spectacle Pond, offers 21 lean-tos and 61 tent sites as well as coin-operated showers. The park is open Memorial Day through Columbus Day. Sites are typically available any time before July 4 or on weekdays thereafter, but may be booked over busy summer weekends. Call ahead to reserve, if possible, for either campground.

Map 10: Navigating The Fen

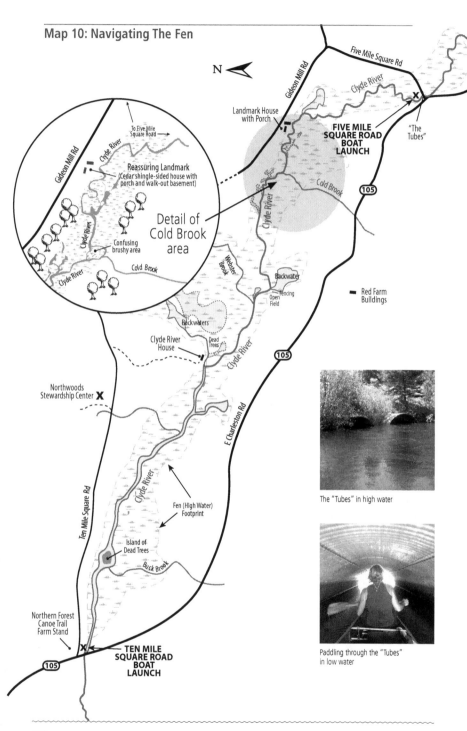

N

Five Mile Square Rd

Clyde River

FIVE MILE SQUARE ROAD BOAT LAUNCH

Gideon Mill Rd

Landmark House with Porch

X "The Tubes"

Cold Brook

105

Detail of Cold Brook area

To Five Mile Square Road →

Clyde River

Gideon Mill Rd

Reassuring Landmark (Cedar shingle-sided house with porch and walk-out basement)

Clyde River

Confusing brushy area

Cold Brook

Clyde River

Webster Brook

Backwater

Fencing

Open Field

Red Farm Buildings

Backwaters

Clyde River House

Dead Trees

Clyde River

105

Northwoods Stewardship Center X

E Charleston Rd

The "Tubes" in high water

Clyde River

Fen (High Water) Footprint

Ten Mile Square Rd

Island of Dead Trees

Buck Brook

Paddling through the "Tubes" in low water

Northern Forest Canoe Trail Farm Stand

105

X

TEN MILE SQUARE ROAD BOAT LAUNCH

THE FEN

Finding your way through the fen between Ten Mile Square Road and Five Mile Square Road is tricky when the channel of the Clyde River is less obvious. A fen is a boggy, wetland area with communities of rare plants into which many secondary streams flow and backwater pools form.

First, be sure to stop and visit the Northern Forest Canoe Trail Farm Stand across the road from the Ten Mile Square Road boat launch. The farm stand is open from mid-May through October. In addition to selling fresh vegetables and frozen ice-cream treats, Bill and Pat offer advice on navigating the fen and where to camp. You can also arrange an overnight stay under a roof at the Clyde River House with them, pending availability.

While water levels could dictate the level of navigational complexity, there are a few landmarks that may help you follow the correct upstream course. Keep in mind wetlands are in a constant state of flux and conditions may be other than described.

Generally speaking, the strongest channel of the fen's central maze-like configuration, and the not-always-obvious Clyde River, weaves between Route 105 and Dolloff Mountain and back again. Attempt to locate and remain within the main channel. Look for signs such as bending aquatic plants or river bottom sand ripples suggesting the path of the strongest current.

Another tip—with the exception of beaver dams—this section of the Clyde River has traditionally been kept free of dangerous obstructions like strainers. Any signs of cut openings is reinforcement that you are paddling the Clyde and not one of the other area feeder streams.

From Ten Mile Square Road follow the Clyde upstream passing large stands of dead trees where ospreys nest. In high water, this area becomes more pond-like. Keep Route 105 on your right, paddling river left.

Once you go by the large island of dead trees, start bearing river right (your left). Staying to the north side of the fen may help prevent you from inadvertently entering dead end backwaters that are more present river left (your right). If the course of the river is not obvious, a loose guideline is to continue choosing left leading channels that will keep you moving along the northern edge of the fen in the direction of Dolloff Mountain.

Look for the screen porch of the two-story Clyde River House on the north shore, west of an area of backwaters. A south-southeast channel "turn-off," river left (your right) is located just before the property. The Clyde now starts weaving back toward the direction of Route 105. Webster Brook will enter river right and in spring and high water, this open area becomes more pond-like. Don't be fooled into thinking this is the river's direction.

The next challenge is locating the main channel as it heads east. The correct "turn" is adjacent to a large backwater pond. The backwater can be identified by an open farm field running along its western edge and bordered by a fence. Route 105 is only .25 miles beyond the field, but out of sight. Red farm buildings can be seen to the south, set back high on a hill across Route 105, opposite the "turn". The river now begins to significantly narrow as it snakes its way through sweet gale and alluvial shrub thickets.

The Clyde may seem to disappear where Cold Brook enters from your right (river left) within a network of connecting channels and fen vegetation. More than one paddler has mistakenly followed Cold Brook in the past. Instead follow the (possibly) less intuitive left channel (river right) through the brushy area.

Your final landmark indicating you are in the home stretch is coming upon a two-story cedar shingle-sided house with a porch facing the river, outbuildings and a large lawn on river right (your left). A dozen or so more twists of the river, and perhaps the sound of vehicles heard on Route 105, and "The Tubes" appear, marking the end of the fen section. "The Tubes" are a pair of huge culverts through which you can paddle under normal to low water conditions at Five Mile Square Road. Early spring paddlers may need to carry around them in high water.

From here, the Clyde winds its way through forests as you head toward Island Pond. After passing the outlet of Oswegatchie Brook, you'll need to bear right three times to get there. The first split appears less than .5 miles after ascending the old dam ruins. Follow the right (river left) channel paddling for about one mile. Look for the next right turn where the river again splits. This is where Pherrins River joins the Clyde. Another .5 miles will get you close to Island Pond and the final right turn that leads a short distance between cattails, under the hotel and out onto the lake. This section is not routinely maintained. Expect beaver dams and the occasional blown down tree.

ACCESSING BRIGHTON STATE PARK AND CAMPGROUND

If you would like to camp at Brighton State Park you'll need to first register at the park office and pay for a campsite. The state park is accessible by two means.

By Foot/ Island Pond Access

One option of getting to the park is by utilizing the take-out listed as part of the original Nulhegan Pond Carry. Paddle across Island Pond and depart from the day use beach area located on the far south end of Island Pond (the left beach of the two beaches seen as you paddle across the lake.). From the beach, turn left and walk .5 miles along Lakeshore Drive to the park's entrance on the right. You'll be adding more road miles this way, but will pass the park office on your way into the park.

By Water/Spectacle Pond Access

The second option is to portage first from Island Pond to Spectacle Pond following the Nulhegan Pond Carry detailed in the next section. The portage originates from the Lakeside Campground beach. Brighton State Park is accessible from the water at the park's swimming beach, which is located in the south end of Spectacle Pond, or from waterside campsites. From the beach, paddlers will need to follow the road for .3 miles to reach the office located well away from the sites, near the park's entrance off of Lakeshore Drive. If comfortable, leave your gear at the beach or at an open campsite instead of hauling it to the office and back again. Early season travelers can paddle right up to a site or lean-to prior to Memorial Day weekend.

PORTAGE DETAILS

#1) Five Mile Square Carry (The Tubes)
Few hundred feet: Carry
Only necessary when water levels are high.

#2) Old Logging Dam Ruins
Few hundred feet: Carry
In high water, the breached dam forms a nice tongue with standing waves that will be difficult to track up. In low water, exposed logs and remnant ruins create a different set of obstacles in which to contend. In either situation, carry around using a river side of your choice.

#3) Boulder Gardens/Rapids
Few hundred yards or more: Carry
The carry route is not maintained. Portage gear around the Class I–II rapids if too difficult to ascend. Higher water and stronger currents may require a longer carry along the brushy shoreline. Be prepared to bushwhack.

POINTS OF INTEREST
- ✯ Large turtle past Pensioner Pond
- ✯ The fen
- ✯ Osprey nests
- ✯ The "Tubes"
- ✯ Paddling under the hotel in Island Pond

SERVICES
The Fen Area (page 223)
Lodging, Camping, Shuttle, Farm Stand

Island Pond, Vt. (page 224)
Grocery Store, Convenience Store, Shuttle, Restaurants, Lodging, Camping, Library, Post Office, Bank, ATM, Hardware Store, NFCT Kiosk

OVERNIGHT OPTIONS AND DISTANCES FROM PENSIONER POND
Stealth ....4–6 miles
Cedar-lined riverbanks between Toad Pond and Cross Road

Ten Mile Square Road..9 miles
Unofficial camping at boat launch

Clyde River House (fen area)...10.75 miles
Lodging (fee) or camping

Five Mile Square Road..14.5–15 miles
Unofficial camping at boat launch
Unused picnic-like area adjacent to Route 105 slightly farther upstream

Island Pond, Vt....18 miles
Lodging

Lakeside Camping ....19.5 miles
Private campground (fee) on far end of Island Pond

Spectacle Pond..20.5 miles
Brighton State Park camping (fee)

Beaver dam near Island Pond (in high water)

NFCT MILEPOST

318.5

NFCT MAP #

Island Pond, Vt., to Debanville Landing, Bloomfield, Vt.

1
2
3
4
5
6
7
8
9
10
11
12
13

NFCT Map: 6
Total Miles: 19.5
Milepost: 318.5
Portages: 4 to 6
Type of Watercourse(s): 3 ponds, 1 downstream river

The Nulhegan River is a unique ecosystem full of wildlife, native trout and great birding, but due to the location, degree of difficulty and/or seasonal low water levels, many Through-Paddlers miss covering part or all of this free-flowing river. While the first half originating out of Nulhegan Pond typically has deep enough water—thanks to numerous beaver dams— there are no services at Wenlock Crossing to assist paddlers around the Class II–IV Upper Nulhegan Gorge or when navigable water is absent before reaching the confluence of the Connecticut River at Debanville Landing.

This segment begins either by first paddling across Island Pond or departing from one of the campgrounds east of the village of Island Pond. The original 3.3-mile portage, described in the first edition guidebook, began at the park's Lakeshore Drive day use area and boat access and followed a dirt road around Spectacle Pond. In 2013, the Island Pond– Nulhegan Pond Carry was rerouted adding Spectacle Pond to the Trail and reducing the distance of the portage following Route 105. The take-out is now located on the east side of Island Pond at Lakeside Camping.

From the put-in on Nulhegan Pond, it can take between four and five hours to paddle the 7.25-mile winding upper portion of the Nulhegan River to Wenlock Crossing. Expect to cross numerous beaver dams as well as blown down trees.

The toughest stretch of the Nulhegan is near the Silvio O. Conte National Wildlife Refuge Visitor Center, about four miles by river from Wenlock Crossing. *Only expert paddlers with the appropriate whitewater skills should consider running the section after Wenlock Crossing.* The center is out of sight at the top of the hill, but adjacent to the Nulhegan, river right. A riverside nature trail provides only a brief reprieve around a few sets of rapids. You can use it for portaging or scouting, but it will not get you around the Upper Nulhegan Gorge.

About three miles past the Wenlock Crossing/Route 105 bridge, the river will start picking up speed and dropping into technical Class II–III boulder fields and rapids. The sight of the first erratics parked in the water indicates you have reached the beginning of technical whitewater. You'll need to use lining skills and/or coaxing your vessel through the boulder gardens where rocks are set too close together to allow paddling.

One-half mile or so, past the erratics and first signs of the rapids, two small islands will split the river into three channels. In high water, expect a few Class II+ situations where the river rejoins and just before it bends sharply left (north). The bend will suddenly reveal an iron trestle railroad bridge signaling the Upper Nulhegan Gorge/Moore portage, a mandatory take-out. The take-out is only about 75 yards downstream from the bridge and just several yards above swiftwater leading to the long Class IV ledge/chute. The bridge crosses the pool in the river and the portage take-out is river left, at the bottom of it. *In high water catching the take-out is must-make maneuver.*

After putting back in below the chute, the river continues for two miles to the next Route 105 bridge crossing. The Lower Nulhegan Gorge/Old Stone Dam portage take-out is located here, river right. Using Route 105 as a portage, paddlers may dodge the lower gorge and Class III-IV rapids.

AVOIDING THE NULHEGAN GORGES OR LOW WATER CONDITIONS BY FOOT

If running the lower Nulhegan exceeds your skill set or is too shallow, you will have to consider a different means of getting ahead to the next section of navigable water, the Connecticut River. Route 105 is a remote, yet busy, two-lane highway that many paddlers use as a portage option from Wenlock Crossing.

From the bridge at Wenlock Crossing the distance to:
- The Nulhegan River (hand carry access) is 5.25 miles
- The East Branch Nulhegan (Route 105 bridge) is 5.4 miles
- Debanville Landing (Connecticut River) is 8 miles

Route 105 also passes by a covered moose viewing platform, 1.75 miles from Wenlock Crossing. The Silvio O. Conte Visitor Center (WiFi, bathroom, water) is another .8 miles beyond the platform.

SHUTTLE SERVICES

There currently are no established shuttle services located within the village of Island Pond, but both Bill Manning (Northern Forest Canoe Trail Farmstand/Clyde River House) and Clyde River Recreation offer service to this area. Arrange for a shuttle prior to departing Island Pond. Cell phone service is unreliable or non-existent.

An *active* railroad parallels the Nulhegan River and Route 105 for several miles—from the beginning of the whitewater section by the Silvio O. Conte Visitor Center to the old Stone Dam (and even beyond to Bloomfield).

There are no services after leaving Island Pond. Plan on camping at one of three official options located within this section. An enclosed timber frame hut and Confluence Campsite was added to the Trail in 2016. It is accessible following the rerouted East Branch Nulhegan (lower Nulhegan Gorge) Portage, a short distance before reaching the Route 105 bridge that crosses over the East Branch Nulhegan River. The second site, the NFCT Nulhegan campsite is located river left, just past the confluence of the East Branch of the Nulhegan on the Nulhegan River. It has a sign-in box and privy. The third is a state-managed site situated in the woods behind the NFCT kiosk at Debanville Landing.

PORTAGE DETAILS

#1) Spectacle Pond Carry

.3 miles: Wheelable

An NFCT medallion is posted near a culvert that extends into the lake from the take-out at Lakeside Camping's beach. The private campground is located on the eastern shore of Island Pond, southeast of Island Pond's island. Follow the markers and arrows through the campground, exiting on Lakeshore Drive. Turn right, following Lakeshore Drive for 150 feet. Turn left on Fishing Village Road following it to the Vermont Fish and Wildlife Spectacle Pond Boat Access. Paddle across the pond for .5 miles in a southeasterly direction, dropping into the lower bay and rounding the small peninsula point that juts out from the east side. Keeping the point on your left, paddle straight toward the shore and the take-out at the signed NFCT portage on state-managed land. No camping is permitted at the take-out.

#2) Nulhegan Pond Carry

2 miles: Not Easily Wheeled (on woods road)/Wheelable (along Route 105)

From the piney take-out on Spectacle Pond, follow the trail/woods road for about .4 miles (it may not be easily wheeled), then cross the railroad tracks. Turn right (east) on Route 105 and walk more than 1.5 miles to the put-in at the culvert where a stream feeds into the pond. Take care portaging along the shoulder of this busy highway. Nulhegan Pond can also be accessed from a dirt road located after passing the airfield. The unsigned dirt road is .3 miles prior to reaching the culvert on Route 105.

Original Island Pond – Nulhegan Pond Carry

This lengthier and buggier 3.3-mile portage is no longer recommended.

Iron railroad trestle at the Nulhegan River's Upper Gorge (in late May after heavy rains), photographed from the nature trail

#3) Snowmobile Trail Bridge
Carry (Seasonal)

This is a low clearance bridge appearing before Wenlock Crossing. In spring or high water you will need to carry around it. In low water, you can paddle under it.

#4) Silvio Carry
.3 miles: Not Wheelable

A riverside nature trail can be utilized for bypassing some of the rapids or for scouting. Take out, river right, where the trail appears. Put back in within sight of the railroad bridge. You will then need to *immediately* and *quickly* *ferry* across the river to the where the trestle crosses the river over a small pool. *This is a must-make maneuver.* The take-out for the Moore Portage (Upper Nulhegan Gorge) is at the end of this pool, river left, *only a very short distance above the Class IV chute.*

#5) Moore Carry (Upper Nulhegan Gorge)
.2 miles Not Wheelable

Mandatory carry around the Class IV chute. The portage starts at the beginning of the upper gorge and ends at the bottom of it. The river left take-out is close to the head of the long Class IV ledge/chute that comes up right after the railroad bridge. *You do not want to miss it.*

The established, but lightly used portage is located within overgrown riverside brush. It may be initially difficult to spot, but is an obvious trail, once found.

Below the put-in at the bottom of the gorge there are still more bony and technical Class II rapids for another .75 miles or so before reaching quieter waters.

#6) Nulhegan Gorge Carry (Route 105 Bridge/Old Stone Dam) or East Branch Nulhegan River

1–1.2 miles: Wheelable (along roads)/Not Wheelable (trail to river)

The improved one mile lower Nulhegan Gorge Portage gets paddlers off busy Route 105 sooner, avoids the notoriously shallow East Branch Nulhegan River and includes access to the enclosed timber frame hut and Confluence Campsite. Take out, river right, upstream of the Route 105 bridge/old Stone Dam. Follow Route 105 .8 miles east to Vermont River Conservancy land with trails leading back to the river, The signed trail, on your right, appears *before* crossing over the East Branch Nulhegan River bridge and includes several hand-carry river access options.

If water levels are high enough, you can also continue another .2 miles along Route 105 and put in at the East Branch Nulhegan bridge. This avoids using the trail, but also misses the Confluence Campsite and hut. Resume paddling on this feeder stream to rejoin the Nulhegan.

POINTS OF INTEREST
- ✶ Wenlock Crossing logging area
- ✶ Remains of the St. Johnsbury Granite Company quarry
- ✶ Silvio O. Conte National Fish and Wildlife Refuge
- ✶ Upper Nulhegan Gorge and iron railroad bridge
- ✶ Moose sightings
- ✶ Debanville Landing NFCT kiosk

NFCT kiosk at Debanville Landing

SERVICES

North Stratford, N.H. (page 225)
Library, Post Office

OVERNIGHT OPTIONS AND DISTANCES FROM ISLAND POND, VT.

Confluence Campsite..16.5 miles
Hand-carry access; enclosed timber frame hut and campsite with picnic table, privy; 12 people/night limit

Nulhegan Campsite...17 miles
(River left just beyond confluence of E. Br. Nulhegan and Nulhegan rivers)
NFCT water-access only primitive site with sign-in box and privy

Debanville Landing..19.5 miles
State-managed primitive campsite, sign-in box

The Nulhegan River at Wenlock Crossing

New Hampshire Overview

NFCT Map 7

```
◄──── Segment 18 ────►
        22 Miles
     Bloomfield
```

New Hampshire is exclusively about river traveling until you reach the town of Errol and cross Umbagog Lake into Maine. The Connecticut and Androscoggin Rivers flow through forests and farmlands and the Upper Ammonoosuc threads its way north of the White Mountains. You'll paddle under picturesque covered bridges in quaint New England villages as well as witness the devastation that a changing economy has brought to this area as you portage around dams in formerly vibrant industrial towns.

Connecticut River

102

Upper Ammonoosuc River

3

Groveton

The first 20 miles is a relaxing paddle down the Connecticut, which is also part of the larger Connecticut River Paddlers' Trail. Then it's back to upstream paddling: 19 miles traveling up the Upper Ammonoosuc River, a 3.8 mile portage along Route 110A followed by a 19-mile segment ascending the Androscoggin.

The railroad will continue to be your companion all the way to West Milan. Anticipate seeing and hearing trains.

The Upper "Ammo" is another body where seasonal water levels may make the river difficult, if not impossible to paddle. You could find yourself frequently needing to get out to pull the boat over sand and gravel bars. There are several ankle-twisting, cobbled areas that will require careful footing especially if algae are present.

The Androscoggin is a larger recreational river. Water is routinely released to create pleasant rafting trips. Unlike the Upper Ammo with its fewer and smaller rapids, the Androscoggin has more than a dozen Class I–II rapids requiring eddy-hopping, tracking, poling or portaging.

There are several towns through which you will be passing over the next few days and it is feasible to plan on sleeping with a roof over your head instead of camping if that appeals to you. The Stark Inn B&B, conveniently located halfway along the Upper Ammonoosuc, is a favorite of paddlers.

Map 11: New Hampshire

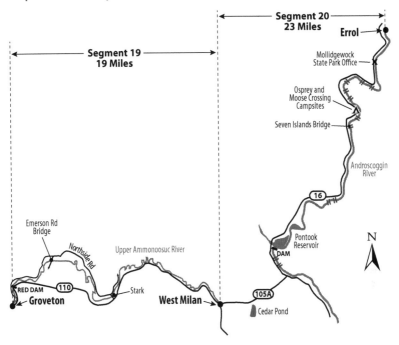

SHUTTLE SERVICE OPTIONS

There are several outfitters and rafting companies that serve the Androscoggin and one in West Milan along the Upper Ammo. Slacking options exist for paddling these two rivers downstream instead of upstream if water levels are too low or if you wish to paddle these river sections of the Trail with, instead of against, the flow.

Note: Paddling any river in a reverse direction or skipping any sections will affect your designation as a Through-Paddler. Please refer to the NFCT Recognition List definitions.

AVERAGE PADDLE TIMES*

Island Pond, Vt., to Errol, N.H.	As little as 3 days/as many as 7 Average 4.5

* Variables include navigable water levels for the Nulhegan and Upper Ammonoosuc Rivers. Late season paddlers often walk or shuttle around these rivers. Some paddlers also have opted to take advantage of paddling the Androscoggin River downstream.

Debanville Landing, Bloomfield, Vt., to Groveton, N.H.

NFCT Map: 7
Total Miles: 22*
Milepost: 340.5
Portages: 0
Type of Watercourse(s): 1 downstream river, 1 upstream river

By this point in the trip, the broad and placid Connecticut River should be easy enough to complete in one day from the state-managed campsite located behind the NFCT kiosk to Groveton, but it is a beautiful stretch of water to leisurely paddle.

The river can be a scratchy near the put-in at the confluence of the Nulhegan and Connecticut Rivers, but the Connecticut soon broadens out with only the occasional gentle rip to break up otherwise flatwater. The river winds through oxbows and around sandbars.

Wildlife is abundant—watch for bald eagles, herons, red fox, deer, otters, mink and ever-present ducks and geese. Ospreys are common and there are nesting platforms located along the river between the two NFCT Connecticut River campsites and the outskirts of Groveton.

Begin your upstream paddle to Groveton on the Upper Ammonoosuc River by literally making a left turn, north, where the two rivers intersect at a "T." The Upper Ammo is decidedly narrower and shallower than the Connecticut. Your speed will significantly decrease and you'll need to get out and pole or track up over smaller rips or pull through areas of stronger current before reaching the Groveton NFCT Normandeau campsite.

Depending on water levels, there may be plenty of sandbars along the Connecticut River where you could presumably pitch a tent, but the locations of the two riverside NFCT sites are at achievable distances where landowners have graciously allowed free camping. Both of these campsites are quite nice with beach areas, although they can be buggy. The Maine Central Railroad Trestle site is located farther away from the river than Samuel Benton, which is perched on a hill under silver maples overlooking the river. The Normandeau campsite is located outside of Groveton .5 miles *before* reaching the first portage, around Weston Dam, on the Upper Ammonoosuc River.

You'll likely hear trains passing by on the opposite bank while camped at any of these sites. If you choose to continue past Groveton, there is no established campsite for another seven miles upstream, almost another full day's "paddle" away. Long-term parking is permitted at the Normandeau campsite for Section-Paddlers.

Groveton offers services including a grocery store, restaurant, motel and Laundromat up to .5 miles away from the kiosk. It also has three dams positioned within the 1.5 mile length of river flowing through the community. Portage instructions are detailed in the next segment.

Plan on camping along the way or staying at the Downhome Motel that can be accessed through the NFCT Normandeau campsite. The NFCT kiosk is located near the covered pedestrian bridge after the Weston Dam Carry.

Mileage for this section is based upon the put-in at the Debanville Landing to Weston Dam, the first dam located on the outskirts of Groveton after passing the NFCT Normandeau primitive campsite.

POINTS OF INTEREST

- ✴ Railroad trestle ruins
- ✴ Osprey platforms
- ✴ Late model tractor and car "riprap" along the banks
- ✴ Groveton covered pedestrian bridge
- ✴ Historic train engine and caboose
- ✴ Groveton NFCT kiosk

SERVICES

Groveton, N.H. (page 225)

Grocery Store, Convenience Store, Restaurants, Lodging, Library, Laundromat, Post Office, Bank, ATM, NFCT Kiosk

Normandeau Clean Drain Dry Station

Treat all waters as though they are infected and follow the Clean Drain Dry protocol when transitioning between the Connecticut River and the Upper Ammonoosuc River.

A signed Clean Drain Dry station with instructions is located at the Normandeau campsite.

OVERNIGHT OPTIONS AND DISTANCES FROM BLOOMFIELD, VT.

Maine Central RR Trestle Campsite ....7 miles
NFCT primitive site

Samuel Benton Campsite ....13 miles
NFCT primitive site

Groveton, N.H. ....22 miles
NFCT Normandeau primitive camping site
Down Home Motel (Access before reaching Groveton through the NFCT Normandeau campsite)

NFCT
MILEPOST

359.5

Groveton, N.H., to West Milan, N.H.

NFCT Map: 7
Total Miles: 19
Milepost: 359.5
Portages: 3 to 4
Type of Watercourse(s): 1 upstream river

It is highly unlikely that most people will be able to paddle this entire section upstream in one day. Past paddlers have ended up stopping at Stark, a charming historic New England village with a B&B but no other services. The NFCT Frizzell campsite, a little more than a mile before reaching Stark, is another practical stopping option after hours of trudging your way upstream.

The tree-lined, fast moving, but shallow, Upper Ammonoosuc River is challenging—primarily due to its depth, or lack thereof. Upstream paddlers could find themselves frequently out of the canoe tracking through boulder fields and rock gardens, and pushing over gravel and sand bars from the Red Dam outside of Groveton to Stark. A good summer rainstorm elevating the water level will help keep you from bottoming out over the scratchy areas.

After the boulder field above Stark, the river is a little deeper, a little less rocky and comparatively a little less challenging to paddle (or track). Gord's General Store, located upstream in West Milan, offers shuttle services if water levels are too low for paddling.

There are three notable areas that will require careful footing for the upstream Through-Paddler. The first section is around a series of braided islands encountered about two miles beyond Red Dam. You might still be out of the boat a lot after Red Dam pushing over low gravel bars and islands, but there are fewer boulders. The current is fast, the rocks many, the trees occasionally blown down. It could take several hours to ascend the few miles to the Emerson Road bridge, which is the second section that will give you pause to reconsider paddling upstream—especially knowing that Emerson Road connects to Northside Road which leads to Stark.

A boulder field creating Class I–II rapids extends from the bridge to the mouth of Nash Stream. Cobblestones are algae covered and slippery. You'll most likely be tracking or poling more than paddling for this stretch, but you will

The Upper Ammonoosuc River above Emerson Road bridge and past Nash Stream

be rewarded for your efforts as you head east past Nash Stream where the river drops to a deeper, sandy bottom flanked by cedars for a few miles of easy paddling.

The river will again grow shallow with the need for more wading. The NFCT Frizzell campsite is located river right (your left) at a bend in the river and in the west shadow of the mountain. Stop here or continue on to the village.

Like the banks of the Connecticut River, more evidence of late model cars and tractors hold back shoreline erosion as you approach Stark. Enter a boulder field, the lower end of the largest set of rapids on this section, passing under the covered bridge. The Stark Inn B&B is on river right (your left) adjacent to the bridge.

The almost mile-long boulder field continues out of Stark, the third and last formidable obstacle on the Upper Ammo. Paddlers may want to consider portaging around the rapids using Route 110 avoiding the need to pick through close set slippery rocks. Paddling can resume above the boulder field from a riverside access area.

From the boulder fields eastward to West Milan, the river meanders through forests and some farmlands, and around sandy beaches that have built up on the inside of the river bends. These provide perfect stopping places for a rest or a quick dip. The river bottom here is far less rocky making wading or tracking easier to manage when you do need to get out and drag over shallow spots.

Approximately 1.5 miles before reaching West Milan, look for the NFCT Cordwell site. It is situated just past the railroad bridge, river left, up a bank on the same side of the river as the railroad tracks. Expect to hear (and feel) passing trains. Another convenient stopping point for many paddlers is the private Cedar Pond Campground located about halfway along the Route 110A/Upper Ammonoosuc to Androscoggin portage after leaving West Milan.

Plan on camping or staying over night at the Stark Inn or Ammo Cabin along the Upper Ammonoosuc River. (Call ahead to confirm availability.)

PORTAGE DETAILS

#1) Weston Dam
150 yards: Carry

Paddle under the railroad bridge into a small cove on your left near the base of the dam. Follow the short path from the marked take-out/put-in, up over the earthen berm and back down to the river on the upper side of the dam.

#2) Mill Dam (Formerly Wausau Papers)
.2 miles: Wheelable

Paddle under both the Main Street bridge and the covered bridge upriver toward the foot of the dam, river left, (your right). Look for signs of an underused path and carry your gear up the steep bank to Brooklyn Street. Wheel or continue carrying past the dam. Put back in on the river upstream of the danger sign. The paddling distance between the old Wausau Papers Dam and Red Dam is relatively short (less than one mile). Some paddlers have opted to continue walking, following Brooklyn Street to Route 110 and putting in after Red Dam.

#3) Red Dam
.1 mile: Carry/Wheelable

This shallow dam may be able to be run when open and traveling downstream, but will need to be portaged around traveling upstream. Both the take-out and nearest put-in are quite steep at Route 110. Either carry and put back in immediately above the old dam or continue portaging down the highway (wheelable) and put in at the end of the guardrail where the banks become less steep, opposite low water gravel islands. Take care walking along the highway's edge where there is little shoulder along the guardrail.

Map 12: Upper Ammonoosuc River

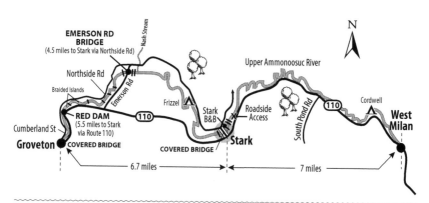

WHAT TO DO WHEN THE UPPER AMMO IS TOO LOW

OPTION 1: PORTAGE

If you intend to miss the entire river, your shortest walk to West Milan from the NFCT kiosk in Groveton follows busy Route 110, a total distance of 13.7 miles. But either Route 110 or Northside Road can get you from Groveton to Stark without paddling.

Northside Road is a less busy unpaved road that parallels the Upper Ammo, river right (your left). There are several opportunities where you can access it from the river.

The first option is from Groveton, taking out by the NFCT kiosk between the highway and covered bridges and following Main Street north to Cumberland Street. Turn right on Cumberland Street. Cumberland becomes Northside Road where the railroad veers right crossing over the river. The distance from the Groveton NFCT kiosk to Stark is 8.3 miles (vs. 6.7 miles via Route 110).

The second option is taking out at the Emerson Road bridge after working your way several miles upstream around the braided islands and through quickwater. The road also appears river right at least twice before the reaching the bridge. The distance from the Emerson Road bridge to the Stark bridge following Northside Road is 4.5 miles.

Northside Road also comes into view before reaching the Frizzell campsite. If you've committed to the upstream paddle, it provides you with another option to leave the river if has turned into a tiring grind.

OPTION 2: SHUTTLE

North Brook Outfitters/Gord's General Store, located in West Milan, rents out kayaks for recreational day trips and keeps several miles of the river free from blown down trees between South Pond Road and West Milan. They also own the Ammo Cabin and offer shuttle services. If you've worked your way up to Stark from Groveton and want to consider a second night at the B&B or at their cabin, you could paddle downstream from West Milan to Stark for a pleasant four or five hour trip. Or if you feel like the river is too low for any upstream paddling, arrange for a pick up in Groveton. The outfitter services all of the Upper Ammonoosuc and the Androscoggin rivers.

Note: Paddling any river in a reverse direction or skipping any sections will affect your designation as a Through-Paddler. Please refer to the NFCT Recognition List definitions.

#4) Stark Carry
.9 miles: Wheelable

Take out at Stark covered bridge and walk along Route 110, putting back in at the riverside access/vehicle turnout area above the boulder fields.

POINTS OF INTEREST
- ☆ The industrial dams of Groveton
- ☆ Covered bridge in Stark
- ☆ Wildlife (black bear have been seen along this section of the Trail)
- ☆ Late model tractor and car "riprap" along the banks
- ☆ Site of a WWII POW Camp
- ☆ Groveton and Stark NFCT kiosks

SERVICES

Stark, N.H. (page 226)
B&B, NFCT Kiosk

West Milan, N.H. (page 226)
Convenience Store, Cabin, Shuttle, ATM

OVERNIGHT OPTIONS AND DISTANCES FROM GROVETON

Frizzell Campsite ....7.2 miles
NFCT primitive site

Stark ....8.5 miles
B&B

Upper Ammo...15 miles
Cabin

Cordwell Campsite ....17.4 miles
NFCT primitive site

Cedar Pond Campground ....21 miles
Private campground (fee)

Arriving in Stark, N.H.

NFCT
MILEPOST

382.5

NFCT MAP #

West Milan, N.H., to Errol, N.H.

NFCT Map: 7
Total Miles: 23
Milepost: 382.5
Portages: 2 or more
Type of Watercourse(s): 1 upstream river

Compared to the Upper Ammonoosuc, the Androscoggin River is a highway. Wider and with generally reliable water levels, the river will be more easily ascended in the areas of calm between the rapids. There are, however, at least a dozen boulder fields and Class I, II and III rapids to portage around, pole or track up.

If you've persevered thus far without using any shuttle services to paddle upstream rivers downstream, and you aren't concerned about the NFCT paddler categories, this is the one river really worthy of slacking by paddling it downstream. The Andro is a popular recreational river with outfitters and shuttle services operating both out of Errol and Milan (off the Trail route). As an upstream paddler, the rapids will provide, at times, a cursed challenge. Paddling them downstream turns them into a joyous ride. The river can be run in one day downstream. Traveling upstream will take at least two days. The Androscoggin can be particularly challenging between the Route 110A Carry put-in and the Pontook Dam.

Route 16 parallels the river almost the entire way from Pontook Dam to Errol. Camping is offered only at Mollidgewock State Park (conditional upon availability).

It is important to note that the Mollidgewock State Park office headquarters is located five miles farther upstream from the location of the first campsite (Osprey) you encounter at the south end of the park. This will make it difficult to register in person. It is recommended that you call in advance to reserve and/or confirm campsite availability. Out of 44 campsites, only sites 1–5 are available on a first-come, first-served basis, and these are located at the north end of the park closest to the office.

The river is deep and broad from Mollidgewock State Park to the Route 26 bridge. The Errol canoe access/boat launch is found at the northeast end of Bragg's Bay before ascending farther up the Andro. An NFCT kiosk is located at the parking area. Both anglers and recreational kayakers frequent this area.

Northern Waters/Saco Bound Outfitters operate a campground along the shores of the Androscoggin River above the Route 26 bridge and across the street from the NFCT kiosk. They generously provide a complimentary night's stay in Errol for Through-Paddlers. If staying here, you can use the campground road as your portage. Northern Waters/Saco Bound also manages the Cedar Stump sites (fee) at the outlet of the Rapid River off of Lake Umbagog. Reserve a site during a stop at Northern Waters if you intend to camp at any of the Cedar Stump sites.

Errol is a larger town with many services including lodging, restaurants and an outfitter. The town, however, is spread out a half mile away from the take-out. Plan on camping or lodging.

PORTAGE DETAILS
#1) Route 110A/Upper Ammonoosuc to Androscoggin
3.8 or 5.4 miles: Wheelable

Paddle under Route 110 and take out at the boat access by the North Branch Upper Ammonoosuc River. Gord's General Store is southeast of the bridge and Route 110A is northeast of it. Follow Route 110A (Muzzey Hill Road) from West Milan, passing the Cedar Pond Campground en route to the Androscoggin River. Take care as these are busy highways. Some paddlers may wish to continue portaging an additional 1.6 miles up the road following Route 16 straight to the Pontook Reservoir Dam. The road shoulder on Route 16 is well maintained and level.

Note: The next two portages are necessary only if rejoining the water directly from the Route 110A portage. Otherwise, continue your paddle from the Pontook Reservoir Dam.

#2) Androscoggin River Trail (Spur Trail)
100 yards: Carry

If not following Route 16 by foot up to the reservoir, cross over Route 16 once your reach the end of Route 110A and follow the painted blue and yellow blazed spur trail 100 yards. Put in on the Androscoggin River where the power lines cross the river. While shallow most of the time, the Andro is subject to big water releases and it may be difficult to ascend this section of river prior to reaching the Pontook Reservoir Dam in heavy current. A second trail exists for scouting and/or avoiding one series of rapids above the put-in. This is a good section to test your poling skills going up the Class II–III rapids. Otherwise track through or portage around the rapids as necessary.

#3) Pontook Dam Reservoir

175 yards: Carry

Carry everything around from the base of the dam, river right (your left) to the reservoir waters above the dam.

#4) Androscoggin River Rapids

Carry (for bushwhacking), Wheelable (if using Route 16)

While some of the rapids can be tracked up, currently there are no established portages around any of them. Some paddlers have left the river where Route 16 becomes easily accessible (Seven Islands bridge has a hand-carry canoe access) and walked or wheeled past the longest and most difficult stretch of rapids (Androscoggin Wayside Park), putting back in at Mollidgewock State Park, a distance of about four miles.

POINTS OF INTEREST
- ✴ Pontook reservoir dam
- ✴ Wildlife sightings (moose, deer, eagles, egrets)
- ✴ Giant Northern Waters "moose"
- ✴ NFCT kiosk

SERVICES

Errol, N.H. (page 226)
General Store, Outfitter, Shuttle, Restaurant, Lodging, Camping, Library, Post Office, ATM, NFCT Kiosk

OVERNIGHT OPTIONS AND DISTANCES FROM WEST MILAN, N.H.

Cedar Pond Campground .... 2 miles
Private campground (fee)

Mollidgewock State Park .... 15–19.5 miles

Osprey primitive campsite .... 15 miles

Moose Crossing primitive campsite .... 16 miles

State park campground and office .... 19.5 miles
(non-reservable sites 1–5) (fee)

Errol, N.H. .... 23 miles
Lodging
Northern Waters/Saco Bound Outfitters (campground)

Maine Overview

NFCT Maps 8, 9, 10, 11, 12 and 13

A **psychological shift occurs** when you depart Errol. 94 percent of the upstream paddling is over and you now are almost halfway done. The rest of the journey will be solely spent paddling through one of the most forested and least populated states in the nation. It's impossible not to feel awestruck at the foot of expansive lakes and rugged mountain ranges.

With the exception of Lake Champlain nestled between New York and Vermont, the largest lakes of the Trail are found in Maine as well as many of the longer portages and the longest river segment. Everything about Maine looms large including the 800' rhyolite cliff of Mount Kineo that climbs straight out of Moosehead Lake and the spectacular 40' Grand Falls on the Dead River, the most impressive of several waterfalls the Trail skirts. Wildlife sightings, as well as the opportunity to see moose—a lot of moose—grow exponentially.

Unlike earlier segments of the Trail where towns, services or obstacles help dictate logical breaks, the mileage segments detailed within this section vary widely. Weather conditions, significant portages, stamina and any sense of urgency are all contributing factors determining the speed at which you will meet or surpass goal distances.

Many paddlers may worry about ascending the remote Spencer and Little Spencer Stream segment as well as the Mud Pond Carry. Both of these areas are challenging but are not comparatively any more difficult than other areas of the Trail you've already traversed, such as the Clyde River or the Grand Portage.

The time of year you travel will also affect whether or not you will be able to paddle the 19-mile section of the South Branch Dead River between Rangeley and Stratton. As early as May, water levels can be exceedingly low and the river impassable. Late summer or fall dam drawdowns can affect the ease of paddling up Umbazooksus Stream out of Chesuncook Lake or the need to walk on a larger area of exposed shoreline on Brassua Lake in order to reach the portage trail.

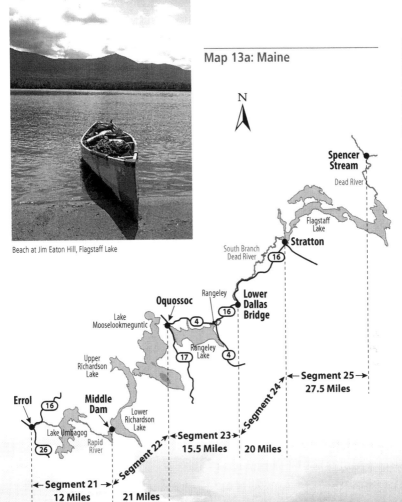

Map 13a: Maine

N

Beach at Jim Eaton Hill, Flagstaff Lake

Spencer
Stream

Dead River

Flagstaff
Lake

South Branch
Dead River   16   Stratton

Rangeley   Lower
Oquossoc   Dallas
                        Bridge
Lake   16
Mooselookmeguntic   4

Upper   Rangeley   4
Richardson   17   Lake
Lake

Errol   Middle   ← Segment 25 →
        16   Dam   27.5 Miles
     Lake Umbagog   Lower
                    Richardson
        26   Lake
              Rapid   Segment 24
              River

              ← Segment 23 →
               15.5 Miles   20 Miles
       Segment 22

← Segment 21 →
   12 Miles   21 Miles

Upper Richardson Lake

Rangeley and Jackman, Maine are common and convenient stopover points offering many services for Through-Paddlers. While there is a small general store located along the Northeast Carry at Mile 564, Jackman is an important stop for resupplying at Mile 512. It is the last on-trail town with a supermarket (grocery store, bakery, meat counter, liquor store) before reaching Fort Kent and the eastern terminus, one to two weeks distant.

There are several lodging options in the towns and villages through which you pass, but once you leave Jackman, your options are much more limited and you'll likely be camping until your arrival in Fort Kent. As you venture farther north, accommodations slant toward resorts or lodges catering to the weeklong vacationer. Some properties require a two-night minimum and pricing often includes the American Plan full meal service (breakfast, lunch and dinner). It's worth inquiring, however, to see if these remote guest houses will let you stay for one night if you are in need of a roof, although the room cost may include an upcharge.

Plan on having enough cash, or bring along checks, to pay for any food, lodging and/or campsites you need along the way. Credit cards may not be accepted and ATMs are scarce or non-existent in some communities.

Campsites are abundant throughout Maine and all but those shown on Map 8 are available on a first-come basis without prior reservations. The lakes on Map 8—Umbagog, the Richardsons and Mooselookmeguntic—are managed by different organizations and sites are characteristically reserved in advance. Sites may or may not be available when you pass through.

While some paddlers have taken the alternative Allagash Lake Loop, one of the more challenging—and many paddlers will admit, most psychologically rewarding—portages of the NFCT is the infamous Mud Pond Carry which you will encounter near the end of your trip, on Map 12. For two miles it alternates between a three-foot wide shallow stream to a mucky, sandal-sucking mire, ending with a lovely stroll through a beaver pool. If it makes you feel any better, know that Henry David Thoreau followed the same portage on his expedition in the mid-1800s sporting woolens and without the benefit of insect repellent. After exhuming the mud out between your toes and from under the arches of your feet, you then paddle into Mud Pond that connects to 16-mile long Chamberlain Lake and the Allagash Wilderness Waterway.

The Allagash Tramway Carry between Chamberlain and Eagle Lakes is unquestionably the most astonishing portage along the entire NFCT. Steel tramway tracks and two commanding steam locomotive train engines are rooted within the forest where they were left after the logging boom died in the early 20th century. You could easily spend hours poking through

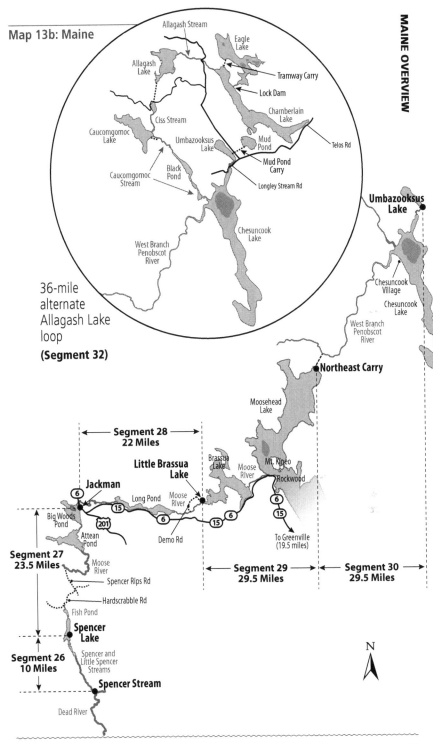

Map 13b: Maine

MAINE OVERVIEW

Allagash Stream

Eagle Lake

Allagash Lake

Tramway Carry

Lock Dam

Chamberlain Lake

Ciss Stream

Caucomgomoc Lake

Umbazooksus Lake

Mud Pond

Telos Rd

Mud Pond Carry

Black Pond

Caucomgomoc Stream

Longley Stream Rd

Umbazooksus Lake

Chesuncook Lake

West Branch Penobscot River

Chesuncook Village

Chesuncook Lake

36-mile alternate Allagash Lake loop **(Segment 32)**

West Branch Penobscot River

Northeast Carry

Moosehead Lake

◄— Segment 28 —►
22 Miles

Little Brassua Lake

Brassua Lake

Moose River

Mt. Kineo

Rockwood

Jackman

⑥

Long Pond

Moose River

Big Woods Pond

⑮

⑥

Attean Pond

㈡⁰¹

Demo Rd

⑮

⑥

To Greenville (19.5 miles)

⑥

⑮

Segment 27
23.5 Miles

Moose River

Spencer Rips Rd

◄— Segment 29 —►
29.5 Miles

◄ Segment 30 —►
29.5 Miles

Hardscrabble Rd

Fish Pond

Spencer Lake

N

Segment 26
10 Miles

Spencer and Little Spencer Streams

Spencer Stream

Dead River

MAINE OVERVIEW • MAPS 8, 9, 10, 11, 12 AND 13

140

the rusting history. Only visitors who arrive by water are able to see these massive artifacts.

Notable for its remoteness, outstanding scenery and wildlife sightings, the Allagash Wilderness Waterway (AWW) was one of the first rivers in the nation designated and preserved for future generations as a wild and scenic river. Set in the middle of a working forest, the Waterway includes a 400- to 800-foot, state-owned, restricted zone within a privately owned forest extending one mile on either side of the watercourse. There are four larger water bodies breaking up the 77-mile long river with occasional swiftwater to keep paddling interesting. Chamberlain Lake north to Churchill Dam is flatwater lake paddling. A few ponds break up paddling on the Allagash River between Umsaskis Lake and Allagash Village, but from here on to the end of the Trail, your trip is almost exclusively river travel. By this point in the journey, it is not unusual for Through-Paddlers to log more than 40 miles in one day.

The 80+ campsite options throughout the AWW are fee-based but available on a first come, first served basis. Photos and information about each site are mapped on Google Earth. Ranger stations are located at Eagle Lake, Allagash Lake (within the Allagash Lake alternate loop), Churchill Dam, Long Lake by American Realty Road, Round Pond and Michaud Farm where camping fees can be paid. You'll pass by another ranger station, located by Chamberlain bridge/Telos Lake, if entering the Allagash by road instead of water.

The 17 miles of the St. John River, at times swiftwater and with the occasional rapid, straddle the United States and Canadian international border as you paddle on to Fort Kent. Savor these last miles and moments knowing that all too soon your arrival at the last kiosk not only heralds the successful completion of paddling across four states and two nations, but also marks re-entering into the life you had before the Trail.

Paddle under the International Bridge and past the mouth of the Fish River to the Riverside Park boat launch, river right, where the eastern terminus and perhaps some friends and family await you at the end of your epic journey.

Plan mostly on camping.

AVERAGE PADDLE TIMES

Errol, N.H., to Jackman, Maine*	As little as 5 days/as many as 12 Average 7
Jackman, Maine, to Fort Kent, Maine	As little as 6 days/as many as 15 Average 9.5

* *Variables include navigable water levels for the South Branch Dead River. Often paddlers need to portage or shuttle past this river.*

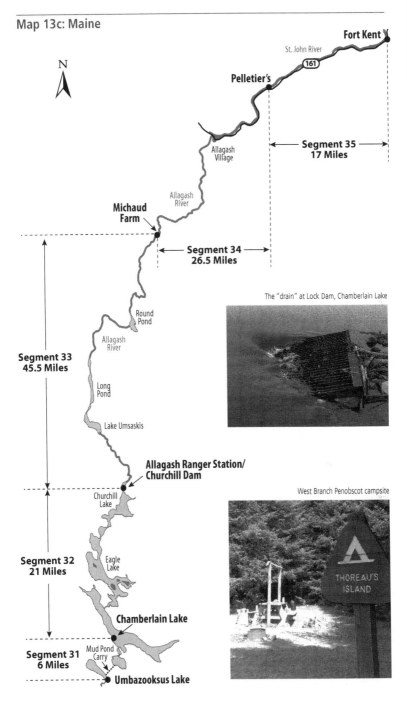

N

Fort Kent

St. John River

161

Pelletier's

Segment 35
17 Miles

Allagash
Village

Allagash
River

Michaud
Farm

Segment 34
26.5 Miles

The "drain" at Lock Dam, Chamberlain Lake

Round
Pond

Allagash
River

Segment 33
45.5 Miles

Long
Pond

Lake Umsaskis

Allagash Ranger Station/
Churchill Dam

West Branch Penobscot campsite

Churchill
Lake

Segment 32
21 Miles

Eagle
Lake

THOREAU'S
ISLAND

Chamberlain Lake

Segment 31
6 Miles

Mud Pond
Carry

Umbazooksus Lake

Errol, N.H., to Middle Dam

NFCT Map: 8
Total Miles: 12
Milepost: 394.5
Portages: 2 or 3
Type of Watercourse(s): 1 upstream river, 1 or 2 lakes

If you are not stopping at Errol for supplies, refreshment, lodging or camping at Northern Waters, you can continue upstream and take out closer to the base of the Errol dam. However, you would first need to ascend several more sets of rapids and some of the bigger waves that are populated with whitewater kayaking and rafting groups. The official portage route is located at the base of the dam, river left (your right). You can also portage from the Errol NFCT kiosk using roads to reach the put-in above the dam.

Current above the Errol Dam on the last upstream portion of the Androscoggin River is negligible. You'll continue to meander to the river's source at Umbagog Lake, a shallow lake home to the Umbagog National Wildlife Refuge. Look for bald eagles that nest in the area.

The time spent traveling this section is going to be more about portaging than paddling. If you haven't camped the night before at the Northern Waters Outfitters Campground in Errol and instead camped on one of the remote campsites on Umbagog Lake, you should be able to make it to the Richardsons. Be aware, however, that all of the trailside campsites on Umbagog, Lower Richardson, Upper Richardson and Mooselookmeguntic are fee-based and reservable. Only a handful of sites are first-come, but are off the trail's west to east direction. See details about these lakes and camping recommendations in next section.

If you intend to stay overnight at any of the Cedar Stump campsites at the outlet of the Rapid River, be sure to check-in first with Northern Waters/Saco Bound in Errol. They manage the sites and a fee is required. All other sites on Umbagog Lake are managed by the New Hampshire State Parks & Recreation and are subject to reservations and fees through ReserveAmerica.

From the Cedar Stump campsites, you'll be trekking along the Carry Road, immortalized by Louise Dickinson Rich's memoir, *We Took To The Woods*. The road passes by points of interest detailed in the book and the family's original "Forest Home." The author's winter home is listed on the National Historic

Registry and you can see the typewriter on which she wrote her book and the other household items described.

You may be sharing the carry with whitewater kayakers who trudge up the same trail lugging their boats in order to surf the rapids at Smooth Ledge. An obvious side trail to the ledge, at about the halfway point of the carry, is on the right and makes for a nice break. A disintegrating vintage car seen along the carry also makes for an interesting photo op.

The Carry Road itself is ungraded, rocky and most parts are not easily wheelable. It becomes sandier and does smooth out as you approach seasonal camps and Forest Home near Pond in the River. You can either continue on this road all the way to Middle Dam or put in by Lower Dam and take a break from portaging by paddling 1.2 miles through Pond in the River. The remains of the steam tug *Alligator* can be found just past Lower Dam on Pond in the River. The pond's shores are studded with forests and few private properties. Take out at the docks and reconnect with the portage trail that joins the road leading to Middle Dam.

Camping is allowed at Middle Dam with permission of the manager who lives there.

PORTAGE DETAILS

#1) Errol Dam Options
FROM NORTHERN WATERS/SACO BOUND CAMPGROUND
.4 miles, short paddle, then .2 miles: Both Wheelable
Whether or not you are camping here for the night, you can follow the campground road north to the end from the Route 26 bridge take-out (and NFCT kiosk). A rafting/kayaker's put-in is above the rapids. Paddle across the pool to the base of the dam and follow the instructions below.

FROM ROUTE 26 BRIDGE BOAT ACCESS
1.2 miles: Wheelable
This put-in avoids paddling the last series of rapids and the pool below the dam and follows roads. From the NFCT kiosk/parking area, cross the bridge over the Androscoggin and follow Route 26 east for a short distance. Turn left on Mountain Pond Road to the Androscoggin River boat access, located at the end of this gravel road.

AROUND THE DAM
.2 miles: Wheelable
If you haven't taken out at the Route 26 bridge, continue ascending the rapids and take out river left (your right) at the base of the dam by the outlet channel. Carry up to the dirt road and walk *past* the trees to the parking area. Do NOT put in immediately above the dam at the grassy area. There is a protective boom downstream of the boat launch that you will have to climb over if you put in too soon. Put in at the Androscoggin River boat launch.

#2) Rapid River Carry/Carry Road
3.2 miles or 4.2 miles: Not Wheelable/Not Easily Wheeled

The portage can begin as early as following the trails and carrying your gear from the Cedar Stump campsites. Trails from the campground connect to the portage. Or, you can paddle a short distance farther to the base of the rapids and pick the portage trail up from there. The portage footpath is rooty and rocky. Wheeling may or may not be possible once you reach the remnants of the old road. This car-wide corridor is not graded and the tracks are eroded with exposed rocks. Wheeling will be challenging and it may be easier to carry your gear than fight with the cart. As you near the seasonal camps and Forest Home, the road levels out and wheeling becomes more viable. The road soon forks after passing Louise Dickinson Rich's "Winter House." The left fork is a sandy continuation of the portage trail and will take you to Middle Dam another mile distant. Staying on this trail omits paddling Pond in the River.

#3) Pond in the River to Middle Dam (Optional)
.7 miles: Not Easily Wheeled

Taking the right fork brings you to a put-in by the remnants of Lower Dam and Pond in the River. If water levels are low, you will need to track through the dam to reach the Pond. Paddle to the boat dock on the north end of the pond. From the dock, follow the rutted boat access road north and take a right on the road that leads to Middle Dam. This sandy road may be soft and difficult to wheel after rains or ruts may be problematic.

POINTS OF INTEREST
- ⚹ Umbagog National Wildlife Refuge
- ⚹ Smooth Ledge along the Rapid River
- ⚹ Rusting late model car along Carry Road
- ⚹ Louise Dickinson Rich's "Forest Home"
- ⚹ Remnants of the steam tug *Alligator* in Pond in the River

SERVICES
None

OVERNIGHT OPTIONS AND DISTANCES FROM ERROL, N.H.

Umbagog Lake ....**4.5–7 miles**
State-managed remote campsites (fee)

Umbagog Lake/Cedar Stump ....**8 miles**
Campsites near Rapid River (managed by Northern Waters/Saco Bound: fee)

Middle Dam ....**12 miles**
With dam manager's permission

Lower Richardson Lake ....**13+ miles**
Reservable campsites (managed by South Arm: fee)

NFCT MILEPOST **415.5**

NFCT MAP #

Middle Dam to Oquossoc, Maine

NFCT Map: 8
Total Miles: 21
Milepost: 415.5
Portages: 2
Type of Watercourse(s): 3 lakes

Beautiful campsites, shoreline beaches and historic fishing camps make paddling these headwaters of the Androscoggin River a pleasure. But they are large lakes. Like other sections within Maine, your amassed mileage may differ today from this section's details. Wind may affect how far you are able to paddle. Mooselookmeguntic Lake in particular can kick up big waves.

Out of the entire trail, this is the one area where stopping for the night without making advance arrangements could be difficult. Like the campsites on Umbagog Lake, all campsites on Lower and Upper Richardson Lakes and Mooselookmeguntic Lake are fee-based, the majority of which are by reservation only. It can be hard to predict what night you will be reaching this area as a Through-Paddler in order to make an advance reservation. One tactic is to contact the management area(s) as you get closer, perhaps while you are in Errol, using a credit card to book an open site.

South Arm Campground manages the Upper and Lower Richardson Lake campsites. Stephen Phillips Memorial Preserve manages Mooselookmeguntic Lake. Be advised that campsites may be completely booked in July and August, especially over the weekends. Reservation names are posted on boards at each Mooselookmeguntic Lake campsite, which is a helpful indication of whether or not the site is booked. Echo Point and Woodyard, two of the smaller-sized campsites along the western shore, are the least popular and less frequently reserved. If you don't see a name with a date posted on a site's board, it is highly likely that site is open. Fees can be paid retroactively.

Of course, when dangerous paddling conditions develop, it is advisable to get off the water as soon as possible taking refuge at any open site.

If there is any time when you need to consider stealth/renegade/bush/wild camping, this may be it. Be a respectful camper and leave no trace and camp out of site. Rangers patrol these waters and will make you move if you are not in an official campsite or camping in a site in which you are not registered. Another more risk-free option is to ask if you can share a campsite with a registered party.

Upper Dam portage to Mooselookmeguntic Lake

There are only two first-come, first-served sites in this entire section. Both are on Mooselookmeguntic Lake and located on the southwest shore. In order to utilize either of these sites, you would need to paddle south from the Upper Dam portage instead of following the Trail north onward to Oquossoc.

From Middle Dam you will be heading through the narrows that separate Lower from Upper Richardson Lakes, passing several beach campsites on the eastern shores. Mind the wind direction when making the crossing to Upper Dam and the portage to Mooselookmeguntic Lake.

On the Upper Dam Carry, you'll pass by several camps and a tribute to fly fishing legend Carrie Gertrude Stevens and her record-setting brook trout. There is an artesian spring just beyond the commemorative plaque. Take time to check out the dam. You may see people trying to beat her 1924 record, fishing within the dam's outflow.

There are two portage options noted on Map 8 that lead to Rangeley Lake. Only one is detailed below. Unless a paddler intentionally wants to see the Rangeley River, a boulder-ridden waterway in which you would be traveling .7 miles upstream, then portaging around a dam, Through-Paddlers access Rangeley Lake via the road to Oquossoc from Haines Landing. The vacationer community has a general store, farm market, restaurants and lodging.

Plan on lodging or camping.

PORTAGE DETAILS
#1) Upper Dam
250 yards: Wheelable

From the marked boat launch, follow the dirt road past several camps, the Carrie Gertrude Stevens marker and the artesian well to the put-in on Mooselookmeguntic Lake.

#2) Carry Road (Haines Landing to Oquossoc)
1.5 mile: Wheelable

Follow the paved road (Carry Road/Route 4) uphill from Haines Landing, passing by summer camps and cabins. The Oquossoc Cove Landing put-in on Rangeley Lake is located after crossing the Route 4 bridge over the Rangeley River. The carry takes you past both the general store and a fine restaurant with an ice-cream counter near the end of the portage just before reaching the intersection of Routes 4 and 17.

POINTS OF INTEREST
* ★ Carrie Gertrude Stevens tribute plaque
* ★ Freshwater spring
* ★ Upper Dam
* ★ Views of Bald Mountain
* ★ Ice cream in Oquossoc, Maine

SERVICES
Lower and Upper Richardson Lakes/Mooselookmeguntic Lake (page 227)
Camping (Fee/Reservations)
Oquossoc, Maine (page 227)
Groceries, Outfitter, Restaurants, Lodging, Post Office

OVERNIGHT OPTIONS AND DISTANCES FROM MIDDLE DAM
The Narrows ....**3 miles**
Campsites between Lower and Upper Richardson Lakes (managed by South Arm: fee)
Whitney Point ....**6.5 miles**
Campsites on Upper Richardson Lakes (managed by South Arm: fee)
Brandy Point ....**11 miles**
Campsites on Mooselookmeguntic Lake
(managed by Stephen Phillips Memorial Preserve: fee)
Woodyard ....**12.5 miles**
Under-used campsite on Mooselookmeguntic Lake, located on
the west shore, between Birch Point and Farrington Island
(managed by Stephen Phillips Memorial Preserve: fee)
Echo Point ....**14 miles**
Under-used campsite on Mooselookmeguntic Lake, located on the northern point,
opposite Shelter Island (managed by Stephen Phillips Memorial Preserve: fee)
Stoney Batter Point ....**17.5 miles**
Campsite on Mooselookmeguntic Lake
(managed by Stephen Phillips Memorial Preserve: fee)
Oquossoc, Maine ....**21 miles**
Lodging (advance reservations and/or confirm availability)

Oquossoc, Maine, to Lower Dallas Bridge

NFCT Map: 8 and 9
Total Miles: 15.5
Milepost: 431
Portages: 3
Type of Watercourse(s): 1 lake, 1 pond

Meeting the mileage listed for this segment will be determined by several factors:

1) Limited camping options;
2) Services available in Rangeley;
3) Staging yourself for paddling (or not paddling) the South Branch Dead River; or
4) Tackling an additional 7- to 20-mile portage* due to low water levels of the South Branch Dead River

* See Segment 24 for more details about condition-dependent paddling and portage options.

If you are traveling in late spring, summer or fall, it is extremely likely that the upcoming section of the Dead River will indeed be dead and too low for paddling. An unfortunate reality is that Through-Paddlers cannot paddle most or any of it. There is no gauge on the river to monitor flow. Unless you hit a period of heavy rain, water levels begin falling after the spring snow runoff, making travel on this rock-ridden, shallow river unfeasible.

For all of these reasons, a stop in Rangeley to assess your next stage will be helpful. You'll find lots of services here. Besides an outfitter who can inform you about the condition of the river and provide a shuttle if necessary, there are restaurants, pubs, a movie theatre, library and a Laundromat. Accommodations range from hostels to hotels. The town is also a crossroad with the Appalachian Trail.

Your first stop should be a visit to Ecopelagicon, an outfitter/nature store with a shuttle service located on Haley Pond, adjacent to the Gull Pond Stream Carry put-in. (In 2013, Haley Pond was added to the Trail which eliminated the Route 16 roadway portage between Rangeley and the forestry museum.) Check the message board posted outside the door and stop in to talk to the staff about your options. Your level of potential misery will guide you. If you cannot paddle, you may need to walk as far as Stratton following Route 16 from Rangeley (or a few miles less if starting from the museum or Kennebago Road bridge), arrange for a shuttle or hope for help from a trail angel.

If water levels are adequate, you still have a 3.4-mile portage along Route 16 between the Maine Forestry Museum (formerly Rangeley Lakes Region Logging Museum) and the put-in on the river at the Lower Dallas Bridge.

Four camping options exist between Oquossoc and the South Branch Dead River within this 15.5-mile segment. The first is the Rangeley Lake State Park located slightly off trail. The ranger station is situated quite a distance away from the campsites. It's easier to paddle to the park's boat launch, walk up the hill, head left and inquire about an available site at the park entrance than it is to walk from the campsites and back again. If you arrive on a weekend, the campground may be full. Past paddlers have been able to negotiate an unofficial spot with the rangers. If no water site is available for easy access, site #28, is a good alternative. The site is adjacent to a trail that leads from the lake and you can stash your boat on the grass instead of hauling it to a site. A camping fee is charged. The state park is several miles away from the village of Rangeley on the south shore of the lake.

Your second and third options are accessible as part of the Gull Pond Stream Carry en route from Haley Pond to the Lower Dallas Bridge put-in. An NFCT lean-to and campsite can be found off a short side trail from the portage before reaching the Maine Forestry Museum. The museum also allows Through-Paddlers to camp by the picnic shelter located here.

Your final option is at the finish of the Dallas Carry. Two free campsites exist near the bridge, but in summer, car campers often use these sites.

Looking at the map, you might be tempted to paddle past Lakeside Park where the NFCT kiosk is located and up a narrow channel that appears to take you to Haley Pond, suggesting a shorter portage distance to town. The outlet is dammed and impassable. Taking out here would get you closer to the village center and the outfitter located on Pond Street, but you would need to cut across a private yard.

1
2
3
4
5
6
7
8
9
10
11
12
13

South Bog, Rangeley State Park

PORTAGE DETAILS

#1) Rangeley (Lakeside Park to Haley Pond)
.3 miles: Wheelable

From the take-out and lakeside NFCT kiosk, follow the park road to Main Street (Route 4) and turn right, following it for several blocks before turning left on Pond Street. Put in at the park on Haley Pond adjacent to Ecopelagicon.

#2) Gull Pond Stream Carry
.4 miles: Not Wheelable

This portage trail was constructed in 2013 allowing another water body (Haley Pond) to be added to the NFCT. It shaves off 1.5 miles of walking along Route 16 from Lakeside Park. From the put-in at the park on Haley Pond, paddle northeast to the far shore of the pond and take out by the marked trail near the outlet of Gull Pond Stream. Follow the trail and boardwalk that leads through the woods and over bog bridges to the Maine Forestry Museum. The access trail to the lean-to appears a little more than halfway along the portage prior to reaching the museum. The carry rejoins Route 16 for the final 3.4 miles to the Lower Dallas Bridge put-in.

#3) Route 16 Carry (Dallas Carry/Lower Dallas Bridge)
3.4 miles: Wheelable

From the Maine Forestry Museum follow Route 16 to the Lower Dallas Bridge put-in. Take care with traffic on this two-lane highway.

SOUTH BRANCH DEAD RIVER/ROUTE 16 PORTAGE ALTERNATIVE

If you are walking all the way to Stratton, pass the Lower Dallas Bridge and continue another 14 miles to Stratton. Watch for moose that frequent this stretch of highway. Turn right on Route 16/27 to access services in Stratton. A hostel, the Stratton Motel, is located here. From the Stratton Motel, you can put in at Stratton Brook, which feeds into Flagstaff Lake.

The NFCT kiosk is located another .75 miles north of the Route 16/27 intersection. The kiosk can be found at the Route 27 public boat access where the South Branch Dead River enters Flagstaff Lake.

SHUTTLE SERVICES

Ecopelagicon offers shuttle services to Stratton. The Farmhouse Inn, located .65 miles south of the grocery store on Route 4, is another option. This interesting hostel has built its business on hikers, but are happy to provide services to paddlers. They also own the Stratton Motel.

Message board at Ecopelagicon

POINTS OF INTEREST
☆ CCC-built stone Rangeley library
☆ Inquire about water levels with the outfitter
☆ Enjoy a restaurant or pub or clean clothes
☆ Rangeley NFCT kiosk
☆ Maine Forestry Museum (Formerly Rangeley Lakes Region Logging Museum)

SERVICES

Rangeley, Maine (page 228)
Grocery Store, Convenience Store, Outfitter, Shuttle, Restaurants, Lodging, Hostel, Library, Laundromat, Post Office, Bank/ATM, Hardware Store, Movie Theater Medical Facility, NFCT Kiosk

OVERNIGHT OPTIONS AND DISTANCES FROM OQUOSSOC, MAINE

Rangeley Lake State Park ....5 miles
State campground (fee)

Rangeley...11 miles
Hotel, motels, inns, hostel

Maine Forestry Museum..13 miles
"Halfway Hilton" lean-to (side trail to lean-to appears prior to reaching the museum); picnic table, privy
Camping (water is available by the building)

Lower Dallas Bridge ....15.5 miles
Primitive campsites

Lower Dallas Bridge to Stratton, Maine/Flagstaff Lake

NFCT Map: 9
Total Miles: 20
Milepost: 451
Portages: 1 to 2
Type of Watercourse(s): 1 downstream river

In low water, this river is impassable. *When spring runoff is running high or when water levels are adequate, paddlers should possess river reading and whitewater skills to navigate this segment.* Like the lower Nulhegan, the South Branch Dead River is a remote water body that includes intermittent sections of Class I–II whitewater, Class III–IV rapids and ledges, and the possibility of deadfalls and strainers. Route 16 will occasionally come into view, river right, for the first half of the distance before the river veers away northward toward Flagstaff Lake.

Some paddlers may wish to consider following the Trail by water at least as far as Kennebago Road—before deciding to portage the rest of the way to Stratton by foot. With the exception of Fansanger Falls looming within the first 2.5 miles, the most challenging sets of rapids appear several miles after the Kennebago Road bridge. There are two take-out options to circumvent the falls, *but only experienced paddlers should attempt paddling beyond the Kennebago Road bridge.* Paddlers will need to line, bushwhack or run the Class III-IV rapids and ledges that begin with Cherry Run. Currently, there are no established portages around these sections of technical whitewater.

If you aren't completely bypassing the South Branch Dead River, put in at the gravel access where the river crosses under Route 16 at Lower Dallas Bridge. After about two miles of moving flatwater, a quick Class II drops into a wide pool. Be on your game, because fastwater now begins and the two take-out portage options around Fansanger Falls will show up within the next .6 miles.

After portaging around the Class IV Fansanger Falls gorge, you'll continue to paddle almost three miles of nearly continuous Class I and II whitewater. You'll pass under two bridges within this stretch. The first bridge is for a private road leading to a quarry. The second bridge is Langtown Mill, after which the river settles down to winding flatwater the rest of the way to the Kennebago Road bridge.

Map 14: South Branch Dead River

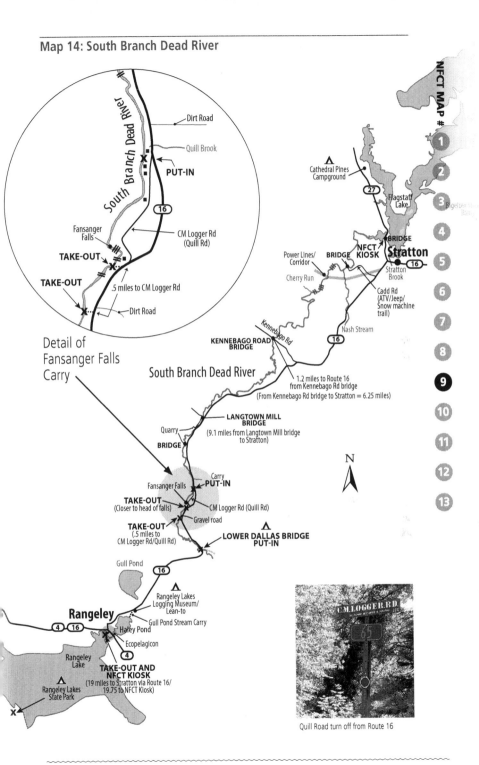

South Branch Dead River

Dirt Road

Quill Brook

PUT-IN

16

Fansanger Falls

CM Logger Rd (Quill Rd)

TAKE-OUT

TAKE-OUT

.5 miles to CM Logger Rd

Dirt Road

Detail of Fansanger Falls Carry

South Branch Dead River

Cathedral Pines Campground

27

Flagstaff Lake

BRIDGE

NFCT KIOSK

Stratton

16

Stratton Brook

Power Lines/ Corridor

BRIDGE

Cherry Run

Cadd Rd (ATV/Jeep/ Snow machine trail)

Kennebago Rd

Nash Stream

KENNEBAGO ROAD BRIDGE

16

1.2 miles to Route 16 from Kennebago Rd bridge (From Kennebago Rd bridge to Stratton = 6.25 miles)

LANGTOWN MILL BRIDGE

Quarry

(9.1 miles from Langtown Mill bridge to Stratton)

BRIDGE

N

Carry

Fansanger Falls

PUT-IN

TAKE-OUT (Closer to head of falls)

CM Logger Rd (Quill Rd)

Gravel road

TAKE-OUT (.5 miles to CM Logger Rd/Quill Rd)

LOWER DALLAS BRIDGE PUT-IN

Gull Pond

16

Rangeley Lakes Logging Museum/ Lean-to

Gull Pond Stream Carry

Rangeley

Haley Pond

4 16

Ecopelagicon

4

Rangeley Lake

TAKE-OUT AND NFCT KIOSK (19 miles to Stratton via Route 16/ 19.75 to NFCT Kiosk)

Rangeley Lakes State Park

X

CM. LOGGER RD

65

Quill Road turn off from Route 16

Unnavigable South Branch Dead River in low water

The river between Langtown Mill and Kennebago Road bridges is deeper and less rocky when navigable, but still prone to dead falls, strainers and sweeping turns.

The first four miles after the Kennebago Road bridge feature faster moving water with an occasional Class I–II rapid. Keep an eye out for Cherry Run Brook immediately after which Class II–III rapids abruptly start and continue until Nash Stream. The first mile after Cherry Run Brook is the most difficult, with many rocks. Medium to low water levels will make this section more technical and difficult.

Just past the Cadd Road ATV/snowmobile bridge is a rocky promontory known as the Barn Doors. Beyond this point, the river gradually quiets, petering out in several Class I ripples meandering around gravel and sand bars before entering the western end of Flagstaff Lake. It is another mile or so to the boat launch at Route 27 outside of Stratton where the NFCT kiosk is located.

Mileage for this section is measured from the Lower Dallas Bridge to the village of Stratton, a distance of 20 miles. Subtract one mile from your overall mileage if continuing onto Flagstaff Lake directly from the South Branch Dead River bypassing Stratton. There are no established campsites along this segment. Plan on stealth camping along the river or lodging in Stratton.

PORTAGE DETAILS
#1) Fansanger Falls
If you can, it is a good idea to scout these take-outs ahead of time.

OPTION 1
1.3 miles: Wheelable (after trail)
The first portage around Fansanger Falls appears about two miles after putting in on the river at Lower Dallas Bridge. After dropping into a wide pool from a Class II rapid, keep your eyes open for the signed take-out, river right, tucked within an eddy in the middle of Class II rapids. Route 16 is accessed from a

short trail leading up a mossy hill from the river. Turn left and follow Route 16, north-northeast, for .5 miles to CM Logger Road (Quill Road). Turn left, leave the busier highway and follow this unmaintained lane to the end. A signed trail, adjacent to a camp, leads you to the put-in where Quill Road rejoins Route 16. You'll have over 1.5 miles of Class I-II rapids before passing under the first (quarry) bridge.

OPTION 2
.8 miles: Wheelable

The second portage option places you much closer to the head of Fansanger Falls. *Do not attempt in high water.* This takeout is located another half mile downriver from the first take-out and the signage is trickier to spot—*especially* in big water. The river will have been gradually curving northward since the previous take-out, then abruptly makes a 90-degree sweeping turn east. Take-out at the bend, within an eddy, river right. *Do not miss this take-out.* Fansanger Falls is only two football field lengths away. Although the river bank is steeper here at this take-out option and you will not be able to see the road, Route 16 is only about 50 feet from the river. CM Logger Road (Quill Road), will be seen as you emerge from the woods. Follow the lane to the put-in described above.

#2) Kennebago Road Bridge to Stratton (Optional)
6.25 miles: Wheelable

Take-out at the bridge and walk 1.2 miles (southeast) to Route 16. Turn left, (east) on Route 16 and walk an additional 5.05 miles to Stratton.

POINTS OF INTEREST

* Waterfall, whitewater and gorges
* Moose
* "Barn Doors"
* Flagstaff Lake NFCT kiosk

SERVICES

Stratton, Maine (page 229)
Grocery Store, Natural Food (Co-op), Shuttle, Restaurants, Lodging, Hostel, Library, Post Office, Bank, ATM, Hardware Store, NFCT Kiosk

OVERNIGHT OPTIONS AND DISTANCES FROM LOWER DALLAS BRIDGE
No official campsites until Flagstaff Lake

Stratton, Maine ....20 miles
Lodging

Flagstaff Lake ....22.5 miles
Trout Brook primitive campsite

Cathedral Pines Campground ....24 miles
Private campground (fee), 4 miles off trail

Stratton, Maine/Flagstaff Lake to Spencer Stream

NFCT Map: 9
Total Miles: 27.5
Milepost: 478.5
Portages: 2
Type of Watercourse(s): 1 lake, 1 downstream river

The 27.5 miles detailed within this section would make for one very long, aggressive day of paddling under the most favorable conditions. The main reason so many miles are covered within this chapter is to help you plan for the next section following Flagstaff Lake—your paddle—or walk—up Spencer and Little Spencer Streams. It will be important for you to end up close to the confluence of Spencer Stream when you begin this segment, as you will want to reach Spencer Lake in one day. But that's the next chapter.

There are several reasons why you might linger in this area including exploring Flagstaff Lake and the two waterfalls found along this section of the Dead River. Or—you may want to take advantage of staying at one or both of the "huts" offered by Maine Huts & Trails. Or—wind and weather can be a factor.

The Flagstaff Lake area is rich in natural beauty and human history. The impressive Bigelow Mountain Range rises from Flagstaff's southern shore. The lake itself was formed when the Dead River was dammed in 1950. Two villages were evacuated to make room for the new reservoir. On windless days, submerged masonry—evidence of the doomed communities—can still be seen lurking in the watery depths west of Jim Eaton Hill.

Like any big body of water along the Trail, Flagstaff Lake can be unpredictable. One party of Through-Paddlers was held up for three days waiting for wind to die down, while others have been able to glide along a glassy surface all the way to the dam at Long Falls in less than a day. Be sure to follow the original course of the Dead River along the north side of the lake to reach Hurricane Island and beyond. The outlet south of the larger island is blocked.

Several campsite options are evenly spaced out along the lake including a group of eight sites located at Round Barn that may even be shared with Appalachian Trail thru-hikers. The Appalachian Trail parallels the south side of Flagstaff Lake as it traverses the ridgelines of the majestic Bigelow Range.

Flagstaff Lake and Grand Falls are home to two stunning backcountry "huts" that opened in 2009 and 2010. True gems, the huts operated by Maine Huts & Trails offer possible stops for paddlers along the Trail. Hostel-like in accommodations, the amenities are anything but. Comfy chairs, cozy common areas and family-style meals welcome visitors in these rustically beautiful, sustainably built lodges. Spartan private and semi-private bunkrooms provide a bed where you can unroll your sleeping bag. And there are showers. Rates include dinner and breakfast.

Flagstaff Hut is on the NFCT route, located about one mile north of the One Mile Beach campsites, and tucked into the bay on the west shore. Grand Falls Hut is located off the NFCT, a one-mile hike past the Spencer Stream turnoff. It is set away from the river, overlooking a valley with dramatic views of Basin Mountain. While not as conveniently placed for paddlers, it still offers exceptional wilderness accommodations. Marked trails lead to the hut from the boat landing and portage route above Grand Falls or from the rafting access/launch area below it.

Don't assume there will be vacancies without calling ahead first, but same-day bookings are accepted pending availability. Lunch is available without reservations. Both facilities have wine, beer, soda and desserts for sale.

After portaging around scenic Long Falls and its gorge, you will paddle the broader and deeper Dead River downstream to spectacular Grand Falls and the confluence of Spencer Stream. The Dead River has many scheduled water releases that produce hydroelectric power as well as providing rafting opportunities. Releases are also subject to change without notice at any time and water levels can rise and flow increase quickly.

The 40' Grand Falls makes for a picturesque break. The recommended portage route follows trails and roads, but be sure to check out the Grand Falls Hiking Trail with its impressive stone steps for viewing this, the largest waterfall along the NFCT, from land. If you are traveling in late June, you may be sharing the area with other paddlers during "Huckfest," an informal extreme whitewater kayaking group that has been running Grand Falls and filming their feats since 2010. The falls are dangerous and CANNOT be run by open canoes or loaded kayaks. Portaging is mandatory.

The recommended portage route has shifted over the years and now utilizes maintained trails developed in partnership with Maine Huts & Trails (MH&T). Camping is still permitted at the original high water take-out, river left, but paddlers are advised to use the Grand Falls Hut boat landing as the preferred portage take-out.

While there are official campsites along the Dead River prior to reaching Grand Falls, it is highly recommended to finish this section by staying near the Grand Falls portage, Spencer Stream confluence or at the Grand Falls Hut.

Please respect the privacy of the cabins and seasonal camps in this area, camping and portaging only where designated.

PORTAGE DETAILS

#1) Long Falls Dam Carry

There are two options here, one of which utilizes an adjacent road; the second follows a footpath along the river, which is the official NFCT portage route. Both options begin with taking out at the well-marked portage trail adjacent to the Long Falls dam on the northwestern (left) end of Flagstaff Lake. Follow the short, not easily wheelable path, through the woods to an open area. The open area leads to a view of the dam to your right and to Long Falls Dam Road on your left (also known as N. Flagstaff Road in the *Delorme Maine Gazetteer*).

OPTION 1A: FOLLOWING THE ROAD
.75 to 1 mile: Wheelable (on road)

To access the road option, turn left at the open area, passing by the large boulders placed to prohibit vehicles from entering and continue north along the road. Put in at the bridge for a Class I–III run, depending on water levels. Otherwise cross over the bridge and continue walking another .25 miles to the low water put-in below the boulder field at the Big Eddy camping area. The camping area is located on Long Falls Dam Road and is a popular fishing spot. Big Eddy (RV-sized) campsites are also very open and very public.

Note: If you use the road for portaging, you will miss seeing the waterfall and gorge that is viewable from the riverside trail.

OPTION 1B: FOLLOWING THE RIVERSIDE TRAIL
.6 to .85 miles: Not Wheelable

This is the official NFCT carry. From the open area, continue straight following the rocky riverside trail. The portage trail ends by the bridge from where you can decide to launch here or continue on to Big Eddy, a quarter-mile further. From the trail you are able to view the gorge and falls, which you will miss if you take the road.

Grand Falls

#2) Grand Falls

Several take-out opportunities exist, but the NFCT maintains and promotes only the high water option using trail infrastructure created by Maine Huts & Trails. There is no barrier above the 40' falls.

HIGH WATER OPTION
.9 miles: Not Easily Wheeled/Wheelable

The official NFCT portage begins at the Grand Falls Hut boat landing, river right, opposite the large island above the old breached Dead River dam. If you paddle past these dam remnants, you have gone too far.

The original take-out was located river left where a foot trail arced around private camps and joined a tangle of snowmobile trails, cross-country ski trails and camp driveways north of the river. The rerouted portage now follows Maine Huts & Trails blazed trails commencing from the river right side at a dock.

After crossing over the Tom and Kate Chappell foot bridge, watch for directional signage leading you northwest away from the falls following wheelable dirt roads and not easily wheeled trails, then looping east back toward the river. The portage and put-in ends at the pool below the falls. An unofficial campsite is located farther along the MH&T trail, near the snowmobile bridge, at the confluence of Spencer Stream.

LOW WATER OPTION
.6 miles: Not Easily Wheeled/Wheelable

This is not a sanctioned take-out. *Use extreme caution* if attempting this option—and <u>only</u> under low water conditions. This route must first be scouted prior to running. *The low water take-out is at the head of the non-barricaded 40' falls and should only be attempted by expert paddlers.* The presence of exposed dam remnants, water levels and water speed are all considerations. Review your portage route and your must-make take-out maneuver in the eddy and pool immediately above the falls before proceeding.

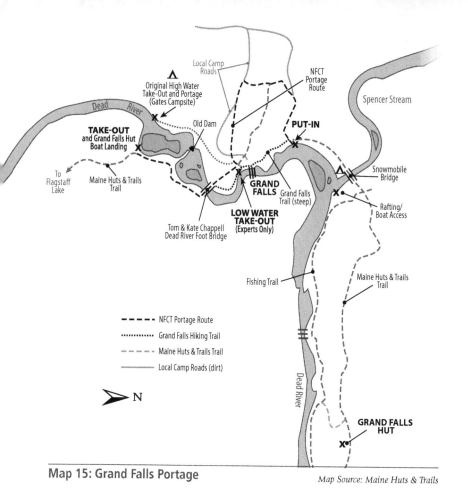

Map 15: Grand Falls Portage

Map Source: Maine Huts & Trails

Begin the run by lining or paddling over the breached dam. After passing the island(s) and riding through a short stretch of swiftwater and rapids under the Tom and Kate Chappell foot bridge (Maine Huts & Trails/NFCT portage route), you'll wind around a blind curve and through Class II rapids to the large eddy and small pool at the head of the falls. *The distance from the bridge to the pool is less than 300 yards.* Take out at the beach area, river left. You'll need to carry gear up the bank to the Grand Falls Hiking Trail that joins the roads and portage trail.

TOM AND KATE CHAPPELL FOOT BRIDGE OPTION
.7 miles: Not Easily Wheeled/Wheelable

The footbridge abuts private property and is suspended over swiftwater and rapids. The banks are steep along the cobbled shoreline. If you take out here, continue following the Maine Huts & Trails trail to the put-in below the falls.

The .3-mile Grand Falls Hiking Trail is not recommended as a portage. While the falls can be viewed from this route and the stone stairway is exquisitely beautiful, the trail is very steep. It still is worth your time to visit and linger. If you miss seeing the falls during the portage, you can paddle back to the base of them from the put-in and view them from the river.

POINTS OF INTEREST

Flagstaff Hut

★ Old Flagstaff Village ruins and history
★ Sandy beaches
★ Long Falls gorge area with NFCT informational sign
★ Grand Falls stairway
★ Grand Falls

SERVICES

Maine Huts & Trails—Flagstaff Lake and Grand Falls (page 230)
Lodging, Meals, Beverages

OVERNIGHT OPTIONS AND DISTANCES FROM STRATTON, MAINE

Flagstaff Lake ....3.5 miles
Savage Farm primitive campsite

Flagstaff Lake ....10.5 miles
Hurricane Island primitive campsite

Flagstaff Lake ....14.5 miles
Round Barn primitive campsites

Flagstaff Lake ....19 miles
Flagstaff Hut

Dead River ....21 miles
Big Eddy primitive campsites

Dead River ....25.3 miles
Philbrick Landing primitive campsite

Dead River...26.5 miles
Gates primitive campsite

Dead River ....27.5 miles
Unofficial Spencer Stream campsite

Dead River ....28.5 miles
Grand Falls Hut

Spencer Stream to Spencer Lake

NFCT Map: 10
Total Miles: 10
Milepost: 488.5
Portages: 1 (not including low water)
Type of Watercourse(s): 2 upstream streams, 1 lake, 3 deadwaters

Regardless of the time of year, heading up Spencer Stream to Little Spencer Stream to Spencer Lake is going to take most of the day, a large part of it poling, tracking or walking instead of paddling. It takes paddlers an average of 6–8 hours, and often longer, to complete 10 miles. Sea kayaks will have even more of a struggle with this section. If you've made it this far with a fiberglass sea kayak, this river will give you another beating as you maneuver over and around boulder fields with no portage options.

A lacework of logging trails exist in this area, but there is no direct roadway alternative getting around this section in order to avoid the upstream work to reach Spencer Lake.

It is best to start your day from the campsite closest to the confluence. (Add another hour if you start from the Grand Falls Hut or have to first portage around Grand Falls.) Spencer Lake is beautiful and you'll want to be able to enjoy the sunset from the sandy beaches of the Sandbar campsites or make it all the way to the Fish Pond campground. Plus, it will be difficult to carve out a stealth camp among the alder thickets, cedar and marshy areas that line the banks of these narrow streams.

As you ascend through this unpopulated area, you need to take special note of the brooks that connect to this route and maintain a northwesterly direction as you head toward Spencer Lake. Use of GPS coordinates or compass readings is helpful. Reassuring green, red and other hull-colored paint "blazes" may be in evidence on the river rocks bearing proof that you are following the route of previous Through-Paddlers.

The area can be buggy, so be prepared with strong repellent, head nets and/ or bug suits. The scenery however, is stunning and a reward for grappling with this relatively short stretch of the trail; lichen-encrusted boulders, firs and cedars line much of the area's shoreline. Watch for dragon and damselflies and signs of moose among the alders. Spencer Mountain rises ahead and to your left as you edge closer toward the lake.

From the Spencer Stream campsite on the Dead River, you'll pass under the snow machine bridge heading up Spencer Stream, which for the first 100 yards or so seems navigable. Boulder fields soon appear. In high water, rocks are slippery and the current strong. In low water, the stream is bony with only the occasional pool deep enough to suggest paddling. It may take as many as two to three hours traveling the first 2.4 miles where Little Spencer Stream joins Spencer Stream from your right.

Initially, the depth of Little Spencer Stream appears promising, but you will soon find yourself poling or out walking and tracking again. If beaver are active, you may also be crossing over a dam or two. The water deepens between Parker Brook and Parker Bog Brook, but from Parker Bog Brook to Spencer Lake there can be waterless rips and/or lots of exposed boulder fields at low water levels. Tracking becomes useless. Boats need to be unloaded and reloaded. Paddling the deadwaters offers a momentary reprieve.

Little Spencer Stream (low water)

In the last of the three deadwaters, an abrupt 30-foot granite cliff, topped with groves of spruce trees, will greet you as you approach the dam that holds back Spencer Lake from Little Spencer Stream. While paddlers sometimes gravitate toward scaling the dam from its base, the landowner requests that paddlers use an unmarked corridor, river left, accessed by one of several small coves located downstream of the dam.

The land around Spencer Lake is privately owned but purposely left largely undeveloped and wild. Paddlers are permitted to camp free at either of the two established campgrounds with advanced registration. The first is located about halfway along the eastern shore on Spencer Lake. Campsite #3 is particularly attractive at the water-access only Sandbar Beach Campground. A second campground is located on the far west shore of Fish Pond. This campground is accessible by car and the road leading from the campground will connect to the same road that is used later to get to Spencer Rips via the NFCT portage route. However, taking out from the Fish Pond will add another two miles to that portage walk. Portage details to Spencer Rips are described in the next section.

PORTAGE DETAILS

#1) Little Spencer Stream to Spencer Lake

OPTION 1: AROUND SPENCER LAKE DAM
About 150 yards: Carry

This is the NFCT-recommended route, but it is unsigned and unblazed per the landowner's request. Small coves are located downstream of the dam, river left, providing access to the portage corridor. With proper scouting you will find an adequate route to get you around the dam following rough trails. Please respect the landowner and ensure you observe Leave No Trace principles.

If you don't utilize this corridor, you'll find yourself needing to lift or drag your boat up onto the ledge of the dam, then maneuvering it over another cliff to the pool above the dam.

OPTION 2: MIDDLE DEADWATER TO SPENCER LAKE
.6 miles: Wheelable (after taking the trail from the water)

This undesignated and unmarked portage can be found on the west shore of Middle Deadwater before entering the Class I–II rapids that connect to Upper Deadwater. It follows a private road from Middle Deadwater to Spencer Lake. A short, lightly used unmarked trail leads from the water's edge through the woods to a parking area that connects to the private gravel road. Turn right (north) on the road and follow it as it turns into a dirt track that leads all the way to Spencer Lake. A cabin will be on your right as you approach the lake. You will miss the beauty of the Upper Deadwater by taking this road, but you'll also avoid the logistics of portaging around the dam.

POINTS OF INTEREST
⭐ Staying on Little Spencer Stream to Spencer Lake
⭐ Looking for other canoe "blazes" in the river bed
⭐ Upper Deadwater cliffs
⭐ Spencer Lake Sandbar Beach Campground

SERVICES
Spencer Lake and Fish Pond (page 230)
Camping

Tracking up Little Spencer Stream

OVERNIGHT OPTIONS AND DISTANCES FROM GRAND FALLS

Dead River ....1 mile
Grand Falls Hut
Spencer Lake ....10 miles
Sandbar Beach campsites (5) free, but by reservation only
Fish Pond ....14 miles
Fish Pond campsites (8) free, but by reservation only

NFCT
MILEPOST

512

NFCT MAP #

Spencer Lake to Jackman, Maine

NFCT Map: 10
Total Miles: 23.5
Milepost: 512
Portages: 2
Type of Watercourse(s): 1 lakes, 3 ponds, 1 downstream river separated
   by Attean Pond

Even though half of the paddling miles described in this section occur on rivers, this segment can take more than one day to complete due to the long, but wheelable portage to the Moose River following Spencer Rips Road. The location of the campsite options may also dictate your travel. There are no services until you reach Jackman, Maine

The original portage directions from Fish Pond to Spencer Rips had paddlers traveling through Whipple Pond. This portage route is no longer maintained and not recommended. Instead paddlers will follow more than five miles of gravel roads to the put-in on the Moose River.

Locating the first portage at the Hardscrabble Road take-out from Fish Pond can be confusing. The map illustrates Fish Pond as a larger body of water, but reeds fill the northern end of the lake from the campground boat landing. The take-out is reached by following the channel opposite Fish Pond Campground that winds its way through the reeds and alders and heads directly north. This sinuous stream passes through areas of beaver activity and the occasional blown-down tree and it can take longer to reach the take-out by the culvert on Hardscrabble Road than you might expect judging by the map.

Hardscrabble (Spencer) Road is one of several logging and backcountry roads crisscrossing this area and you need to keep track of intersections and pay attention to signage. While this portage is long and slightly uphill, the roads are level, easy for wheeling and intermittently marked with blue and yellow painted blazes.

Just beyond the put-in by Spencer Rips, there are several huge boulders erratically placed within the river that you paddle among and around on the placid Moose River. For the next seven miles, you meander east, then north to Attean Pond.

After running or portaging around the Class I–II Attean Falls rapids, island-studded Attean Pond opens up as you emerge from the Moose River. Sally Mountain rises ahead. Re-enter the Moose River from the upper northeast corner passing Attean Landing. Paddle under the railroad bridge and enter Big Wood Pond hugging the east shoreline and past waterside camps as you make your way toward Jackman.

Camping along the Moose River and Attean Pond is available on a first-come basis. Attean Falls has at least five well-used campsites spread along both sides of the river. Several beach sites are located on the far north shore of Attean Pond in the shadow of Sally Mountain.

Jackman, the self-dubbed "Switzerland of Maine," is a larger town with several restaurants, stores, camping and lodging options, but the services are spread out over a mile along Route 201. This is your last reliable town for restocking supplies before reaching Fort Kent, nearly 200 miles distant.

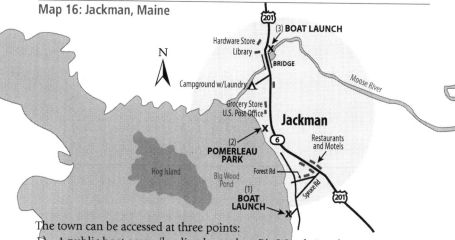

Map 16: Jackman, Maine

The town can be accessed at three points:

1) A public boat access/landing located on Big Woods Pond appears first, before reaching the Pomerleau Park. It provides the closest access to most restaurants and motels that are found at the intersection of Route 201 and Spruce Road following less busy roads.

2) Pomerleau Park is the most centrally located waterside access and closest to the grocery store and post office. The majority of restaurants and motels, however, are located ½ to ¾ mile south of Pomerleau Park along Route 201.

3) The library (with Internet service), a hardware store and a lodging option are located north of the park close to the boat access at the Moose River/ Route 201 bridge just after leaving Big Woods Pond. Private Jackman Landing Campground (with coin-op washing machines) is located riverside, before reaching the Route 201 bridge.

PORTAGE DETAILS

#1) Fish Pond to Spencer Rips

There are two options out of Fish Pond, both wheelable, but one longer than the other.

OPTION 1: FISH POND TO SPENCER RIPS VIA HARDSCRABBLE (SPENCER) ROAD
5.5 miles: Wheelable

The shorter of the two options out of Fish Pond, this portage takes you through the reedy and rush-filled north end of the lake following an increasingly narrowing channel, through alders and over beaver dams and fallen trees until you reach the culvert over which the road passes.

Unload and head east (right) for a short distance, then north-northeast following Hardscrabble (also known as Spencer) Road for about two miles until coming to the marked intersection of Spencer Road and Spencer Rips Road. Turn left (north) on Spencer Rips Road, where Whipple Bog, a skinny and shallow body of water parallels the road for a short distance. Stay on this road for three miles, passing by the occasional camp, to the dead end at the Moose River and the Spencer Rips put-in.

OPTION 2: FISH POND CAMPGROUND TO SPENCER RIPS
7.25 miles: Wheelable

Take out at the campground on the west shore of Fish Pond. Follow the rough dirt road out of the campground (.7 miles) to Hardscrabble Road. Head east (right) on Hardscrabble (Spencer) Road and follow the same directions listed above.

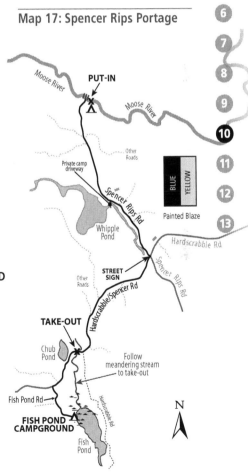

Map 17: Spencer Rips Portage

#2) Attean Falls

Few hundred yards: Not Easily Wheeled

There are two portage options on either side of the falls if you don't run them. Both are short trails and it will be more efficient to carry your gear than try to maneuver the wheels over the bumpy path. Campsites are accessed from these trails as well.

POINTS OF INTEREST
* ✯ Spencer Road and Spencer Rips Road signage indicating the portage route
* ✯ Large boulders plunked down in the Moose River and in Attean Pond
* ✯ Moose
* ✯ Blueberries (in season)

SERVICES

Jackman, Maine (page 230)
Grocery Store, Convenience Store, Outfitter, Shuttle, Restaurants, Lodging, Camping, Library, Laundromats, Post Office, Bank, ATM, Hardware Store, Medical Facility

Spencer Rips Road turn-off signage

IMPORTANT RESUPPLY NOTICE

Rockwood is a smaller town with fewer services. While there is a small general store along the Northeast Carry, Jackman is the last trail town with the largest grocery store.

OPTIONS AND DISTANCES FROM SPENCER LAKE SANDBAR CAMPSITES

Fish Pond ....5 miles
Fish Pond primitive campsites (8) free, but by reservation only

Spencer Rips ....10.5 miles
Primitive campsite

Attean Falls ....17.5 miles
Primitive campsites

Attean Pond ....21 miles
Sally Mountain primitive campsites

Jackman, Maine ....24 miles
Cabins, motels, Jackman Landing Campground (fee)

Long Lake ....31.5 miles
Last Resort campsites and rustic cabins

NFCT MILEPOST

534

NFCT MAP #

Jackman, Maine, to Little Brassua Lake

NFCT Map: 10
Total Miles: 22
Milepost: 534
Portages: 1 or 2
Type of Watercourse(s): 1 downstream river separated by 1 lake

While sparsely populated with largely undeveloped shorelines, an active railroad shadowing you along the Moose River from Jackman to Little Brassua Lake and a highway along the south shore of Long Pond ensures you won't feel completely far from civilization. The second of three NFCT water bodies named "Long" this one lacks the protection of mountains and wind can be a factor—either to your favor or detriment. Many Through-Paddlers have experienced success "sailing" when the lake has given them prevailing winds out of the Northwest.

From Jackman, paddle the gentle, meandering Moose River to Long Pond. Look for moose as you emerge onto the reedy west end of the lake. The Moose River picks up more steam as you exit Long Pond. Ride over, line or portage around Class I–II rapids until you reach Demo Road bridge and the river gauge painted on a huge shoreline boulder, river left.

A portage option was added in 2015 that helps paddlers get around the most technically dangerous rapids found below the Demo Road bridge without needing to leave the Moose River corridor. *However, only experienced paddlers should attempt running the next two mile stretch of Class II–III rapids and ledges to Little Brassua Lake.* Like the South Branch Dead River, paddlers must possess river reading and whitewater skills in order to safely navigate this river section. Heed the gauge recommendations noted in the NFCT map and guidebook. If in doubt, follow the original Demo Road portage to Little Brassua Lake.

Campsites are widely spaced out within this section. The last official campsite before reaching Demo Road is 10 miles back on Long Pond. The next nearest one is at the Moose River's outlet, just beyond the Demo Road portage put-in on Little Brassua Lake. Camping and rustic cabins are also available at a private resort located in the northwest cove on Long Pond.

PORTAGE DETAILS

#1) Demo Road or Demo Road Bridge/Elbow Carry

From the take-out on the Moose River, river left, at the river gauge (painted on the large boulder), carry all your gear up the hill to Demo Road. Depending on your whitewater skills, follow one of the two portage options.

OPTION 1: DEMO ROAD
3.6 miles: Wheelable (on roads) and Not Wheelable (on trail sections)

This longer route avoids running any of the technical Class II–IV rapids that appear after the Demo Road Bridge on this section of the Moose River. Like the Spencer Rips Carry, Demo Road is also marked with reinforcing blue and yellow painted blazes. Follow Demo Road, north, taking care to watch for logging trucks that regularly use it. Demo Road will bear right at the intersection of Moose River Road, about .5 miles from the bridge. Stay on Demo Road for another 1.85 miles crossing over two small brooks—Stony Brook and Demo Brook—before turning right (southeast) on the old and overgrown, NFCT-signed, logging road. Beware of earlier false trails that turns right, just after passing the turnoff to Stony Brook Road on your left. You must cross over Demo Brook in order to locate the correct, yet seldom used, overgrown old road (better described as a track) that is part of the Demo Road portage. Follow this signed track for about .75 miles, watching for another NFCT medallion indicating the .3-mile turnoff trail through the dark woods. The sign is posted higher on a tree trunk where branches have been known to partially obscure it. It is easily missed if you are carrying a canoe or walking with your head down. The old road will continue for some time before fading into a grassy area and woods after passing the marked turn-off trail to Little Brassua Lake. If you start experiencing an increasingly overgrown track, retrace your steps and search for the forest path. You'll need to carry your gear over this last piece of rough trail to the put-in on Little Brassua Lake.

OPTION 2: DEMO ROAD BRIDGE/ELBOW CARRY
150 yards: Carry + .7 miles

Expert paddling skills are required to paddle this river section. This shorter carry allows paddlers more river time while avoiding the most difficult Class III–IV rapids, ledges and hydraulics that appear under and just beyond the Demo Road and snowmobile trail bridges. Instead of following Demo Road north, cross over it, and follow the river left shoreline trail to a put-in at the base of the rapids. You still will face two miles of Class II–III rapids before reaching Little Brassua Lake. Elbow Carry, a rough, underutilized .7-mile path with elevation changes, was added in 2016. It is located river right, about one mile downstream of the bridge, helping paddlers circumvent a run of rapids on either side of the of Stony Brook outlet.

Note: The mileage detailed within this segment is measured from Pomerleau Park in Jackman to the put-in on Little Brassua Lake after completing the Demo Road or Demo Bridge portage.

POINTS OF INTEREST
* River gauge and rapids at Demo Road
* Whitewater paddling
* Wildlife sightings

SERVICES
Long Lake (page 231)
Lodging

OVERNIGHT OPTIONS AND DISTANCES FROM JACKMAN, MAINE

Long Lake ....7.5 miles
Last Resort campsites and rustic cabins

Long Lake ....12 miles
Primitive campsites at the Lower Narrows

Little Brassua Lake ....22-22.5 miles
Primitive campsite(s)

Brassua Lake ....28 miles
NFCT primitive site on island

Map 18: Demo Road and Demo Road Bridge Portage Options

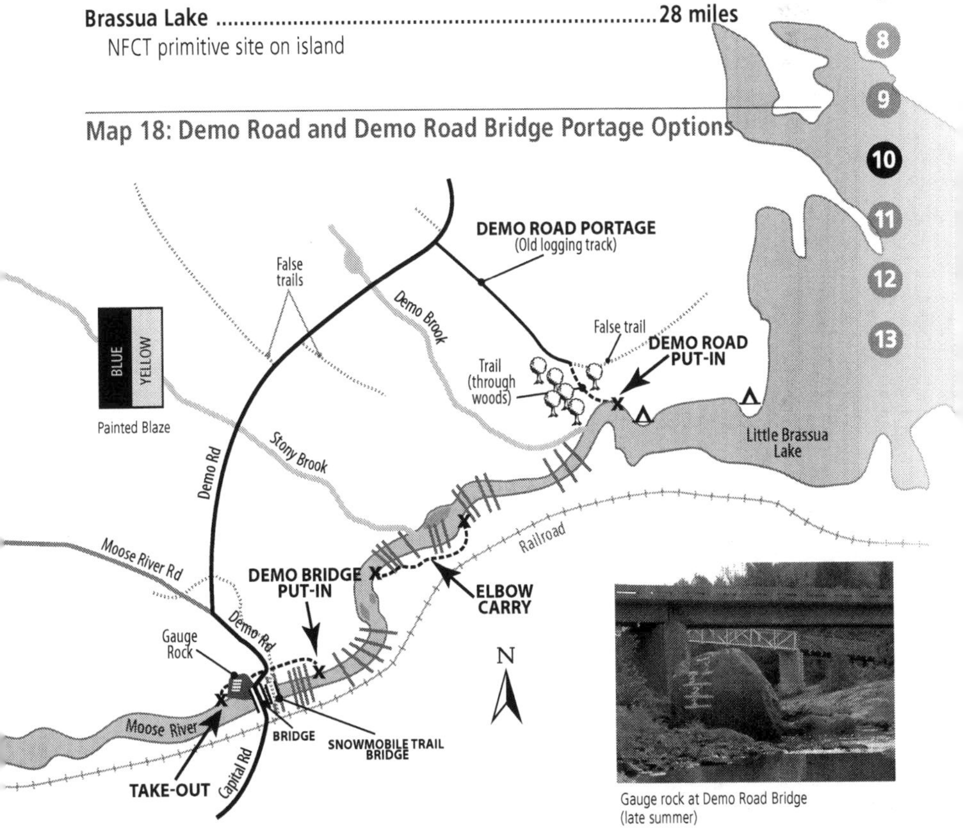

DEMO ROAD PORTAGE
(Old logging track)

False trails

Demo Brook

False trail

DEMO ROAD PUT-IN

BLUE
YELLOW

Painted Blaze

Trail (through woods)

Stony Brook

Demo Rd

Little Brassua Lake

Moose River Rd

Railroad

DEMO BRIDGE PUT-IN

Demo Rd

ELBOW CARRY

Gauge Rock

N

Moose River

BRIDGE

Capital Rd

SNOWMOBILE TRAIL BRIDGE

TAKE-OUT

Gauge rock at Demo Road Bridge
(late summer)

NFCT
MILEPOST

563.5

Little Brassua Lake to Northeast Carry

NFCT Map(s): 10 and 11
Total Miles: 29.5
Milepost: 563.5
Portages: 1
Type of Watercourse(s): 3 lakes, 1 downstream river

From the put-in on Little Brassua Lake, paddle east toward Brassua Lake. Beware of strong winds, especially as you round the point heading southeast to the take-out adjacent to the Brassua Dam. Shorelines are undeveloped until nearing the dam. Keep an eye out for eagles and osprey that live here.

After portaging around the dam, rejoin the Moose River as it flows into Moosehead Lake. Just after the put-in, Class 1 rapids will carry or bump you along, depending on the water level. The river then settles down and camps and cottages begin appearing along either side of the river. The distinctive outline of the dramatic rhyolite Mount Kineo cliff, rising straight out of the water, takes shape before you as the Moose River widens and empties into Moosehead Lake. Moosehead Lake is a clear, beautiful natural freshwater lake with smooth pebble beaches.

Although Rockwood is one of the last trail towns, it is primarily a community of camps, resorts and marinas with services limited mostly to accommodations for the Through-Paddler. Options range from cabins to lodges contingent on availability. The Birches Resort (cabins or lodge rooms) is located lakeside, about one mile northwest of the Moose River outlet. They also operate a restaurant. You can even stop in just to buy a hot shower, if that's all you need. Another option is staying at Rockwood Cottages. The small cluster of white bungalows is located lakeside, just south of the river's outlet.

Rockwood had once been a reliable resupply town, but with the closing of the trailside Moose River Country Store in 2014, services in Rockwood are fewer and farther away. The larger city of Greenville offers many services, but is located 17 miles off-trail, at the south end of Moosehead Lake. While a convenience store and restaurant/bar is located about .75 miles distant from the NFCT kiosk at the Kineo Launch, this would be a good town to consider a mail drop if you are dependent on a resupply before reaching Fort Kent. The U.S. post office is across the street from the Kineo boat launch and ferry entrance, but confirm hours of operation. It is not open daily.

View of Mount Kineo from the mouth of the Moose River

10

11

Moosehead Lake is the largest lake in Maine and one of the biggest unimpeded stretches of open water found along the Trail, second only to Lake Champlain. The ability to paddle the entire lake in one day from Rockwood to the Northeast Carry is completely dependent on the weather. If you haven't made it to Farm Island or Hardscrabble Point the day before (or even if you have), be sure to be up before dawn in order to take advantage of calmer water. Sudden high winds can be unpredictable and dangerous when crossing the two mile stretch of open water between the mouth of the Moose River to Hardscrabble Point. In general, plan on staying close to shore for your entire paddle to the Northeast Carry. Consider taking breaks throughout the day or even waiting until evening to put on miles when winds die down.

If time permits, there are two means of visiting Mount Kineo and the summit. One option is by taking the ferry (pontoon boat ride) from the Kineo Launch to Kineo Township (or paddling the .75 miles passage.) The second option is by following the signed trail from the campsites located at Hardscrabble Point.

From Hardscrabble Point you will be paddling through another open stretch of water until reaching the protection of Deer Head Farm's shoreline. Prevailing northwesterly winds can still present a danger for pushing you into the shore. The western shore may offer more protection from wind, but all of the shoreline is privately owned and camping isn't available until Seboomook Point, nearly 14 miles from Rockwood. By contrast, within the first eight miles after passing Farm Island and Hardscrabble Point, there are free primitive campsites located at Kelly's Wharf and Big Duck Cove along the eastern shoreline. Sites are available on a first-come, first-served basis.

On a clear day, the far north shoreline, where the Northeast Carry lies, first appears as a faint smudge on the horizon looking out from Hardscrabble Point. As you paddle closer, a row of houses with different colored roofs, begins to materialize. Scan the shoreline for a large white house with a woodsy area to its left. To the right of the large white house is a cabin with a green roof. Next to the cabin is another white building with a red roof. Aim toward these landmarks. The blue-signed public boat access is adjacent to the large white house and this is the start of the carry.

The Northeast Carry portage from Moosehead Lake to the West Branch Penobscot River is the most direct Trail route as you make your way east. To date, no Through-Paddlers have reported using the more distant Northwest Carry.

Camping for Through-Paddlers is permitted, but not encouraged, on the grassy area to the west of the boat landing. It borders a wetland and can be soggy and buggy. Keeping the lights off after dark may help prevent the no-see-ums from finding you. An outhouse is located at the parking area.

If you have made good time or started this segment somewhere beyond Rockwood, you may be able to push on further to the Penobscot River where your first campsite opportunity following the Trail is Thoreau Island, another 4.5 miles beyond the put-in on the river. This also means first taking the almost two-mile Northeast Carry, which is detailed in the next section.

Located a half-mile from the Moosehead Lake take-out, and along the carry, is the last general store before the end of the Trail. Besides selling basics (including beer), Raymond's Country Store bakes fresh loaves of bread each morning and offers a shuttle service for a fee.

Plan on lodging and/or camping.

PORTAGE DETAILS

#1) Brassua Dam Carry

.2 miles: Not Easily Wheeled

The portage is marked and identifiable from a distance by the stacked, washed-up, weather-beaten wood known as dri-ki left of the dam. If the lake has been drawn down, the trail will be farther away from the water requiring a longer walk over more of the exposed cobblestone shoreline. While the portage is well used and the first few hundred yards could be wheeled, it

Brassua Dam Carry during draw down

will probably be just as easy to carry everything. By now you should be pretty strong and the portage should present little problem. There are several put-in options once you get beyond the dam along the downstream riverbank. Be sure to put in well away from any eddies, especially during high water levels, that could pull boats up into the hydraulic hole at the base of the dam.

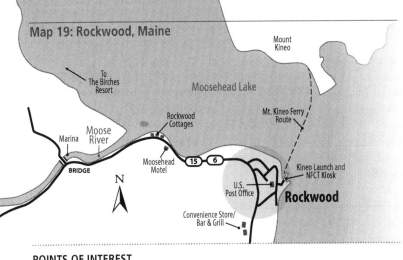

POINTS OF INTEREST

★ The interesting stacked dri-ki by the Brassua Dam portage
★ Mount Kineo
★ Last chance for eating at a restaurant before reaching Allagash Village
★ Smooth pebble Moosehead Lake beaches
★ Rockwood NFCT kiosk

SERVICES

Rockwood, Maine (page 231)
Convenience Store, Restaurants, Lodging, Post Office, Ferry (pontoon boat) to Mount Kineo, NFCT Kiosk

Northeast Carry (page 232)
General Store, Shuttle

OVERNIGHT OPTIONS AND DISTANCES FROM LITTLE BRASSUA LAKE
(Note: Distances include traveling from the Kineo Launch and NFCT kiosk)

Brassua Lake..**6 miles**
Poplar Hill Island campsite
Rockwood..**10–12 miles**
Cabins, resort rooms
Moosehead Lake ....**14.5–22 miles**
Hardscrabble Point primitive campsites ....14.5 miles
Farm Island primitive campsites ....14.5 miles
Kelly's Wharf campsite..17.75 miles
Big Duck Cove campsites ....23.5 miles
Northeast Carry ....**29.5 miles**
Public land/boat access
West Branch Penobscot River ....**36 miles**
Thoreau Island campsite
Lobster Lake ....**37 miles**
Ogden Point campsites

Northeast Carry to Umbazooksus Lake

NFCT Map: 11
Total Miles: 29.5
Milepost: 593
Portages: 1 or 2 (dependent on water levels)
Type of Watercourse(s): 1 downstream river, 2 lakes,
**   1 upstream creek (if water levels are normal)**

This section begins with the two-mile Northeast Carry and covers the entire length of the West Branch Penobscot River, through Chesuncook Lake and into Umbazooksus Stream to Umbazooksus Lake. Umbazooksus Stream begins as an arm of Chesuncook Lake before narrowing at the Longley Stream Road bridge on its north end. In late summer or early fall, water may be drawn down from the dam on Chesuncook Lake affecting the stream's water levels and the need to portage by road into Umbazooksus Lake. Otherwise, the stream flowing out of Umbazooksus Lake can be ascended.

Part of paddling this segment of the NFCT is about staging yourself (or not) for the upcoming Mud Pond Carry out of Umbazooksus Lake. The almost 30 miles detailed within this section are intended to help you with that planning. Upon reaching Chesuncook Lake, you will be faced with a few choices about the infamous carry. Some paddlers may opt for avoiding it by using roads as an alternative portage route or instead paddling the Allagash Lake Loop that completely bypasses the Mud Pond Carry. There is no established shuttle service for getting around it.

The Allagash Lake Loop is considered a challenging section that includes a three-mile long, but less muddy, portage and Class I–II rapids. Taking this loop will add overall mileage and upstream paddling to your journey.

Be aware that by mid-summer, water levels may be low in Upper Caucomgomoc Stream and Allagash Stream ensuring that this route is even tougher.

Allagash Lake is the most remote lake in the Allagash Wilderness Waterway (AWW) and the route provides increased solitude, great fishing and the opportunity to explore ice caves. The directions for taking the Allagash Lake Loop are detailed in the next section as one of the alternatives to using the Mud Pond Carry.

While there are two portages that will convey paddlers to the West Branch Penobscot River, the Northeast Carry is the most direct. In addition to the Northwest Carry being longer, choosing it adds another portage (around the Seboomook dam) to your trip as well as presenting you with additional Class II-III rapids and ledges downstream of the dam. It will also add miles to your cumulative trip total.

From the shore of Moosehead Lake, the Northeast Carry follows a gravel road until crossing the Lobster Trip Road. You'll continue along a dirt track to the put-in at Penobscot Farm on the West Branch Penobscot River. Beaver activity in the area may affect the sogginess of the last hundred yards just before reaching it. There is a spring (untested) on the left, just after passing through the intersecting roads that locals use for water. Raymond's Country Store, located about a half-mile away from the take-out on Moosehead Lake, offers shuttles for a fee, and will sell you water and other last-minute supplies.

From Penobscot Farm, the West Branch Penobscot River is another beautiful stretch of lazy river where it is easy to add up the miles. Henry David Thoreau paddled this area in the mid-1800s and camped at the island that bears his name today. Campsites along the Penobscot are plentiful, the fishing is good and Lobster Lake offers a nice side trip option. You may not want to blast through all the miles in one day.

The West Branch Penobscot River flows into Chesuncook Lake, the third largest fresh-water body in Maine. The skinny 22-mile long lake is subject to prevailing winds. Take extreme care when crossing open areas.

Looking back at Mount Kineo from the Northeast Carry

Since 1971, the tiny village of Chesuncook (population of less than a dozen full time residents) has been a popular destination for paddlers looking for homemade fudge and root beer sold at "The Store." Due to the declining health of the owner, the continued presence of this family business is questionable.

At one time this bustling community had a school, post office, stores, hotel and a boarding house and more than 100 year-round residents. Today, paddlers can wander through the historical graveyard and visit the restored church.

Chesuncook Village can be reached by beaching your boat on Graveyard Point. As of 2012, logging operations affected the footpath leading from Boom House campsite on the West Branch Penobscot to the village.

From spring through July, travelers will find water levels generally high enough within the armlike section of Chesuncook Lake (Umbazooksus Stream) to paddle up and under the Longley Stream Road bridge. From here the stream narrows and a slight current is discernible. Pass through the permanently open dam at the head of Umbazooksus Stream and onto Umbazooksus Lake. At the end of a long day, this may be tiring work. There is no opportunity to camp along the open meadows and marshlands bordering the stream until reaching the Umbazooksus Lake.

Late season Through-Paddlers may find lower water and the need to pole up, track over or portage around the rocky areas between the Longley Stream Road bridge and Umbazooksus Lake. You may also need to portage around the small dam (short carry up and over the earth berm) leading onto Umbazooksus Lake. Beavers frequent the pool created by the dam.

If the lake water has been drawn down and is too low to even reach the bridge by vessel, it will be easier to instead utilize the road that accesses Umbazooksus Lake. Paddle as far as you can up Umbazooksus Stream, then walk along the exposed shoreline to reach Longley Stream Road (also known as Umbazooksus Road) at the bridge. From the bridge, turn right (east) and follow Longley Stream Road to the first old road that turns left off of it. A sign indicates Umbazooksus Lake and this short, overgrown track will take you to the lake.

There are no official campsites on Umbazooksus Lake. However, there is room to pitch a tent, if necessary, on the gravel clearing along the track that leads to and from Longley Stream Road. The lakeside spot is within walking distance of the Umbazooksus Stream outlet.

All designated and signed campsites in this area are fee-based. Fees and permits would be typically be collected when driving through local roadway entry points, a scenario that doesn't work for the Through-Paddler arriving by water. North Maine Woods collects fees for the two Umbazooksus Stream sites and the Penobscot River Corridor (PRC) gathers fees (cash or check only) for sites located along the river and on Chesuncook Lake. Use a self-registration station at a PRC site where they exist, settle up with a field ranger or pay retroactively. Penobscot campsites can also be paid at the Michaud Farm Ranger station as you exit the Allagash. All sites are available on a first-come, first-served basis.

If double portaging, tomorrow's Mud Pond Carry will likely take you most of the day to cover. Try to camp at one of the two North Maine campsites located on Umbazooksus Stream before reaching Longley Stream Road bridge or on Umbazooksus Lake the night before. There is also a campsite located about 1/4 mile along the Mud Pond Carry, but it's in dark woods and not near the water.

PORTAGE DETAILS

#1) Northeast Carry
2 miles: Wheelable

Take out by the marked boat access area on Moosehead Lake keeping to the left of the private property that borders it. The carry follows a gravel road and passes by Raymond's General Store, a half-mile from the take-out. Cross a triangular intersection (Lobster Trip Road) and continue northeast on the dirt track leading to the river. There may be issues with muck or even standing water due to beaver activity close to the put-in at Penobscot Farm.

NORTHEAST CARRY SHUTTLE OPTION

Raymond's General Store, located less than one half mile from Moosehead Lake, offers a shuttle for a fee.

#2a) Umbazooksus Carry (Optional)
.4 miles: Not Wheelable (only necessary if water levels are too low)

An underutilized trail is present river right (your left) assisting paddlers between stream and lake when water levels are low, but not absent.

#2b) Longley Stream Road via Bridge or
North Maine Woods Campground(s) (Optional)
1 – 2 miles: Wheelable (only necessary if water levels are too low)

If you can reach the bridge, take out here, turn right and follow Longley Stream Road east for about one mile to the Umbazooksus Lake turn-off. Otherwise, you can utilize either of the North Maine Woods campground locations for road access.

One North Maine Woods campground is located on the west shore and another is located farther north on the east shore. Follow the driveway away from either campground to Longley Stream Road and continue north and eastward. Look for a sign indicating the turn-off to Umbazooksus Lake from Longley Stream Road. The distance from the west shore campground to Umbazooksus Lake is about two miles and you will cross the bridge over Umbazooksus Stream. From the east shore campground, the distance is 1.7 miles. See Map 20 on page 183.

Sign from Longley Stream/Umbazooksus Road

POINTS OF INTEREST
☆ Raymond's General Store
☆ Stopping at Thoreau Island to walk where Thoreau once camped
☆ Lobster Lake side trip
☆ Chesuncook Village

SERVICES

Chesuncook Village (page 232)
Lodging/Cabins (Confirm availability prior to arrival. Cell phone service unreliable/ non-existent en route.)

OVERNIGHT OPTIONS AND DISTANCES FROM THE NORTHEAST CARRY

Penobscot River ....6.5 miles to 20 miles
Many campsite options along all 20 miles of river (fee)

Lobster Lake ....7.5 miles
Ogden Point campsites (fee)

Chesuncook Village ....22.5 miles
Chesuncook Lake House (Cabins)

Chesuncook Lake ....23 miles
Gero Island campsites (fee)

Umbazooksus Stream ....27.5–28 miles
North Maine Woods Umbazooksus West Campsite (fee)
North Maine Woods Umbazooksus East Campsite (fee)

Umbazooksus Lake .... 29.5 miles
Unofficial site

Umbazooksus Lake to Chamberlain Lake

NFCT Map: 12
Total Miles: 6
Milepost: 599
Portages: 1 or 2
Type of Watercourse(s): 2 lakes, 1 pond, 1 downstream brook
 (with enough water)

Because this guide is written following the most direct trail route from the western terminus, it means traversing the Mud Pond Carry as you progress east. So today is all about portaging. And getting muddy. And it can be one of the biggest senses of accomplishment experienced on the Trail.

The historic portage begins about a mile from the Umbazooksus Stream outlet on the opposite shore. A beautiful rock cairn reconstructed by Team Moxie in 2011, marks the location and a noticeable entry into the woods from where a small stream emerges. Some paddlers have been confused that this is only a stream outlet, but this is the take-out—and starting point—for the Mud Pond Carry. The take-out is not easily seen from afar. If in doubt, paddle north along the eastern shoreline from the lake's southern end.

The carry follows the shallow stream crossing private land and you will be spending the majority of your carry walking in it. Expect your shoes to get wet and encased with mud. It is advisable to wear sturdier shoes that won't get sucked off. Crocs® are not a viable option for this portage.

A short way into the trail, there is a primitive campsite located in a dark clearing, but away from the water. Likewise, there is an unofficial spot with just enough room by the Mud Pond put-in at the end if you find yourself in desperate need of a campsite for one or two small tents. However, the goal should be to complete the carry and get on to Chamberlain Lake, where there are several developed, fee-based AWW campsites.

The amount of water and mud on the trail and any plague of deer flies, black flies and/or mosquitoes

Mud Pond Carry cairn

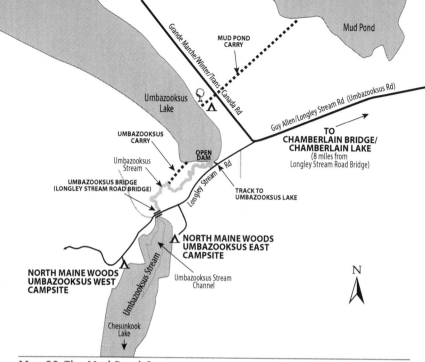

Map 20: The Mud Pond Carry

will depend on the time of year of your paddle. Retain a sense of humor. Marvel at the mushrooms. Fawn over the ferns.

Once the carry is completed, and after you've congratulated yourself on making this character building or soul-destroying portage, you'll need to get yourself out of Mud Pond. Again, water levels may affect how much muck, or not, you'll need to wade, push or pole through the pond's enveloping mudflat before reaching deeper water.

Mud Pond officially marks the beginning of the Allagash Wilderness Waterway for Through-Paddlers entering via this carry.

Mud Brook is almost directly across from the put-in on the northern shore. While narrow and boulder-strewn, it can be navigable in normal to high water. If you haven't had a chance to get most of the mud off of you, this happy little stream will help. Barring any beaver activity or downed trees, shorter kayaks may be able to paddle the most or all of it, but canoes will have a tougher time avoiding the rocks. As you line and wade, you will almost certainly be taking a few refreshing dips stepping around boulders and into holes.

When water levels are too low to even float your boat on Mud Brook, you will instead need to portage about one half mile across a rough and overgrown

Midway on the Mud Pond Carry

snowmobile trail that accesses Chamberlain Lake. At the source of Mud Brook, look for signs of the trail to the right (southeast) that cuts through the woods.

Mud Brook opens onto a small cove on Chamberlain Lake. Depending on how much farther you wish to paddle, you will be able to find four campsite options with seven places to camp, The 6 miles suggested in this day includes the passage across Umbazooksus Lake, the 1.8 mile Mud Pond Carry (which you may be retracing three times), Mud Pond, Mud Brook and about 2–3 miles paddling into Chamberlain Lake. You may be able to put on more miles today. Or less. Chamberlain Lake is another big lake and subject to strong wind and waves.

In 2012, a solo kayaker paddled from one of the Umbazooksus Stream campsites on Chesuncook Lake all the way to Eagle Lake via the Mud Pond Carry. Other paddlers have collapsed at the end of the carry and stopped for the day at the first open campsite opportunity.

In addition to AWW campsites, Nugent's Sporting Camps is located on the far shore, just south of the Mud Pond campsite. They offer a single night's accommodation subject to availability, but care must be taken crossing the lake. Paddling up along the east shore of Chamberlain Lake can be more difficult than the utilizing the wind shadow offered by the west shoreline.

PORTAGE DETAILS

#1) The Mud Pond Carry

1.8 miles: Not Wheelable

Unless drought conditions would exist, the Mud Pond Carry connecting Umbazooksus Lake to Mud Pond consists of a shallow, two-three foot wide stream that you follow the entire way. Wheeling is impractical. The carry will pass by a wooded—and potentially insect-thronged—campsite clearing situated between Umbazooksus Lake and Grande Marche (aka Winter or Trans-Canada) Road. This backcountry road, also accessible from Umbazooksus Road, is still used by lumber trucks. Cross over this evidence of civilization, then plunge back onto the muddy trail for the rest of the portage. In places there are still remnants of an old "corduroy" road. The first half of the trail is the muddiest. The mud can be thick and viscous and you may find yourself sinking up to your calves. At times there is a semblance of a firmer path along the side of the stream, but often it is easier to just remain walking within it. Lace-up boots or shoes are recommended. Crocs or loose sandals can easily get sucked off your feet. Wearing socks inside your water shoes or sandals may offer more of a barrier to the mud, but you will find yourself digging it out from around your ankles from time to time. Without socks, mud will accumulate between your toes. Any downed trees along the carry present further obstacles.

The carry is notoriously buggy.

The second half of the portage is almost heavenly by comparison. The less deep, clearer, cooler water flows downstream on a firmer gravelly base. Thick ferns carpet the forest floor around you and trilliums or fungi abound depending on the time of year. Blown-down trees, though, may still remain to maneuver over, under or around. Beaver have historically been active in the area just before reaching Mud Pond and a large pool may be present with thigh-high water. The shallow lake beckons just beyond. In low water, you may still need to trudge through the shoreline muck of Mud Pond in order to reach navigable waters.

#2) Mud Brook (Optional)

.5 miles: Not Wheelable

As of 2010, this waterway was open but if dry weather or beaver activity has reduced this brook to a trickle, look for signs of an underused trail on the right bank that originate near the head of the brook, along the southeastern shoreline. The portage trail is used as a winter snow machine trail and may be overgrown and strewn with rocks and roots.

AVOIDING THE MUD POND CARRY?

Many paddlers believe that portaging the historic Mud Pond Carry is a rite of passage and should not be avoided. Others may be interested IN avoiding it. Here are two options, neither of which are less time-consuming, but are potentially less muddy.

LONGLEY STREAM ROAD
8 miles: Wheelable

Instead of using Longley Stream Road to access Umbazooksus Lake, continue to follow it east, all the way to Chamberlain bridge on Telos Road. The Chamberlain Ranger Station is located here. This significant hike of at least eight miles follows a gravel road and passes by the marked turnoff to Umbazooksus Lake when accessing the road from the Longley Stream Road bridge at Umbazooksus Stream. Paddle seven miles northward from the Chamberlain Lake bridge toward Eagle Lake to resume the route of the NFCT.

ALLAGASH LAKE LOOP

This 36-mile segment follows Caucomgomoc Stream out from Chesuncook Lake to the undeveloped shorelines of Black Pond, Ciss Stream, Round Pond and Allagash Lake.

Rather than heading northeast up Umbazooksus Stream, paddlers instead will round the northwest point coming off the West Branch Penobscot River, paddling up the connected waterways of Caucomgomoc Stream and Black Pond. The current becomes noticeably harder above Black Pond as the river narrows back to Caucomgomoc Stream and a mile of Class I–II rapids. Like Little Spencer Stream, this is an upstream slog. The .75-mile long portage trail is located to the left (river right) by a ledge where brush has been cleared and the path is traversable to the dam. Although a logging road parallels the stream from the campsite located halfway between Black Pond and the dam, as of 2012, beaver activity has made the trail from the campsite to the road difficult and virtually impassable. This road, however, will also lead to the Caucomgomoc Dam portage trail.

Paddle up through the marshy outlet of Ciss Stream that snakes its way toward Round Pond. Down trees may be present. Take out at the north end of Round Pond by a campsite. The portage to Allagash Lake follows logging roads and is wheelable for the first two miles to the gate. After passing beyond the gate, you have two options for the last mile. The left fork will take you along a wheelable road to the ranger station; the signed right fork follows a rougher path that can be muddy and not easily wheeled.

Beautiful and remote Allagash Lake is the only completely non-motorized lake in the AWW. It is subject to strong northern winds that can produce large waves. Allagash Stream is accessed by Outlet campsite in the northeast corner 4.5 miles way from the put-in.

You now are back to downstream paddling. Allagash Stream contains Class I–II ledges and rapids and the occasional overhanging or blown-down tree to contend with. The first mile or so is steady Class I. After portaging around the ledges at the Little Round Pond outlet and Little Allagash Falls, there are three paddling obstacles that require scouting downriver. Depending on the water levels or your willingness to take an unplanned swim; run, line or portage around two sets of ledges and a third obstacle—a set of rapids—that begins just before reaching the Narrow Pond Road logging bridge. The river quiets as you continue toward Chamberlain Lake. Pass between the supports of the old railroad trestle at the river's outlet and pick up the Trail again north to Eagle Lake via the Tramway Carry.

Note: Water levels may be too low on Upper Caucomgomoc and Allagash Streams in late summer, creating bonier or unnavigable paddling.

Campsites are evenly spaced out throughout this route.

POINTS OF INTEREST
- ☀ Looking up to appreciate the flora along the Mud Pond Carry
- ☀ Mount Katahdin appearing on the south/southeast horizon from Chamberlain Lake

SERVICES

Allagash Wilderness Waterway (page 232)
(Chamberlain Lake) Lodging

OVERNIGHT OPTIONS AND DISTANCES FROM UMBAZOOKSUS LAKE

Mud Pond Carry...1/4 mile
Primitive site near the beginning of the carry

Chamberlain Lake..4+ miles
Beginning with the Mud Brook site, there are four camping areas within 5 miles to Lock Dam AWW campsites (fee)

Chamberlain Lake..7 miles
Nugent's Sporting Camps (cabins), located on the far southeast shore (Prior arrangements are recommended for overnight stay.)

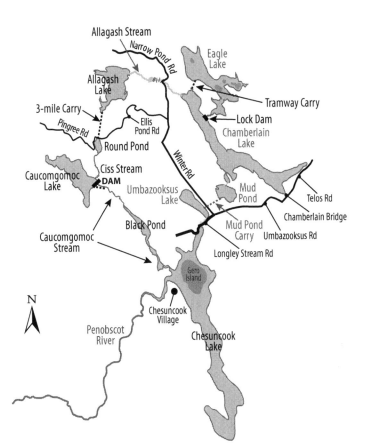

Map 21: The Allagash Lake Loop

SHUTTLE SERVICES

Check with the NFCT website trip planning tools to confirm if any shuttle options are available for this region. In the past, some area lodges have provided shuttles around the Mud Pond Carry, but low demand has restricted or eliminated the service. Shuttles also tend to be expensive and not easy to coordinate due to location and limited or non-existent phone service.

In addition to avoiding the Mud Pond Carry, a shuttle will bypass several bodies of NFCT water, most likely part or all of Chesuncook Lake, Umbazooksus Stream, Umbazooksus Lake, Mud Pond and Mud Brook. If you find a ride, paddling resumes from the far south end of Chamberlain Lake and the boat landing located at Chamberlain bridge on Telos Road.

Chamberlain Lake to Churchill Dam

NFCT Map: 12
Total Miles: 21
Milepost: 620
Portages: 1
Type of Watercourse(s): 3 lakes, 1 pond

Chamberlain Lake is a long, deep and cool water lake that connects with the popular Allagash Lake Loop and is home to some interesting pieces of logging history. You may have the chance to visit one or both sites at Lock Dam and the Tramway Carry, although weather may dictate which shore and carry you'll be using. The elongated lake can produce high waves when winds pick up and the Allagash Wilderness Waterway has seen a few groups capsize here under dangerous conditions. Paddling along the west shore is considered safer.

Paddlers who are looking to put on miles can make it to Churchill Dam if wind conditions are favorable, but with stops to visit the historical sites, ample campsites and the possibility of being stalled by headwinds, this segment can easily end up taking two days to complete.

If you are visiting or using the Lock Dam portage and have camped on the west shore the night before, plan on starting your day early in order to make the one mile crossing to the east side of the lake. However, if winds are high, do not attempt to cross the lake.

The shorter of the two portage options from Chamberlain Lake to Eagle Lake is at Lock Dam. It is easily located. Several spacious campsites are here. The fascinating "vortex" adjacent to boat landing is worth a quick look even if you intend to use the Tramway Carry, the other portage option, to get to Eagle Lake.

Lock Dam was built in 1841 and together with the Telos Dam located south, diverted water from Chamberlain and Telos Lakes through a man made canal and into the Penobscot River drainage. In the 1850's the dam was redesigned to include a series of locks that were used to float groups of logs from Eagle Lake to Chamberlain Lake, allowing them to be driven south to the Bangor sawmills. It was abandoned in the early 1900s as a log moving method in favor of the mechanically powered Tramway.

The corrugated steel culvert spillway is still present draining water out of Chamberlain Lake and creating the unusual vortex.

The longer .75-mile Tramway Carry is more difficult to initially find, but it literally offers a walk back in time. Steel tramway tracks and massive steam locomotives are rooted within the forest. A large boiler rests near the Chamberlain Lake take-out and the two imposing train engines are located close to Eagle Lake, right along the portage trail. There is a reconstructed tramway display as well as quite of bit of logging-era debris to explore within the area. You could easily spend hours poking around through the rusting history.

If you've taken the shorter Lock Dam portage and want to take a look at the Tramway engines, be sure to paddle deep into the southwest corner of Eagle Lake south of Hog Island looking for a recessed piece of shoreline in a wide cove facing Hog Island. As of 2011, a beaver lodge was located next to the trail access, which is a helpful marker. This narrow, somewhat hidden waterway channel leads to the carry. It's only a short walk up a hill, over the track to the grassy opening where the trains are permanently parked. Paddling into the channel is key to finding the well-worn portage trail and the engines from Eagle Lake.

Eagle Lake has many pretty campsites and a ranger station adjacent to a Warden camp. Farm Island was the site of an historic homestead and several spacious campsites are located here where you can still see fieldstone walls. Expect to hear owls if you camp at the Pump Handle site.

As a NFCT Through-Paddler, you will be paddling through two of the three Allagash water bodies named Round Pound. (A fourth, "Little" Round Pond, is found in the Allagash Lake Loop). Paddle under John's bridge from Round Pond and into Churchill Lake. Many campsite options are available on Churchill Lake as well as at the Churchill Dam Campground. Think about where you want to stage yourself for the next segment that begins with Chase Rapids. Water is only released in the mornings and you'll want to arrive and register well before noon if you are intending on running the Class II rapids beyond the Churchill Dam.

Moose are commonly seen in the marshy area by the McCluskey Brook outlet near Churchill Dam on Heron Lake. Take out at the dock on the west shore, left of the dam.

Plan on camping. Fees for staying at the sites located between Chesuncook and Churchill Dam can be paid for when you check in at Churchill Dam. Be sure to have enough cash or bring a check. Credit cards are not accepted.

PORTAGE DETAILS

#1a) Lock Dam
.1 mile: Carry

Carry around the dam on Chamberlain Lake to the short stream that connects to Eagle Lake.

OR

#1b) Tramway Carry
.75 miles: Wheelable (if dry)

The carry is tucked into the northwestern corner of the most northeasterly bay on Chamberlain Lake. Several paddlers have reported difficulty finding the take-out that is located deep within this marshy end of the lake. The map suggests this is a water body. Instead it is a cartographic illustration indicating the overall wetlands footprint of the entire bay and interpreted as water. There are western and eastern points that jut out much farther than the map shows, creating a smaller opening through which you pass to the rush-filled and marshy "bay" beyond. Look for an open water pathway cutting through the rushes as you paddle into the far end of the lake. When it doubt, take compass or GPS readings.

The take-out is obvious once located. Although improvements in 2011 produced a more level trail, parts may still be wet making for "sticky" wheeling. Moose like using this trail too.

Map 22: The Tramway Carry

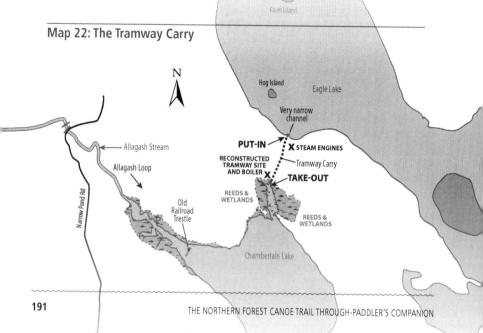

THE NORTHERN FOREST CANOE TRAIL THROUGH-PADDLER'S COMPANION

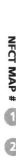

The Tramway Carry

POINTS OF INTEREST

★ Vortex "drain" by Lock Dam
★ Reconstructed tramway site and boiler
★ Locomotives and logging relics along Tramway Carry
★ Historic settlement remnants on Chamberlain and Eagle Lakes
★ The nighttime song of barred owls at the Eagle Lake Pump Handle campsite
★ Looking for moose in the marsh grass near Churchill Dam

SERVICES
None

OVERNIGHT OPTIONS AND DISTANCES FROM CHAMBERLAIN LAKE

Chamberlain Lake..4 miles
Western shore campsites north of Lock Dam (fee)

Eagle Lake ....8–12 miles
AWW campsites (fee)

Churchill Lake ....16–20 miles
AWW campsites (fee)

Churchill Dam ....21 miles
AWW campsites (fee)

Churchill Dam to Michaud Farm

NFCT Maps: 12 and 13
Total Miles: 45.5
Milepost: 665.5
Portages: 1 or 2
Type of Watercourse(s): 1 downstream river, 2 lakes, 1 pond

This segment has been lumped together because you are now on the home stretch passing through the truest wilderness section of the entire trip and in complete control about how you want to spend the next few days. Without any towns or services providing natural stopping points and no serious portages to plan around, your days are spent paddling and your biggest decision is where to camp each night. Stumbling upon feeding moose and watching soaring eagles continue to be highlights of each day.

The Allagash Wilderness Waterway has usage restrictions including a noteworthy one that regulates boat size. Generally speaking, canoes will have no problem, but some kayaks, particularly shorter river or recreational models, will not meet the requirements. Search the maine.gov website for official information about the Allagash when planning your trip. Sails are also not permitted.

Paddlers who avoided the Mud Pond Carry should have already paid their camping fees when they entered the AWW from Chamberlain bridge at Telos Road. Otherwise, every person is required to check-in and pay camping fees at Churchill Dam for the nights they intend to be staying within the Allagash. As you exit the Allagash a few days later, you are required to check out at Michaud Farm. Allow a little time to visit the Churchill Depot History Center before leaving Churchill Dam.

There are several untested springs found in the AWW that some visitors use. Springs (sometimes flagged) can be found on the west shore of Umsaskis Lake and just past the ranger station on Round Pond as well as at the Thoreau campsite on Pillsbury Island and Ziegler, Scofield Cove and Lost Popple campsites. Use your discretion about drawing water from these sources. Potable water is available at Churchill Dam.

The first decision to make is whether or not to run Chase Rapids, portage around the worst part of the rapids or take the inexpensive shuttle provided by the rangers bypassing them. Water is released daily from 8 a.m. to noon to provide a Class II run, which is the most difficult sets of rapids on the Allagash, but not necessarily on the entire NFCT. The lower Saranac River, Nulhegan and South Branch Dead River have similar, if not more difficult whitewater. Still, the Allagash is more remote than any of the other rivers you've traversed and while the end of your journey is now in sight, you've still got over a hundred more miles to go before reaching Fort Kent.

If you decide to run the rapids, the shuttle can still transport your gear for you. Or, it can take your gear and you to the point where the trip continues from the former Bissonnette bridge. Or, you can carry around the most difficult section of Chase Rapids following a maintained 1.5 mile trail leading from Churchill Dam to the first major pool below it. Put in on the Allagash River here at "Big Eddy" and paddle Class I–II rapids to the shuttle access at the former bridge site.

Besides Churchill Dam, the only other portage within this section is the Long Lake Dam, which is short and can easily be knocked off any time of the day.

If you are Tolkien fan, you'll enjoy seeing the "Shire-like" stands of elm trees just prior to entering the second named Round Pond in the Allagash along the NFCT. These trees survived the Dutch elm disease that decimated the species throughout most of the United States in the 1950s and '60s.

From Round Pond to the Musquacook Deadwater, there are continuous rips. Short stretches of Class I whitewater reappear by the Five Finger Brook campsites.

Like the Tramway Carry, more rusting lumber-era antiquities can be seen a few miles before reaching Michaud Farm. Two fenced-in Lombard log haulers rest a short walk from the river's edge.

Location and availability of a campsite will be the determining factor of where to end each day. The sites are well maintained and easily recognizable by the picnic tables with tarp poles, fireplaces and cut grass. Rangers regularly mow the campsites to help reduce the level of annoying bugs and you may even experience the irony of seeing a lawn mower being transported by canoe.

Stop at the Michaud Farm ranger station to check out of the Allagash before continuing. A clipboard with instructions will be left on the porch for self-checkout if no one is around.

PORTAGE DETAILS

#1) Churchill Dam (If not using shuttle service)
Few hundred yards to 1.5 miles: Carry

From the dock, put back in beneath the dam. If you used the shuttle service to transport your gear, stop at former Bissonnette bridge site to pick it up. You can bypass most of the serious whitewater by continuing to portage farther along the riverside portage trail to Big Eddy, 1.5 miles downstream from the dam. Inquire at the ranger station for advice or additional details.

#2) Long Lake Dam
.1 mile: Carry

Approaching the ruins, the horizon line drops indicating the old dam. Paddle river right toward the banks, taking out by the campsites. (Better yet, plan on camping here and then you need not even count this as a portage.) It's just a short carry through the campsites and not worth using the wheels. Some paddlers have lined or run this hazard in high water. Scouting is highly recommended. Boaters beware: Submerged remnant spikes are present that can damage your vessel.

POINTS OF INTEREST
* ✵ Churchill Depot History Center
* ✵ Lombard Log Haulers
* ✵ Elm trees by Round Pond
* ✵ Springs

SERVICES

Allagash Wilderness Waterway/Churchill Dam (page 232)
Shuttle, NFCT Information Sign

OVERNIGHT OPTIONS AND DISTANCES FROM CHURCHILL DAM
Many campsite options (fee) throughout the AWW (sites can be viewed using Google Earth with the photo layer checked)

American Realty Road/Umsaskis Lake ....12 miles

Long Lake Dam...19 miles

Round Pond ....29 miles

Michaud Farm..45.5 miles

Michaud Farm to Pelletier's

NFCT Maps: 13
Total Miles: 26.5
Milepost: 693
Portages: 1
Type of Watercourse(s): 2 downstream rivers

This segment reflects a somewhat aggressive distance, primarily because river miles tend to paddle faster than lakes and you also may be starting to feel a sense of urgency knowing the end is near. Or you may not want the trip to end at all. But after a week or more on the Trail since seeing the last general store along the Northeast Carry, one of your goals today may be hitting Allagash Village to eat at the diner.

After stopping at the Ranger Station in Michaud Farm to check out of the Allagash, the river threads through a series of grassy islands before the mandatory portage around 40' Allagash Falls. A highlight of this area, the falls puts you about 13 miles from the Allagash River's outlet at the St. John River.

You aren't done with whitewater just yet. Intermittent rips and Class I and II rapids are present from the falls all the way to Saint Francis on the St. John River. The Michaud Farm Road follows the river on your left and houses begin to appear along the banks near Eliza Hole Rapids, a few miles beyond the wilderness boundary.

Paddle around the bend in the river approaching the village of Allagash, and look for a steep path up the bank leading to Route 161 and the diner that beckons just beyond, before reaching Casey Rapids. The taxidermy-filled Two Rivers Lunch diner is a popular destination for Through-Paddlers but is only open for breakfast and lunch and closes by mid afternoon. Remember to have cash on hand—they do not accept credit cards. If the day is getting late, consider stopping here to camp at one of the two primitive campsites in the area.

Up until 2012, taking out at Allagash Village, river left, just before the Route 161 bridge, meant meeting nonagenarian Evelyn McBreairty. The

feisty woman charged paddlers a modest fee for landing and accessing the village through her yard. She passed away in 2012 at age 94, but her daughter Deborah still maintains her mother's tradition where camping on their land is still a bargain. McBreairty's also offer a lodging option.

Pass under the Route 161 bridge and join the last waterway of the Trail, the St. John River that will take you to the end of the Trail.

The St. John River is wider with areas of grassy or gravelly flood plains along its shore. Route 161 accompanies you river right for the duration of the trip. Near the confluence of the Allagash and St. John Rivers, just outside of Allagash, look for evidence of a record high flood—mangled canoes, a late model car or two and other evidence proving the mighty force of water, are perched along the steep banks river right.

Pelletier's is an outfitting business with a shuttle service that runs a small, private campground just south of the village of Saint Francis. You will see a broad grassy area from the river, red garbage barrels and covered picnic tables signifying the last campground on the Trail. There are no shower facilities, but a convenience store is located at the top of the driveway adjacent to the road entrance to Pelletier's.

Whether you make it to Pelletier's or stop somewhere earlier, barring any unforeseen issues, this is likely your last night on the Trail.

Plan on lodging or camping.

PORTAGE DETAILS

#1) Allagash Falls
.3 miles: Not Easily Wheeled

The well-worn path travels past the campsites and around the falls. It starts out as an uneven dirt trail, turns into a path of wooden planks and ends up back as dirt. This is your last official portage. If your wheels have held up to this point, and you don't mind all the maneuvering, go for it. However, unless someone is meeting you in Fort Kent, and you intend to stay at the Northern Door Inn, you will have one last mile-long portage through the streets of Fort Kent, Maine that you may want to save those wheels for.

POINTS OF INTEREST
- ✱ Checking out of the Allagash at Michaud Farm
- ✱ Two Rivers Lunch diner (closes at 3 p.m. and takes cash or checks only)
- ✱ Flood evidence

SERVICES

Allagash (page 232)
Convenience Store (unreliable hours/inventory), Shuttle, Restaurant, Lodging, Camping

Saint Francis (page 232)
Convenience Store, Shuttle, Camping, Post Office

OVERNIGHT OPTIONS AND DISTANCES FROM MICHAUD FARM

Allagash River ....< 5.5 miles
Seven AWW campsites (fee) between Michaud Farm and McGargle Rocks

North Maine Woods campsite (fee)..9.5 miles
Three in the area of Twin Brook Rapids (fee)

Michaud Inn Campsite..13 miles
NFCT primitive site (first official site dedicated in 2003)

Allagash Village..16 miles
Primitive camping
- McBreairty property camping (river left, access before Route 161 bridge) (fee)

Pelletier's...26.5 miles
Private campground (fee)

Pelletier's to Fort Kent, Maine

NFCT Maps: 13
Total Miles: 17
Milepost: 709
Portages: 0 or 1
Type of Watercourse(s): 1 downstream river

This segment is your last day.

After all the planning, all the paddling, all the portaging, this is it. The eastern terminus, and perhaps some friends and family, await you at the end of your epic journey at Riverside Park in Fort Kent.

Any number of emotions may bombard you. A sense of pride. A sense of wonder. A sense of relief. You are a different person than you were a few weeks or months ago. You most certainly are stronger—physically, if not emotionally.

From Pelletier's, the St. John River continues to thread its way between Canada and the United States. To avoid any international incidents, make sure to paddle closer to the United States shore and to the right of any mid-river islands that separate the two countries. It is illegal to land on the Canadian shores of the St. John River as a U.S. citizen or visitor to the U.S. without first going through customs.

Take time to notice your surroundings. Even though increasing signs of civilization are appearing along the shores, there are several nice rock formations and ledges that make for picturesque paddling. A few spots of foam suggest some more rips, but there are none of the bigger rapids to paddle through like the ones found at Cross Rock and Golden Rapids. If the water level is low, you may find yourself needing to drag your boat one last time over gravel bars for the last few yards to Riverside Park.

Paddle under the International Bridge and past the mouth of the Fish River to the Riverside Park boat launch area, river right. The last remaining trail marker and the eastern terminus/NFCT kiosk are visible from this final take-out.

Tent camping is available behind the Fort Kent Block House that is located on the opposite side of Fish River and Riverside Park, but almost all Through-

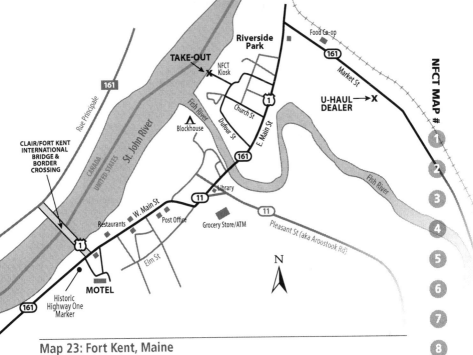

Map 23: Fort Kent, Maine

Paddlers, not being met by a welcoming party, will make one last portage through Fort Kent to the Northern Door Inn, a motel located a mile away from the park.

It's time to take more pictures, celebrate with family and friends and reflect on the unique opportunity and life event you just accomplished by completing a Through-Paddle of the Northern Forest Canoe Trail.

PORTAGE DETAILS

#1) Only if you are headed to the Northern Door Inn

1 mile: Wheelable

This final portage follows city streets. The motel is actually closer to the Claire/Fort Kent International Bridge, but you can't disembark from the river at this controlled border crossing. Plus you'll want to get that ending photo at the terminal kiosk.

From Riverside Park, head southeast on Dufour Street or Church Street, both of which connect to Main Street. Take Main Street west, walking over the Highway 1/Route 161 Fish River bridge, past the Fort Kent Blockhouse (unless you are camping here) and through town to the inn which is set back on a hill behind a gas station.

POINTS OF INTEREST
⭐ Photo op/sign-in: eastern terminus NFCT kiosk
⭐ Highway 1 mile start marker

SERVICES

Fort Kent, Maine (page 233)
Grocery Store, Convenience Store, Restaurants, Lodging, Camping, Library, Laundromat, Post Office, Bank, ATM, Medical Facility, U-Haul, NFCT Kiosk

OVERNIGHT OPTIONS AND DISTANCES FROM PELLETIER'S

Fort Kent, Maine..**17 miles**
Lodging or camping (Overnight parking and recreational vehicle camping is permitted at Riverside Park and tent camping available behind the Fort Kent Block House)

Eastern terminus, Fort Kent, Maine

SUPPORTING THE NORTHERN FOREST CANOE TRAIL

Have you just experienced a meaningful and possibly life-changing journey? Want to help ensure that other paddlers have the same opportunity?

Northern Forest Canoe Trail Inc. is a member-supported, non-profit 501(c)(3) organization. **Sustaining a membership** through your annual dues allows the NFCT to carry out its mission and strategic program areas including waterway stewardship, rural economic development and connecting people and place.

As an internationally regarded preeminent water trail organization in North America, the NFCT continuously works to provide trail access, trail mapping, trail construction and stewardship. In addition, the organization offers a depth of programs and involvement within local communities such as rural tourism development and youth paddling programming.

Pay It Forward

Designated gifts are another way to show appreciation. Your continued support will make a significant difference for future generations of Through-Paddlers.

THE NFCT TRAIL FUND
The organization's primary focus is the responsible stewardship of the 740-mile waterway. In spring, the NFCT opens existing campsites, replaces trail markers, and inspects access areas and portage paths. Throughout the summer, the organization manages interns and volunteers who provide maintenance. Waterway Work Trips and Adopt-A-Segment Programs are outreach initiatives engaging volunteers with place.

Donations to the Trail Fund supports the ongoing work to keep the Trail well-maintained for Through-Paddlers and hundreds of other recreational paddlers, watercraft racers, anglers, birders and visitors to the region.

Visit the NFCT website online at *NorthernForestCanoeTrail.org > Donate* for more details about the Trail Fund and other areas that sustain the work of the organization.

West Branch Penobscot River

Ending Reflections

By now you have recognized that the total mileage has not added up to 740. The official trail represents all of the miles that the NFCT encompasses including a few options for reaching the same point. For example, there are two signed portages out of the north end of Moosehead Lake, the Northeast and Northwest Carries, the second of which accounts for an extra 14 miles. This guide suggests paddlers follow the Northeast Carry, which is the only cumulative mileage counted. Lake Champlain is another section that includes two route options, an inner and outer passage, both of which are counted as part of the total trail mileage.

Reported trip mileages vary from paddler to paddler. Even those who use GPS devices reveal disparate results. Of course, if water levels affected your ability to paddle, you may have put on more miles by foot or fewer miles by shuttle.

Regardless of whether you just completed 709, 702, 720 or 740 miles, you are now part of a select group of people who have been able to experience a contiguous route of mapped waterways propelled under their own power.

You have arrived. You've done it. Finishing the Trail is powerful and emotional but very few people will completely appreciate the grand adventure you've just accomplished. Even among other paddlers, you'll likely hear something along the lines of: "Well that must have been fun..." never fully understanding what you mentally and physically went through. It's as though you have this secret no one else knows about—and indeed no one but you fully knows what it was like paddling and living the Trail. Simply put, it has been your journey and your adventure only.

Mostly you'll find yourself wishing you were still on the Trail—getting lost in the rhythm of your paddle strokes and the songs of that internal radio station broadcasting in your head. You'll wonder when living and sleeping outdoors became normal and will miss the silences and the need to observe the weather. You'll find yourself still looking at clouds even when you've returned to your "ordinary" life.

And now it's time to plan your next adventure...

PART 3

Towns and Services

Services At A Glance (Charts)

Towns and Services

The services detailed within this section include those commonly utilized along the Trail by Through-Paddlers and in business at the time of publication. It does not include detailed directions on how to get to them, but does indicate approximate walking distances. Unless otherwise noted, *all distances are estimated from the NFCT kiosk located in each community.*

The charts shown on pages 208 and 210 provide a quick visual overview of what you can expect to find in each of the towns located along the Trail.

If you intend to visit any of these businesses, it is recommended that you confirm ahead of time for hours of operation or even if the business is operational. Some paddlers have looked forward to stopping at Owls' Head Boulangerie in Mansonville, Québec or the Two Rivers Lunch in Allagash Village, for example, only to discover it is closed on the day or time they arrive.

Inclusion in this guidebook does not constitute an endorsement and these businesses do not pay for advertising although many do offer discounts to NFCT members and are Trail supporters. If you use any of these services, be sure to let them know you are paddling the Trail.

The NFCT website and trip planner pages contain the most up-to-date, comprehensive listing of all of the services found along the Trail by state. Notices of additions, changes or errors are welcome.

Services at a Glance

CITY/KEY	Grocery Store	General Store	Natural Food (Co-op)	Convenience Store	Outfitter	Shuttle	Restaurants	Lodging	Camping	Library	Laundromat	Post Office	Bank	ATM	Hardware	Medical Facility	NFCT Kiosk
Old Forge, N.Y.	●			●	●	●	●	●	▲	●		●	●	●	●		●
Inlet, N.Y.	●						●	●		●	●	●		●	●		
Raquette Lake, N.Y.		●					●	●		●		●					●
Long Lake, N.Y.		●		●	●	●	●	●		●		●	●	●	●		●
Saranac Lake, N.Y.	●		●	●	●	●	●	●		●	●	●	●	●	●	●	●
Redford N.Y.				●													
Picketts Corner, N.Y.				●					▲								●
Plattsburgh, N.Y.	●		●	●			●	●	▲	●	●	●	●	●		●	●
North Hero, Vt.		●					●	●	▲	●		●					●
Swanton, Vt.	●			●		●	●	●		●	●	●	●	●	●		●
Highgate Center, Vt.		●					●			●		●			●		
Sheldon Springs, Vt.				●													
Sheldon Junction, Vt.							●										
Enosburg Falls, Vt.	●		●	●	●	●	●	?	▲	●	●	●	●	●	●		●
Richford, Vt.	●			●			●	●	▲	●		●	●	●			●
Glen Sutton, Qué.						●			▲								
Highwater, Qué.									▲								
Mansonville, Qué.	●			●			●	?		●		●	●		●		●
Perkins Landing, Qué.		●															
Newport, Vt.	●		●	●	●	●	●	●	▲	●		●	●	●	●	●	●
I-91 Interchange	●			●			●	●						●	●		
Derby Center, Vt.	●			●			●			●		●	●				
Salem Lake									▲		●						
West Charleston, Vt.		●				●			▲								
The Fen						●		●	▲								
Island Pond, Vt.	●			●			●	●	▲	●		●	●	●	●		●

Services at a Glance: Definitions

Grocery Store
Supermarkets offering fresh produce, meats, and packaged foods.

General Store
Usually located in a rural area, a store that sells a wide variety of merchandise, including food, clothing and hardware but is not divided into departments. It sometimes features a deli or lunch counter.

Natural Food Store or Food Co-op
A grocery store that offers organic foods and local produce. Many items may be available in bulk.

Convenience Store
A small retail store most often associated with gasoline stations, that is open long hours and sells staple groceries and snack items.

Outfitter
A business that provides camping and paddling equipment and supplies. Some outfitters also offer shuttle services.

Shuttle
A person or business that provides transportation for you and/or your vessel when water levels are too low (or too high).

Restaurants
Options in trail towns where prepared food is offered that can range from ice cream stands offering basic snack items to fine dining.

Lodging
Any type of accommodation where you pay to sleep in a bed with a roof over your head. Includes motels, B&Bs, inns and/or hostels.

Additional options (not documented) may be available through CouchSurfing.com or AirBnB.com.

Camping
Campground options located within or near a trail town. Most, but not all, are privately owned and fee-based. Some may offer additional services such as hot showers, Laundromats, a swimming pool or camp store.

Library
Public libraries offering free use of computers and WiFi service. Hours of operation vary by town.

Laundromat
Coin-operated self-service laundry businesses.

Post Office
U.S. locations where mail drop boxes can be sent.

Bank
Financial institutions where money can be obtained using debit cards or credit card cash advances.

$ ATM
Cash machines where money can be drawn using debit cards or bank account transfers.

Hardware Store
Businesses that may have parts or other gear-fixing items available as well as some basic outdoor supplies.

Medical Facility
Urgent care or hospital emergency rooms located along or near the Trail.

NFCT Kiosk
Official NFCT informational kiosks that have been installed in trail towns and public access points throughout the length of the Trail. The kiosks typically include a map of the local section, historical facts and listings of nearby services. Many paddlers take photos at each of the locations documenting their arrival at these notable structures.

? Uncertain Service
Services in these towns have been available to Through-Paddlers in the past, but do not count on them. The business may or may not be open or services are limited.

Other (not noted on chart)
Services such as ferries, farm stands or U-Hauls that are limited to specific towns. These services are listed in more detail by community or town within the individual mileage segments.

Services at a Glance

CITY/KEY	Grocery Store	General Store	Natural Food (Co-op)	Convenience Store	Outfitter	Shuttle	Restaurants	Lodging	Camping	Library	Laundromat	Post Office	Bank	ATM	Hardware	Medical Facility	NFCT Kiosk
North Stratford, N.H.				✓			✓			✓		✓					✓
Groveton, N.H.	✓						✓	✓		✓	✓	✓	✓	✓			✓
Stark, N.H.								✓									✓
West Milan, N.H.		✓				✓			✓					✓			
Milan, N.H. (off trail)						✓											
Errol, N.H.		✓			✓	✓	✓	✓	✓	✓		✓		✓			✓
Oquossoc, Maine	✓				✓		✓	✓				✓					
Rangeley, Maine	✓			✓	✓	✓	✓	✓		✓	✓	✓	✓	✓	✓	✓	✓
Stratton, Maine	✓		✓			✓	✓	✓		✓	✓	✓	✓	✓	✓		✓
Maine Huts & Trails							✓	✓									
Spencer Lake/Fish Pond									✓								
Jackman, Maine	✓	✓		✓		✓	✓	✓	✓	✓	✓	✓		✓	✓	✓	
Long Lake								✓	✓								
Rockwood, Maine				✓			✓	✓				✓					✓
Northeast Carry		✓				✓											
Chesuncook Lake								✓									
Chamberlain Lake								✓									
Churchill Dam						✓											✓
Allagash, Maine				?		✓	✓	✓	✓								
Saint Francis, Maine				✓		✓			✓			✓					
Fort Kent, Maine	✓		✓	✓			✓	✓	✓	✓	✓	✓	✓	✓	✓	✓	✓

NEW YORK

State Campgrounds

Pre-registration is managed by Reserve America at newyorkstateparks.reserveamerica.com.

If a site appears open upon arrival, you can do either of the following:
- Visit the campground registration area or office and pay for the site in person; or
- Call the local number listed below, confirm site availability and use a credit card to pay for your stay.

Alger Island	(315) 369-3224
Eighth Lake	(315) 354-4120
Browns Tract*	(315) 354-4412
Tioga Point	(315) 354-4101 or
	(315) 354-4230
Golden Beach*	(315) 354-4230
Forked Lake	(518) 624-6646
Saranac Lake Island	(518) 891-2841
(Middle and Lower Saranac Lakes)	
Cumberland Bay	(518) 563-5240

* *These campgrounds are not on the direct route but are accessible on the same bodies of water through which the Trail passes.*

Primitive Camping

Unless marked by a "No Camping" sign, primitive camping is permitted on all DEC lands. In addition to established campsites and lean-tos shown on the maps, you may also find campsites designated with a yellow "Camp Here" marker.

OLD FORGE, N.Y. 13420

oldforgeny.com

GROCERY STORE
Diorio's (IGA) Supermarket
.8 miles
> 2938 Main Street
> Old Forge, N.Y. 13420
> (315) 369-3131
> dioriossupermarket.com

CONVENIENCE STORE
Several options (gas stations)

OUTFITTER
Mountainman Outdoor Supply Company
1.1 miles
> 2855 State Route 28
> Old Forge, N.Y. 13420
> (315) 369-6672
> mountainmanoutdoors.com

SHUTTLE
Mountainman Outdoor Supply Company
1.1 miles
> 2855 State Route 28
> Old Forge, N.Y. 13420
> (315) 369-6672
> mountainmanoutdoors.com

Raquette River Outfitters
raquetteriveroutfitters.com

Central Location:
Tupper Lake (65.5 miles)
> 1754 New York 30
> Tupper Lake, N.Y. 12986
> (518) 359-3228

Satellite Location:
Long Lake (45.1 miles)
> 1265 Main Street
> State Route 30
> Long Lake, N.Y. 12487
> (518) 624-2360

St. Regis Outfitters
Saranac Lake (88.5 miles)
> 73 Dorsey Street
> Saranac Lake, N.Y. 12983
> (888) 775-2925 or
> (518) 891-1838
> canoeoutfitters.com

RESTAURANTS
Many options located within walking distance of the visitor center
oldforgeny.com

LODGING
Many options located within walking distance of the visitor center
oldforgeny.com

CAMPING
Nicks Lake Campground (DEC)
6.6 miles
278 Bisby Road
Old Forge, N.Y. 13420
(315) 369-3314
reserveamerica.com/camping/
Nicks_Lake_Campground

Old Forge Camping Resort
1 mile
3347 State Route 28
Old Forge, N.Y. 13420
(315) 369-6011
oldforgecamping.com

LIBRARY
Old Forge Public Library
.3 miles
220 Crosby Blvd.
Old Forge, N.Y. 13420
(315) 369-6008
oldforgelibrary.org

POST OFFICE
Old Forge Post Office
.5 miles
2992 State Road 28
Old Forge, N.Y. 13420
(315) 369-3414

BANK/ATM
Adirondack Bank
1 block
108 Codling Street
Old Forge, N.Y. 13420
(315) 369-3153

Community Bank
.1 mile
3102 State Route 28
Old Forge, N.Y. 13420
(315) 369-2764

HARDWARE STORE
Old Forge Hardware
.2 miles
104 Fulton Street
Old Forge, N.Y. 13420
(315) 369-6100
oldforgehardware.com

INLET, N.Y. 13360
inletny.com
(Distance from Arrowhead Park)

GROCERY STORE
Kalil's Adirondack Grocery
.2 miles
169 State Route 28
Inlet, N.Y. 13360
(315) 357-3603

RESTAURANTS
Many options located within walking distance of Arrowhead Park
inletny.com

LODGING
Many options located within walking distance of Arrowhead Park
inletny.com

LIBRARY
Inlet Public Library
.2 miles
162 State Route 28
Inlet, N.Y. 13360
(315) 357-6494
townofinlet.org
(click on Community Services and Organizations tab for library hours and info)

LAUNDROMAT
Inlet Laundromat .4 miles
246 State Route 28
Inlet, N.Y. 13360
(315) 357-3904

POST OFFICE
Inlet Post Office
.2 miles
166 State Route 28
Inlet, N.Y. 13360
(315) 357-2012

ATM
.2 miles
172 State Route 28
Inlet, N.Y. 13360

HARDWARE STORE
Inlet Department Store/Ace Hardware
.2 miles
167 State Route 28
Inlet, N.Y. 13360
(315) 357-3636

RAQUETTE LAKE, N.Y. 13436

mylonglake.com/raquette-lake

GENERAL STORE
Raquette Lake Supply Co., Inc.
Lakeside
1 Main Street
Raquette Lake, N.Y. 13436
(315) 354-4301

RESTAURANTS
Raquette Lake Hotel & Tap Room
1 block
4 Main Street
Raquette Lake, N.Y. 13436
(315) 354-4581

LODGING
Raquette Lake Hotel & Tap Room
1 block
4 Main Street
Raquette Lake, N.Y. 13436
(315) 354-4581

LIBRARY
Raquette Lake Library
2 blocks
1 Dillion Road
Raquette Lake, N.Y. 13436
(315) 354-4005
directory.sals.edu/library.php?lib=RAQ

POST OFFICE
Raquette Lake Post Office
2 blocks
185 Main Street
Raquette Lake, N.Y. 13436
(800) 275-8777

LONG LAKE, N.Y. 12847

mylonglake.com/long-lake

GENERAL STORE
Northern Borne (Seasonal)
1 block
1236 Main Street
Long Lake N.Y., 12847
(518) 624-3271

CONVENIENCE STORE/ATM
Kickerville Station
.8 miles
1383 Tupper Road
Long Lake, N.Y. 12847
(518) 624-2178
kickervillestation.com

OUTFITTER AND HARDWARE STORE
Adirondack Outfitters and Hardware
.1 mile
1222 Main Street
Long Lake, N.Y. 12847
(518) 624-5998

OUTFITTER AND SHUTTLE
Raquette River Outfitters
Satellite Location: Across the street
from town beach
1265 Main Street
Long Lake, N.Y.
(518) 624-2360
raquetteriveroutfitters.com

RESTAURANTS
Adirondack Hotel
Across street
1245 Main Street
Long Lake, N.Y. 12847
(518) 624-4700
adirondackhotel.com
ATM

The Long Lake Diner/Owl's Head Pub
.4 miles
State Route 30 (Main Street)
Long Lake, N.Y. 12847
(518) 624-3941

LODGING
Adirondack Hotel
Across street
1245 Main Street
Long Lake, N.Y. 12847
(518) 624-4700
adirondackhotel.com

Motel Long Lake and Cottages
.3 miles by road or
paddle to eastern shore
> 51 Dock Lane
> Long Lake, N.Y. 12847
> (518) 624-2613
> motellonglake.com

LIBRARY
Long Lake Public Library
.3 miles
> 1195 Main Street
> Long Lake, N.Y. 12847
> (518) 624-3825
> directory.sals.edu/library.php?lib=LGL

POST OFFICE
Long Lake Post Office
.7 miles
> 1095 Deerland Road
> Long Lake, N.Y. 12847
> (518) 624-4567

BANK/ATM
Community Bank
.3 miles
> 1199 Main Street
> Long Lake, N.Y. 12847
> (518) 624-5161

SARANAC LAKE, N.Y. 12983

There are two access points to different
services located in Saranac Lake:
a) Distance from NFCT kiosk
   (Lake Flower Carry take-out)
b) Distance from Flower Avenue Park
   (east shore of lake by adjacent to Route 86)

GROCERY STORE
Grand Union Family Markets
a) .4 miles
> 156 Church Street
> Saranac Lake 12983
> (518) 891-4345
> gufamilymarkets.com

Aldi
b) .3 miles
> 587 Lake Flower Avenue
> Saranac Lake, N.Y. 12983
> (630) 879-8100

NATURAL FOOD (CO-OP)
Nori's Village Market
a) .4 miles
> 138 Church Street
> Saranac Lake, N.Y. 12983
> (518) 891-6079
> norisvillagemarket.com

CONVENIENCE STORE
Several options (gas stations) throughout
Saranac Lake

OUTFITTER AND SHUTTLE
St. Regis Canoe Outfitters
a) .3 miles walking OR riverside
access after portaging
> 73 Dorsey Street
> Saranac Lake, N.Y. 12983
> (888) 775-2925 or
> (518) 891-1838
> canoeoutfitters.com

Boat storage and showers are available to
Through-Paddlers.

Adirondack Lake and Trails Outfitters
b) .2 miles
> 541 Lake Flower Avenue
> Saranac Lake, N.Y. 12983
> (800) 491-0414 or (518) 891-7450
> adirondackoutfitters.com

RESTAURANTS AND LODGING
Saranac Lake offers many options (motels,
B&Bs) within walking distance from either
take-out, including several motels accessible
from the north shore of Lake Flower.

Check the kiosk and/or NFCT website for
the most current information.

LIBRARY
Saranac Lake Free Library
a) .3 miles
> 109 Main Street
> Saranac Lake, N.Y. 12983
> (518) 891-4190
> saranaclakelibrary.org/

LAUNDROMAT
Warehouse Coinwash & Carwash
a) .4 miles
> 78 Woodruff Street
> Saranac Lake, N.Y. 12983
> (518) 891-1214

POST OFFICE
Saranac Lake Post Office
a) .3 miles
> 51 Broadway
> Saranac Lake, N.Y. 12983
> (518) 891-4390

BANK AND ATM
Adirondack Bank
a) .2 miles
67 Main Street
Saranac Lake, N.Y. 12983
(518) 891-2323

Community Bank
b) .3 miles
588 Lake Flower Avenue
Saranac Lake, N.Y. 12983
(518) 891-3817

ATMs are available in many locations throughout the village.

HARDWARE STORE
Auburn Hardware
a) .8 miles
258 Broadway
Saranac Lake, N.Y. 12983
(518) 891-4478
aubuchon.com

MEDICAL FACILITY
Adirondack Medical Center
a) 1.7 miles
2233 State Route 86
Saranac Lake, N.Y. 12983
(518) 891-4141
amccares.org

REDFORD AREA

CONVENIENCE STORE (GAS STATION)
Maplefields Redford Mobile
.3 miles from Ore Bed Road bridge/put-in: not immediately accessible from river. It can be seen from the river.) Go over bridge and turn right on Route 3. Station is on the left.
4340 State Route 3
Redford, N.Y.
(518) 293-7100

PICKETTS CORNER, N.Y. 12981

(Distance from Bakers Acres Campground)

COUNTRY/CONVENIENCE STORE AND LUNCH COUNTER
Saranac Country Store
.4 miles
3346 State Route 3
Saranac, N.Y. 12981
(518) 293-1234

CAMPING
Bakers Acres Campground
Riverside access
3233 State Route 3
Saranac, N.Y. 12981
(518) 293-6471
Swimming pool, showers, laundry

PLATTSBURGH, N.Y. 12901

cityofplattsburgh-ny.gov/Tourism/
(Many services are not immediately accessible from the water.)

GROCERY STORE
Cumberland Bay Market
.2 miles from Cumberland State Park
1544 Cumberland Head Road
Plattsburgh, N.Y. 12901
(518) 561-4411

NATURAL FOOD (CO-OP)
North Country Food Co-op
.3 miles
25 Bridge Street
Plattsburgh, N.Y. 12901
(518) 561-5904
northcountryfoodcoop.com

CONVENIENCE STORE
Express Lane Convenience Store
.5 miles
20 Broad Street
Plattsburgh, N.Y. 12901
(518) 561-5644

Stewart's Shops
2.5 miles by road, but closer access is .4 miles by paddling north to Cumberland Bay and accessing road via Cumberland State Park Beach/Beach Road.
7137 State Route 9
Plattsburgh, N.Y. 12901
(518) 562-1083
stewartsshops.com

RESTAURANTS
Many options within a .5 mile walk
of NFCT kiosk

LODGING
Golden Gate Lodging
Accessible from water on northwest end of
Cumberland Bay prior to reaching state park OR
1.2 miles by road from NFCT Green Street kiosk.
432 Margaret Street
Plattsburgh, N.Y. 12901
(518) 561-2040

Rip Van Wrinkle Motel
2.2 miles by road, but closer access paddling
.5 miles north to Cumberland Bay and accessing
road via Cumberland State Park Beach/Beach
Road. The motel is near Cumberland Bay State
Park, but not on the water.
15 Commodore Thomas MacDonough Hwy.
Plattsburgh, N.Y. 12901
(518) 324-4567
ripvanwinklemotel.com

Plattsburgh Super 8 Motel
2.4 miles by road but closer access .7 miles
by paddling north to Cumberland Bay and
accessing road via Cumberland State Park
Beach/Beach Road.
7129 State Route 9 North
Plattsburgh, N.Y. 12901
(518) 562-8888
super8.com

CAMPING
Cumberland Bay State Park
**Accessible by water or 2.2 miles by
road from kiosk**
152 Cumberland Head Road
Plattsburgh, N.Y. 12901
(518) 563-5240
Showers

LIBRARY
Plattsburgh Public Library
.5 miles
19 Oak Street
Plattsburgh, N.Y. 12901
(518) 563-0921
plattsburghlib.org

LAUNDROMAT
Clinton Oak Corner Laundromat
.5 miles
75 Clinton Street
Plattsburgh, N.Y. 12901
(518) 561-1307

POST OFFICE
Plattsburgh Post Office
.4 miles
10 Miller Street
Plattsburgh, N.Y. 12901
(518) 563-1450

BANK
Community Bank/Walmart
.4 miles
25 Consumer Square
Plattsburgh, N.Y. 12901
(518) 561-0051

Champlain National Bank
.4 miles
32 Cornelia Street
Plattsburgh, N.Y. 12901
(518) 562-1776

TD Bank
.4 miles
136 Margaret Street
Plattsburgh, N.Y. 12901
(518) 561-9730

Adirondack Regional FCU
.4 miles
135 Margaret Street
Plattsburgh, N.Y. 12901
(518) 565-4764

ATM
.4 miles
89 Margaret Street
Plattsburgh, N.Y. 12901

MEDICAL FACILITY
CVPH Medical Center
1.3 miles
75 Beekman Street
Plattsburgh, N.Y. 12901
(518) 561-2000
cvph.org

OTHER
Walmart Supercenter
.4 miles
25 Consumer Square
Plattsburgh, N.Y. 12901
(518) 561-0195

Grand Isle Ferry (Lake Champlain)
820 Commodore Thomas MacDonough Hwy.
Plattsburgh, N.Y. 12901
(802) 864-9804
ferries.com

VERMONT

NORTH HERO ISLAND/ LAKE CHAMPLAIN AREA 05474

(Kiosk is located at North Hero Island Visitor Center)

GENERAL STORE AND DELI
Hero's Welcome General Store
Access from City Bay marina (across the street.)
3643 U.S. Route 2
North Hero, Vt. 05474
(800) 372-HERO or (802) 372-4161
heroswelcome.com

RESTAURANTS
The North Hero House Inn & Restaurant
With in walking distance from City Bay marina
3643 U.S. Route 2
North Hero, Vt. 05474
(888) 525-3644 or (802) 372-4732
northherohouse.com

LODGING
Shore Acres Inn and Restaurant
East Shore of North Hero Island between
The Gut and City Bay; 10 miles north of
Gordon's Landing and 1.1 mile south
of City Bay.
237 Shore Acres Drive
North Hero, Vt. 05474
(802) 372-8722
shoreacres.com

The North Hero House Inn & Restaurant
With in walking distance from City Bay marina
3643 U.S. Route 2
North Hero, Vt. 05474
(888) 525-3644 or (802) 372-4732
northherohouse.com

AquaVista Cabins
Accessible from water, located just north of
City Bay on North Hero Island
3821 U.S. Route 2
North Hero, Vt. 05474
(802) 372-6628

Holiday Harbor Motel
Accessible from the water via Alburg Passage,
south of U.S. Route 2 bridge on North Hero Island
8369 U.S. Route 2
North Hero, Vt. 05474
(802) 372-4077
holidayharborlodge.com

CAMPING
North Hero State Park
North Hero State Park has become a day use park,
but Through-Paddlers are permitted to camp in
the unmaintained campsites, accessible from the
water between Bull Rush and Stony Point. A trail
leads through the woods to the old campground
loops and the sites closest to the take-out on the
west shore. No ranger on duty.
3803 Lakeview Drive
North Hero, Vt. 05474
(802) 372-8727
vtstateparks.com/htm/northhero

Knight Island State Park
Open Memorial Day weekend—Labor Day.
Knight Island State Park's seven campsites, six
of them with rustic log lean-tos, are situated
approximately equidistant around the 2½- mile
shoreline, and are connected by a trail system.
Camping is by reservation only on designated
sites. A permit may be obtained at the caretaker's
residence on the west shore, and is necessary
before setting up. Reservations are handled
through Burton Island State Park. No potable
water supply. Fires are permitted in designated
fire rings.
1 Knight Island
North Hero, Vt. 05474
(802) 524-6353
vtstateparks.com/htm/knightisland

The Lake Champlain Paddlers' Trail
Additional campsite options.
lakechamplaincommittee.org

Lakewood Campground
Accessible from water; northeast of North Hero
Island across Lake Champlain
122 Champlain Street
Swanton, Vt. 05488
(802) 868-7270

Campbell's Bay Campground
Accessible from water around Donaldson's
Point/adjacent to Charcoal Creek; look for
boat dock and beach area
200 Campbell Bay Road
West Swanton, Vt. 05488
(802) 868-0405
campbellsbayvermont.com

LIBRARY
North Hero Public Library
.5 miles City Bay Marina
3195 U.S. 2, North Hero, Vt. 05474
(802) 372-5458
northherovt.com/library.php

POST OFFICE
Adjacent to General Store, City Bay
3537 U.S. Route 2
North Hero, Vt. 05474
(802) 372-5071

SWANTON, VT. 05488

GROCERY STORE
Swanton Hannaford Supermarket
.9 miles
139 1st Street
Swanton, Vt. 05488
(802) 868-2637
hannaford.com

CONVENIENCE STORE/ATM
Champlain Farms/Gulf Gas Station
.1 miles
2 Canada Street
Swanton, Vt. 05488
(802) 868-3823
champlainfarms.com

SHUTTLE
Montgomery Adventures
Services all of the Missisquoi River
from Swanton to Richford, Vt.
262 Deep Gibou Road
Montgomery Center, Vt. 05471
(802) 370-2103
montgomeryadventures.com

RESTAURANTS
Swanton House of Pizza
Two blocks
32 Merchants Row
Swanton, Vt. 05488
(802) 868-3085

Several francise restaurants are also located
near the Hannaford Supermarket by I-89.

LODGING
Swanton Motel
.8 miles
112 Grand Avenue
Swanton, Vt. 05488
(802) 868-4284
swantonmotel.com

LIBRARY
Swanton Public Library
.2 miles
1 1st Street
Swanton, Vt. 05488
(802) 868-7656
swantonlibrary.org

LAUNDROMAT
Great Laundromat, LLC
.1 miles
23 Broadway Street
Swanton Vt. 05488
(802) 868-7975

POST OFFICE
Swanton Post Office
.2 miles
21 Grand Avenue
Swanton, Vt. 05488
(802) 868-4188

BANK/ATM
People's United Bank
.2 miles
15 Canada Street
Swanton, Vt. 05488
(802) 868-3329
peoples.com

TD Bank
.25 miles
13 York Street
Swanton, Vt. 05488
(802) 868-7323
tdbank.com

HARDWARE STORE
Aubuchon Hardware
.2 miles
26 Canada Street
Swanton, Vt. 05488
(802) 868-7884
hardwarestore.com

HIGHGATE CENTER, VT. 05459

(Distance from NFCT Highgate Falls Dam
Carry campsite)

GENERAL STORE
Desorcie's Market
.7 miles
9 Saint Armand Road
Highgate Center, Vt. 05459
(802) 868-4409

BAKERY/RESTAURANT
Joey's Junction Bakery and Café
.4 miles
(Reopened as of 2016)
2865 State Route 78
Highgate Center, Vt. 05459
(802) 868-7600

LIBRARY
Highgate Public Library
.8 miles
> 17 Mill Hill Road
> Highgate Center, Vt. 05459
> (802) 868-3970
> highgatelibrary.wordpress.com

POST OFFICE
Highgate Post Office
.7 miles
> 38 Saint Armand Road
> Highgate Center, Vt. 05459
> (802) 868-2576

HARDWARE STORE
O C McCuin & Sons True Value
1 mile
> 3337 State Route 78
> Highgate Center, Vt. 05459
> (802) 868-3261

SHELDON SPRINGS, VT. 05485

CONVENIENCE STORE/LUNCH COUNTER
Pauline's Quick Stop
2.2 miles from Sheldon Springs
Hydro Dam low water take-out
> 682 Mill Street
> Sheldon Springs, Vt. 05485
> (802) 933-4810

CONVENIENCE STORE/ATM
Sheldon Mini Mart
1.9 miles from Sheldon Springs
Hydro Dam low water take-out
> 2824 State Route 105
> Sheldon Springs, Vt. 05485

SHELDON JUNCTION, VT. 05483

RESTAURANTS
Papa Noel's Pizzeria
(formerly known as Chur-Chillin's and
Devyn's Creemee Stand & Deli)
Riverside access from Route 105 bridge
> 4232 State Route 105
> Sheldon, Vt. 05483
> (802) 933-7272
> papanoels.com

The Abbey Restaurant
Access along Missisquoi River Valley Trail
or riverside just above Abbey Rapids
> 6212 State Route 105
> Enosburg Falls, Vt. 05450
> (802) 933-2223
> theabbeyrestaurant.net

ENOSBURG FALLS, VT. 05450

GROCERY STORE
Hannaford Supermarket & Pharmacy
1 mile
> 71 Jayview Drive
> Enosburg Falls, Vt. 05450
> (802) 933-6657

NATURAL FOOD/COOP
Wood Meadow Market
.5 miles
> 342 Main Street
> Enosburg Falls, Vt. 05450
> (802) 933-2256

CONVENIENCE STORE/ATM
Kevin's Korner Market
.2 miles
> 127 Main Street
> Enosburg Falls, Vt. 05450
> (802) 933-4545

OUTFITTER
The Great Outdoors
.3 miles
> 162 Main Street
> Enosburg Falls, Vt. 05450
> (802) 933-4815
> greatoutdoorsvermont.com

SHUTTLE
Montgomery Adventures
Services all of the Missisquoi River
from Swanton to Richford, Vt.
> 262 Deep Gibou Road
> Montgomery Center, Vt. 05471
> (802) 370-2103
> montgomeryadventures.com

RESTAURANTS
Many options within a .5 mile walk of NFCT kiosk

The Flying Disc
.5 miles
> 342 Main Street
> Enosburg Falls, Vt. 05450
> (802) 933-2994
> facebook.com/TheFlyingDisc
> Internet cafe, ice cream, music

LODGING
Options within a .7 mile walk of NFCT kiosk

Somerset Inn
> (802) 933-7771 • somersetinnvermont.com

1906 House (B&B)
> (802) 933-3030 • the1906house.com

Enosburg Inn & Suites
> (802) 933-4403

CAMPING
Lawyer's Landing NFCT Primitive Campsite
.2 miles
Located above the dam/Bridge of Flowers and
Light off of West Enosburg Road (no facilities)

LIBRARY
Enosburg Falls Public Library
.4 miles
241 Main Street
Enosburg Falls, Vt. 05450
(802) 933-2328
enosburghlibrary.org

LAUNDROMAT
Main Market Place
.3 miles
154 Main Street
Enosburg Falls, Vt. 05450
(802) 933-4117

POST OFFICE
Enosburg Falls Post Office
.4 miles
34 School Street
Enosburg Falls, Vt. 05450
(802) 933-2206

HARDWARE STORE
Green's Ace Hardware
.5 miles
6 Railroad Street
Enosburg Falls, Vt. 05450
(802) 933-7500

BANK/ATM
Peoples Trust Co.
.3 miles
140 Main Street
Enosburg Falls, Vt. 05450
(802) 933-9000
ptcvt.com

Merchants Bank
.5 miles
371 Main Street
Enosburg Falls, Vt. 05450
(802) 933-4386
mbvt.com

RICHFORD, VT. 05476

GROCERY STORE
Mac's Market
.25 miles
44 Main Street #100
Richford, Vt. 05476
(802) 848-9891

CONVENIENCE STORE/ATM
Wetherby's Quick Stop
.4 miles (adjacent to put-in)
75 Main Street
Richford, Vt. 05476
(802) 848-3550

RESTAURANTS
The Hot Spot Diner
.2 miles
24 River Street
Richford, Vt. 05476
(802) 848-7791

Claude's Riverside Pub
.3 miles
11 River Street
Richford, Vt. 05476
(802) 848-3855

The Crossing
.35 miles
14 Province Street
Richford, Vt. 05476
(802) 848-3393

LODGING
Grey Gables Mansion B&B
Across the street from Davis Park
122 River Street
Richford, Vt. 05476
(800) 299-2117
greygablesmansion.com

CAMPING
Davis Park
Primitive camping is permitted at Davis Park

LIBRARY
Arvin A. Brown Library
.4 miles
88 Main Street
Richford, Vt. 05476
(802) 848-3313
aabrown.org

POST OFFICE
Richford Post Office
.4 miles
80 Main Street Suite 101
Richford, Vt. 05476
(820) 848-7742

BANK/ATM
TD Bank
.5 miles
93 Main Street
Richford, Vt. 05476
(802) 848-7772

QUÉBEC

GLEN SUTTON, QUÉ. G0E 2K0

SHUTTLE AND CAMPING
Canoe & Co.
Riverside access 2 miles past Glen Sutton
Chemin bridge
 1121 Chemin Burnette
 Glen Sutton, Québec G0E 2K0
 +1 (450) 538-4052
 canoecosutton.com

HIGHWATER, QUÉ. J0E 1X0

CAMPING
Camping Nature Plein air/O'Kataventures
(formerly Camping Carrefour)
.25 miles from riverside take out
 2733 Chemin de la Vallée-Missisquoi
 Potton (Mansonville, Québec, J0E 1X0
 +1 (450) 292-3737 or
 Toll Free: (888) 746-4140
 campingnaturepleinair.com
 Camp store, showers, laundromat

MANSONVILLE, QUÉ. J0E 1X0

GROCERY STORE
Marché Richelieu Épicerie
Jacques Ducharme
Adjacent to Secteur Nautique
put-in entrance
 340 Rue Principale
 Potton, Québec J0E 1X0
 +1 (450) 292-5252

CONVENIENCE STORE
Euro-Deli Du Village
.4 miles
 295 Rue Principale
 Potton, Québec J0E 1X0
 +1 (450) 292-5544

BAKERY
Boulangerie Owl's Bread
.5 miles
 299 Rue Principale
 Mansonville, Québec J0E 1X0
 +1 (450) 292 3088
 owlsbread.com

RESTAURANTS
Tea Room/Café Internet
.6 miles
 302 Rue Principale
 Mansonville Québec J0E 1X0
 WiFi

Trattoria Sofia
.6 miles
 304 Rue Principale
 Mansonville Québec J0E 1X0

LIBRARY
Legion Memorial
.4 miles
 2 Rue Vale Perkins
 Mansonville, Québec J0E1X0
 potton.ca/potton

POST OFFICE
.4 miles
 9 Rue Vale Perkins
 Mansonville, Québec J0E 1X0

HARDWARE STORE
Giroux & Giroux
.5 miles
 300 Rue Principale
 Mansonville, Québec J0E 1X0
 +1 (450) 292-3696
 www.rona.ca/en/Giroux-giroux-mansonville

PERKINS LANDING, QUÉ. J0E 1X0

GENERAL STORE
Jewett General Store
Accessible from portage
 3 George R Jewett
 Mansonville, Québec J0E 1X0
 +1 (450) 292-5245

VERMONT

NEWPORT, VT. 05855

vtnorthcountry.org
(Distance from marina/U.S. customs video phone)

GROCERY STORE
Vista Foods
.7 miles
 21 Waterfront Plaza
 Newport, Vt. 05855
 (802) 334-8661

NATURAL FOOD (CO-OP) AND RESTAURANT
Newport Natural Foods and
Montgomery Café
.2 miles
 194 Main Street
 Newport, Vt. 05855
 (802) 334-2626
 newportnatural.com

CONVENIENCE STORE
Cumberland Farms
1.2 miles
535 E. Main Street
Newport, Vt. 05855
(802) 334-3091
cumberlandfarms.com

OUTFITTER AND SHUTTLE*
The Great Outdoors
.7 miles
59 Waterfront Plaza
Newport, Vt. 05855
(802) 334-2831
greatoutdoorsvermont.com
* Shuttle service subject to availability.

SHUTTLE
Clyde River Recreation
2355 State Route 105
West Charleston, Vt. 05872
(802) 895-4333
clyderiverrecreation.com

RESTAURANTS
Several options in the downtown area

Eastside Restaurant & Pub
1 mile OR Accessible from water OR
.8 miles from Prouty Beach Campground
47 Landing Street
Newport, Vt. 05855
(802) 334-2340
eastsiderestaurant.net

LODGING
Newport City Motel
1.2 miles
444 East Main Street
Newport, Vt. 05855
(802) 334-6558
newportcitymotel.net

CAMPING
Prouty Beach City Campground
Accessible from water prior to marina
386 Prouty Beach Road
Newport, Vt. 05855
(802) 334-7951
newportrecreation.org/
prouty-beach-campground

LIBRARY
Goodrich Memorial Library
.1 mile
202 Main Street
Newport, Vt. 05855
(802) 334-7902
goodrichlibrary.org

POST OFFICE
Newport Post Office
.3 miles
59 Coventry Street
Newport, Vt. 05855
(802) 334-2420

BANK
Passumpsic Savings Bank
.2 miles
119 Main Street
Newport, Vt. 05855

ATM
.2 miles
266 Main Street
Newport, Vt. 05855

.7 miles
9 Waterfront Plaza
Newport, Vt. 05855

HARDWARE STORE
Pick & Shovel
.6 miles
54 Coventry Street
Newport, Vt. 05855
(802) 334-8340
pickandshovel.doitbest.com

MEDICAL FACILITY
North Country Hospital
1.9 miles
189 Prouty Drive
Newport, Vt. 05855
(802) 334-7331
nchsi.org

I-91 INTERCHANGE

GROCERY STORES
Price Chopper
56 Commons Drive
Derby, Vt. 05829
(802) 334-1475

Shaws
4340 U.S. Route 5
Derby, Vt. 05829
(802) 334-8466

CONVENIENCE STORE
Champlain Farms Shell
3923 U.S. Route 5 (and West Street)
Derby, Vt. 05829

RESTAURANTS
Several franchises and other options

Derby Four Seasons
    4412 U.S. Route 5
    Newport, Vt. 05855
    (802) 334-1775
    derbyfourseasons.com

BANK/ATM
Community National Bank
    4811 U.S. Route 5
    Derby, Vt. 05829
    (802) 334-7915
    communitynationalbank.com

HARDWARE STORE
Poulin Lumber Inc. (Ace)
(en route to Derby Center, by foot)
    3639 U.S. Route 5
    Derby, Vt. 05829
    (802) 766-4971

DERBY CENTER, VT. 05829
(Distance from Bridge Street canoe carry access. If portaging using U.S. Route 5, you'll pass by these services.)

GROCERY STORE
Derby Village Store
.2 miles
    483 Main Street
    Derby, Vt. 05829
    (802) 766-2215

CONVENIENCE STORE
Derby Corner Mini Mart
.7 miles
    3131 U.S. Route 5
    Derby, Vt. 05829
    (802) 766-5141

RESTAURANTS
Derby Cow Palace
.7 miles
    3111 U.S. Route 5
    Derby, Vt. 05829
    (802) 766-4724
    derbycowpalace.com

LIBRARY
Dailey Memorial Library
.3 miles
    101 Junior High Drive
    Derby, Vt. 05829
    (802) 766-5063
    daileymemoriallibrary.org

POST OFFICE
Derby Post Office
(Between 1-91 and Route 105)
    U.S. Route 5
    Derby, Vt. 05829

OTHER
Sweet Scoops Ice Cream Stand (seasonal)
(In front of North Country Union Jr High)
    57 Jr High Drive
    Derby, Vt. 05829

SALEM LAKE

CAMPING
Char-Bo Campground
Private campground is located between Salem Lake and Little Salem Pond, but not immediately accessible from the water.
    347 Hayward Road
    Derby, Vt. 05829
    (802) 766-8807
    char-bo-campground.com
    Showers, laundry and small camp store

WEST CHARLESTON, VT. 05872

GENERAL STORE
Scampy's Country Store and Deli
Passed en route when using Route 105 as a portage to the West Charleston Pond put-in.
    1155 State Route 105
    West Charleston, Vt. 05872
    (802) 895-4400

SHUTTLE
Clyde River Recreation
Riverside Access
    2355 State Route 105
    West Charleston, Vt. 05872
    (802) 895-4333
    clyderiverrecreation.com

THE FEN

LODGING, CAMPING OR SHUTTLE
Bill Manning/The Clyde River House
    170 Dolloff Mountain Road
    Island Pond, Vt. 05846
    (802) 723-4534 or (609) 865-3627 (cell)

OTHER
Northern Forest Canoe Trail Farm Stand and Ice Cream Treats
(Seasonal from mid-May — October)
Ten Square Mile Road Boat Access

North Woods Stewardship Center
Located off trail, but near the "fen" and a source of information for Nulhegan River levels
154 Leadership Drive
East Charleston, Vt. 05833
(802) 723-6551
northwoodscenter.org

ISLAND POND, VT. 05846

Island Pond Welcome Center
Adjacent to inlet of the Clyde River
11 Birch Street Island Pond, Vt. 05846
(802) 723-9889
islandpondchamber.org

GROCERY STORE
Kingdom Market
.1 mile
12 Railroad Street
Island Pond, Vt. 05846
(802) 723-5464

CONVENIENCE STORE/ATM
Lakefront Express Mart
1 block
127 Cross Street
Island Pond, Vt. 05846
(802) 723-6178

OUTFITTER
Simon the Tanner
2 blocks
2 Main Street
Island Pond, Vt. 05846
(802) 723-4452
simonthetanner.com

SHUTTLE
Bill Manning/The Clyde River House
170 Dolloff Mountain Road
Island Pond, Vt. 05846
(609) 865-3627 (cell)

Clyde River Recreation
2355 State Route 105
West Charleston, Vt. 05872
(802) 895-4333
clyderiverrecreation.com

RESTAURANTS
Essex House & Tavern
2 blocks
138 Cross Street
Island Pond, Vt. 05846
(802) 723-9888
essexhouseandtavern.com
(Formerly known as the Clyde River Hotel/ Newly remodeled in 2016)

KT Rays On The Pond
1 block
69 Cross Street
Island Pond, Vt. 05846
(802) 723-4590

LODGING
Lakefront Inn & Motel
1 block
127 Cross Street
Island Pond, Vt. 05846
(802) 723-6507
thelakefrontinn.com

Essex House & Tavern
2 blocks
138 Cross Street
Island Pond, Vt. 05846
(802) 723-9888
essexhouseandtavern.com
(Formerly known as the Clyde River Hotel/ Newly remodeled in 2016)

CAMPING
Lakeside Camping
2 paddling miles (far side of Island Pond)
1348 Route 105, East Brighton Road
Island Pond, Vt. 05846
Summer: (802) 723-6649
Winter: (802) 723-6331
lakesidecamping.com

Brighton State Park
2.5 paddling miles and one portage
Open Memorial Day through Columbus Day.
To reserve a site 14 days or more in advance:
– Reserve online or call (888) 409-7579
– If less than 14 days, call the campground number listed above or register upon arrival
(802) 723-4360
vtstateparks.com

LIBRARY
Island Pond Public Library
.25 miles
49 Mill Street
Island Pond, Vt. 05846
(802) 723-6134

POST OFFICE
Island Pond Post Office
.1 miles
  32 Main Street
  Island Pond, Vt. 05846
  (802) 723-5995

BANK
Passumpsic Savings Bank
.1 mile
  49 Mill Street
  Island Pond, Vt. 05846
  (802) 723-4100
  passumpsicbank.com

Community National Bank
.2 miles
  23 E Brighton Road
  Island Pond, Vt.
  (802) 723-4356
  communitynationalbank.com

HARDWARE STORE
Gervais Ace Hardware
1 block
  62 Cross Street
  Island Pond, Vt. 05846
  (802) 723-6138

NEW HAMPSHIRE

NORTH STRATFORD, N.H. 03590
(Distance from NFCT kiosk at Debanville Landing)

RESTAURANTS
Claudette and Dean's Place
.7 miles (Daniel Webster Hwy South)
  1858 Route 3
  North Stratford, NH 03590
  (603) 922-3299

LIBRARY
Stratford Public Library
.5 miles
  74 Main Street
  North Stratford, N.H. 03590
  (603) 922-9016
  stratfordnhlibraries.com

POST OFFICE
North Stratford Post Office
.4 miles
  79 Main Street
  North Stratford, N.H. 03590
  (603) 922-3819

GROVETON, N.H. 03582

GROCERY STORE
North Country Shop & Save
(Hannaford Supermarket)
.35 miles
  25 State Street
  Groveton, N.H. 03582
  (603) 636-6081

RESTAURANTS
North Country Family Restaurant
.3 miles
  12 Main Street
  Groveton N.H. 03582
  (603) 636-1511

LODGING
Down Home Motel
.6 miles from kiosk, but accessible across
U.S. Route 3 from NFCT Normandeau
riverside campsite
  129 Lancaster Road
  Groveton N.H. 03582
  (603) 636-2898
  downhomemotel.com

LIBRARY
North Umberland Public Library
.4 miles
  31 State Street
  Groveton, N.H. 03582
  (603) 636-2066
  northumberlandpubliclibrary.org

LAUNDROMAT
Groveton Laundry Center
.3 miles
  8 State Street
  Groveton, N.H. 03582

POST OFFICE
Groveton Post Office
.3 miles
  59 Church Street
  Groveton, N.H. 03582
  (603) 636-1610

BANK
Passumpsic Bank
.3 miles
  40 State Street
  Groveton, N.H. 03582
  (603) 636-1223
  passumpsicbank.com

MEDICAL FACILITY
Weeks Medical Center/ER
10.6 miles from Groveton, N.H.
  173 Middle Street
  Lancaster, N.H. 03584
  (603) 788-4911
  weeksmedical.org

STARK, N.H. 03582
LODGING AND SHUTTLE ASSISTANCE
Stark Inn Bed & Breakfast
Riverside access
16 Northside Road
Stark, N.H. 03582
(603) 636-2644

Ammo Cabin
(Operated by Gord's Corner Store)
Note: Riverside cabin is between Stark and West
Milan, N.H. Call ahead to reserve.
434 Stark Hwy
(603) 449-2236
gordscorner@yahoo.com

WEST MILAN, N.H. 03588
(THESE SERVICES ARE ACCESSED ALONG THE
CARRY)

GENERAL STORE/LUNCH COUNTER/ATM
Gord's Corner Store
1156 West Milan Road
Milan, N.H. 03588
(603) 449-2236

SHUTTLE
North Brook Outfitters
Gord Roberge
1156 West Milan Road
Milan, N.H. 03588
(603) 449-2236
Services the Upper Ammonoosuc and
the Androscoggin.

CAMPING
Cedar Pond Campground
265 Muzzy Hill Road Route 110A
Milan, N.H. 03588
(603) 631-5753
cedarpondcamping.com

MILAN, N.H. 03588
(Off-trail)

SHUTTLE
North Woods Rafting
Off trail
308 Milan Road
Route 16, Milan, N.H. 03588
(603) 449-BOAT (2628)
northwoodsrafting.com

ERROL, N.H. 03579
Umbagog Area Chamber of Commerce
(603) 482-3906

GENERAL STORE/ATM
Errol General Store
.2 miles
76 Main Street
Errol, N.H. 03579
(603) 482-3235

OUTFITTER/ATM
LL Cote Sports Center
.3 miles
25 Main Street
Errol, N.H. 03579
(603) 482-7777

SHUTTLE
Northern Waters
Across the road from kiosk
3579 Upton Road
Errol, N.H. 03579
(603) 482-3817
beoutside.com

North Woods Rafting
Off trail
308 Milan Road
Route 16, Milan, N.H. 03588
(603) 449-BOAT (2628)
northwoodsrafting.com

RESTAURANTS
Northern Exposure Restaurant
and Bear Pub
.3 miles
12 Main Street
Errol, N.H. 03579
(603) 482-3468

Subway
.3 miles
25 Main Street
Errol, N.H. 03579

LODGING
Errol Motel
.1 mile
132 Main Street., Route 26
Errol, N.H. 03579
(603) 482-3256
errol-motel.com

150 Main Street Lodging
.2 miles
150 Main Street
Errol, N.H. 03579
(603) 482-3150

CAMPING
Mollidgewock State Park
3.5 miles before reaching the NFCT kiosk
1437 Berlin Road, Route 16
Errol, N.H. 03579
(603) 482-3373
nhstateparks.org/explore/state-parks/
mollidgewock-state-park

Northern Waters
Across the road from kiosk
In Errol, riverside campsites are provided free to
Through-Paddlers. Northern Waters also manages
Cedar Stump campsites located by the Rapid River
Carry. Reserve and pay for these fee-based sites
with Northern Waters.
3579 Upton Road
Errol, N.H. 03579
(603) 482-3817
beoutside.com

Umbagog Lake Campsites
First come, first-served welcome, pre- and
post-season or if sites are available, but need
to contact the park office to confirm before
setting up. Sites are reservable through
reserveamerica.com.
Route 26, Errol, N.H. 03579
P.O. Box 18, Errol N.H. 03579
(603) 482-7795 or
Toll-free (877) 674-2757
nhstateparks.org

LIBRARY
Errol Public Library
.2 miles
67 Main Street
Errol, N.H. 03579
(603) 482-7720

POST OFFICE
Errol Post Office
.3 miles
25 Main Street #1
Errol, N.H. 03579
(603) 482-7764

ATM
Cardtronics
.3 miles
6 Main Street
Errol, NH 03579

MEDICAL FACILITY
Androscoggin Valley Hospital
29 miles south of Errol, N.H.
59 Page Hill Road
Berlin, N.H. 03570
(603) 752-2200
avhnh.org

MAINE

RICHARDSON LAKES AREA

CAMPING
South Arm Campground
Richardsons Reservations
62 Kennett Drive
Andover, Maine 04216
(207) 364-5155
camp@southarm.com
southarm.com

MOOSELOOKMEGUNTIC LAKE

CAMPING
Steven Phillips Memorial Preserve
Mooselookmeguntic Lake Reservations
P.O. Box 21
Oquossoc, Maine 04964
(207) 864-2003
stephenphillipswildernesscamping.com
Note: The Echo and Woodyard sites are least
used and more likely to be available when
passing through.

OQUOSSOC, MAINE 04964
(These services are accessed along the carry)

GROCERY STORE
Oquossoc Grocery
75 Carry Road, Route 4
Oquossoc, Maine 04964
(207) 864-3662

Farmers Daughter
13 Rumford Road
Oquossoc, Maine 04964
(207) 864-2492

OUTFITTER
Rivers Edge Sports
38 Carry Road
Oquossoc, Maine 04964
(207) 864-5582
riversedgesports.com

RESTAURANTS
The Gingerbread House
55 Carry Road
Oquossoc, Maine 04964
(207) 864-3602
gingerbreadhouserestaurant.net

Four Seasons Cafe
92 Carry Road
Oquossoc, Maine 04964
(207) 864-2020

LODGING
Loon's Nest
274 Shore Drive
Oquossoc, Maine 04964
(207) 670-8391
loonsnestrangeley.com

POST OFFICE
Oquossoc Post Office
92 Carry Road
Oquossoc, Maine 04964
(207) 864-3685

RANGELEY, MAINE 04970

GROCERY STORE
IGA Foodliner
1 mile
2185 Main Street
Rangeley, Maine 04970
(207) 864-5089

CONVENIENCE STORE
Lakeside Convenience
.3 miles
2582 Main Street
Rangeley, Maine 04970
(207) 864-9004
lakesideonrangeley.com

OUTFITTER
Ecopelagicon
.3 miles
7 Pond Street
Rangeley, Maine 04970
(207) 864-2771
ecopelagicon.com

Rangeley Region Sport Shop
.2 miles
2529 Main Street
Rangeley, Maine 04970
(207) 864-5615
rangeleysportshop.com

SHUTTLE
Ecopelagicon
.3 miles
7 Pond Street
Rangeley, Maine 04970
(207) 864-2771
ecopelagicon.com

The Farmhouse Inn and Hostel
(Town and Trail shuttles)
2057 Main Street
Rangeley, Maine 04970
(207) 864-3113
thefarmhousemaine.com

RESTAURANTS
Many options within .5 miles of kiosk

LODGING
The Farmhouse Inn and Hostel
1.8 miles (will pick up/shuttle)
(Bunkhouse and private rooms. The Farmhouse Inn also operates The Stratton Motel and Hostel.)
2057 Main Street
Rangeley, Maine 04970
(207) 864-3113
thefarmhousemaine.com

Town & Lake Motel
.5 miles from kiosk, but accessible from Rangeley Lake
2886 Main Street
Rangeley, Maine 04970
(207) 864-3755
rangeleytownandlake.com

Rangeley Inn
.4 miles
2443 Main Street
Rangeley, Maine 04970
(207) 864-3341
rangeleyinn.com

CAMPING
Rangeley Lake State Park
6 miles before reaching Rangeley
In Maine: (800) 332-1501 or
Outside Maine: (207) 624-9950
maine.gov/doc/parks/index.html
Showers

LIBRARY
Rangeley Public Library
.3 miles
7 Lake Street
Rangeley, Maine 04970
(207) 864-5529
rangeleylibrary.com

LAUNDROMAT
Village Scrub Board
.5 miles
2391 Main Street
Rangeley, Maine 04970
(207) 864-3390

POST OFFICE
Rangeley Post Office
.2 miles
2517 Main Street
Rangeley, Maine 04970
(207) 864-2233

Camden National Bank
.25 miles
2484 Main Street
Rangeley, Maine 04970
(207) 864-3321
camdennational.com

ATM
Cardtronics
.2 miles
2775 Main Street
Rangeley, Maine 04970

HARDWARE STORE
Rangeley Lakes Builders Supply
.7 miles
2742 Main Street
Rangeley, Maine
(207) 864-5644
rangeleybuilderssupply.com

MEDICAL
Rangeley Family Medicine
1.4 miles
42 Dallas Hill Road
Rangeley, Maine 04970
(207) 864-3303
healthreachchc.org/center

STRATTON, MAINE 04982

(Distance from the intersection of
Routes 27 and 16)

The NFCT kiosk is located adjacent to the
Route 27 bridge and boat launch .75 miles north
of the village of Stratton. The village of Stratton is
bypassed when following the Trail north from the
S. Branch of the Dead River onto Flagstaff Lake.

GROCERY STORE
Fotter's Market and Hardware
1 block
157 Main Street
Stratton, Maine 04982
(207) 246-2401
fottersmarket.com

NATURAL FOOD (CO-OP)
The Coplin Co-op .5 miles
ME-16/27. 134 Main Street
Stratton, Maine 04982
(207) 491-4979

SHUTTLE
The Stratton Motel and Hostel
1 block
162 Main Street (Route 27)
Stratton, Maine 04982
(207) 246-4171 or (207) 670-5507
rangeleyfarmhouse.wix.com/thestrattonmotel

RESTAURANTS
The White Wolf Inn
.1 mile
146 Main Street (Route 27)
Stratton, Maine 04982
(207) 246-2922
thewhitewolfinn.com

The Stratton Plaza Hotel
.1 mile
(Closed Sundays and Mondays)
149 Main Street
Stratton, Maine 04982
(207) 246-2000
strattonplazahotel.com

LODGING
The Stratton Motel and Hostel
1 block
162 Main Street (Route 27)
Stratton, Maine 04982
(207) 246-4171 or (207) 670-5507
rangeleyfarmhouse.wix.com/thestrattonmotel
or thestrattonmotel.com

The Stratton Plaza Hotel
.1 mile
149 Main Street
Stratton, Maine 04982
(207) 246-2000
strattonplazahotel.com

The White Wolf Inn
.1 mile
146 Main Street
Stratton, Maine 04982
(207) 246-2922
thewhitewolfinn.com

Tranquillity Lodge
.6 mile (or .1 mile from NFCT kiosk)
310 ME-27
Eustis, Maine 04982
(207) 246-2122
tranquillitylodge.com

CAMPING
Cathedral Pines Campground
Off-trail: 3.6 miles from Stratton, but
accessible from water
945 Arnold Trail/ME-27
Eustis, Maine 04936
(207) 246-3491

LIBRARY
Stratton Public Library
.4 miles
88 Main Street
Stratton, Maine 04892
(207) 246-4401
stratton.lib.me.us

LAUNDROMAT
.4 miles
> In lower walk-out level of two-story building opposite Camden National Bank on School Street

POST OFFICE
Stratton Post Office
.4 miles
> 95 Main Street
> Stratton, Maine 04982
> (207) 246-6461

BANK
Camden National Bank
.4 miles
> 9 School Street
> Stratton, Maine 04982
> (207) 246-2181
> camdennational.com

ATM
Cardtronics
.1 mile
> 152 Main Street
> Stratton, Maine 04982

HARDWARE STORE
Fotter's Market and Hardware
1 block
> 157 Main Street
> Stratton, Maine 04982
> (207) 246-2401
> fottersmarket.com

MAINE HUTS & TRAILS

LODGING AND MEALS
24 hour advanced reservations are necessary for overnight accommodations and meal planning July – October.
> mainehuts.org
> (207) 265-2400

OTHER
Dead River Water Release
amcbostonpaddlers.org/DeadRiverReleases

SPENCER LAKE AND FISH POND

CAMPING
Free camping with advanced reservation at Sandbar Beach on Spencer Lake or Fish Pond Campground.
> (207) 243-3020

JACKMAN, MAINE 04945
jackmanmaine.org

Services for Jackman are spread out for a mile along Route 201. Distances shown are calculated from Pomerleau Park, unless otherwise noted.

GROCERY STORE
Mountain Country Supermarket
.2 miles (north)
> 554 Main Street
> Jackman, Maine 04945
> (207) 668-5451

SHUTTLE
Cry of the Loon Outdoor Adventures
> P.O. Box 238
> Jackman, Maine 04945
> (207) 668-7808
> cryoftheloon.net

RESTAURANTS
Several diners and restaurants are located south of Pomerleau Park, up to ¾ mile distant and clustered around Route 201 and Spruce Road. The first boating landing provides slightly closer access.

LODGING
Sally Mountain Cabins
Waterside just past the Wood Lake boat access
> 9 Elm Street
> Jackman, Maine 04945
> (800) 644-5621 or (207) 668-5621
> sallymtcabins.com

Jackman Motel (and Taxidermy)
.5 miles (south)
> 450 Main Street
> Jackman, Maine 04945
> (207) 668-5051
> jackmanmotel.com

Bishops Motel
.4 miles (south)
> 461 Main Street
> Jackman, Maine 04945
> (207) 668-3231
> bishopsmotel.com

CAMPING
Jackman Landing Campground
Accessible from water OR
.4 miles north from park
> 582 Main Street/Route 201
> Jackman, Maine 04945
> (207) 668-3301
> Laundromat, showers, WiFi

LIBRARY
Jackman Public Library
.6 miles north from park OR
1 block north from Route 201/6 bridge and boat access point on the Moose River
> 604 Main Street
> Jackman, Maine 04945
> (207) 668-2110
> maine.gov/msl

LAUNDROMAT
Jackman Landing Campground
.4 miles
> 582 Main Street/Route 201
> Jackman, Maine 04945
> (207) 668-3301

POST OFFICE
Jackman Post Office
.5 miles
> 552 Main Street
> Jackman, Maine 04945
> (207) 668-7771

ATM
Cardtronics
.4 miles
> 407 Alternate Main Trail
> Jackman, ME 04945

HARDWARE AND SPORTING GOODS STORE
Jackman True Value Hardware and U-Haul
.6 miles north from park OR
1 block north from Route 201/6 bridge and boat access point on the Moose River
> 598 Main Street
> Jackman, Maine 04945
> (207) 668-5151

MEDICAL FACILITY
Jackman Regional Health Center
.8 miles from park OR
.6 miles from boat access
> 376 Main Street
> Jackman, Maine 04945
> (207) 668-4300
> PCHC.com/Jackman

LONG LAKE
LODGING/CAMPING
The Last Resort
Lakeside access/north shore of Long Lake after emerging from Moose River. Single night stays are available at the cabins before mid-July and after mid-August. Campsites and showers.
> 11 Last Resort Road
> Jackman, Maine 04945
> (207) 668-5091
> lastresortmaine.com

ROCKWOOD, MAINE 04478
(Distance from NFCT kiosk unless otherwise noted)

CONVENIENCE STORE
Rockwood Convenience Store
.75 miles
> Route 15
> Rockwood, Maine 04478
> (207) 534-7352

RESTAURANTS
Rockwood Bar & Grill
.75 miles
> Route 15
> Rockwood, Maine 04478
> (207) 534-0202

The Birches Resort
Waterside access, about one mile north of Moose River outlet
> 281 Birches Road
> Rockwood, Maine 04478
> (800) 825-9453
> birches.com

LODGING
Rockwood Cottages
Lakeside access before reaching the NFCT kiosk
> P.O. Box 176
> Rockwood, Maine 04478
> Summer Tel. (207) 534-7725
> mooseheadlakelodging.com

The Birches Resort
Waterside access, about one mile north of Moose River outlet
> 281 Birches Road
> Rockwood, Maine 04478
> (800) 825-9453
> (207) 695-8927
> birches.com

POST OFFICE
Rockwood Post office
.1 mile
> 62 Village Road
> Rockwood, Maine 04478
> (207) 534-2277

MEDICAL FACILITY
Charles A. Dean Memorial Hospital
20 miles south of Rockwood, Maine
> 364 Pritham Avenue
> Greenville, Maine 04442
> (207) 695-5200
> cadean.org

THE NORTHEAST CARRY

(This service is accessed along the carry)

GENERAL STORE AND SHUTTLE SERVICE
Raymond's Country Store
642 NE Carry Road
Rockwood, Maine 04478
(207) 557-5348

CHESUNCOOK VILLAGE 04441

LODGING
Chesuncook Lake House
Lakeside access
Confirm availability prior to arrival.
Under new management.
Pine Stream Road, Route 76
Chesuncook Village, Maine 04441
(207) 745-5330
chesuncooklakehouse.com

ALLAGASH WILDERNESS WATERWAY

CAMPING
Allagash Wilderness Waterway
Search the government website for "Allagash Wilderness Waterway" to obtain information about boat sizes regulations and camping fees. All of the Allagash Wilderness Waterway's campsites can all be virtually viewed using GoogleEarth.
maine.gov/doc/parks

LODGING
Nugent's Camps
Lakeside Access on Chamberlain Lake
No minimum night stay, but subject to availability without advance reservations. Best chances are mid-week in July and August. Important note: Camp is located on far east side of Chamberlain Lake and crossings can be dangerous. Most Allagash paddlers stick to the west shore.
(207) 944-5991
nugentscamps.com

SHUTTLE
Churchill Dams Ranger Station
Modest fee to shuttle you and/or your gear around the Chase rapids.

ALLAGASH, MAINE 04774

GENERAL/CONVENIENCE STORE
A basic store with irregular hours and questionable inventory is located off Hwy 161, east of the bridge.

OUTFITTER/SHUTTLE
Allagash Guide Service
928 Allagash Road
Allagash, Maine 04774
(877) 815-8165
(207) 398-3418
allagashguideservice.com

Tylor Kelly Camps
77 Dickey Rd
Allagash, Maine 04774
(207) 398-4478
allagashhunting.com

RESTAURANTS
Two Rivers Lunch
Accessible from river
75 Dickey Road
Allagash, Maine 04774
(207) 398-3393
allagashhunting.com

LODGING OR CAMPING
Tylor Kelly Camps
77 Dickey Rd
Allagash, Maine 04774
(207) 398-4478
allagashhunting.com

McBreairty Point Lodge and Camping Site
AFTER CASEY RAPIDS, ACCESS AT THE BOAT LAUNCH, RIVER LEFT, BEFORE BRIDGE
(207) 398-6062 or (207) 398-3245
No facilities and no campfires are permitted

SAINT FRANCIS, MAINE 04774

(Distance from Pelletier's campground)

GENERAL STORE
Joe's Country Store
Up the driveway from
Pelletier's Campground
1005 Main Street
Saint Francis, Maine 04774
(207) 398-4172

CAMPING AND SHUTTLE
Pelletier's Campground
Riverside access
P. O. Box 67, Main Street
Saint Francis, Maine 04774
(207) 398-3187
mainerec.com/pellcamp

POST OFFICE
Saint Francis Post Office
.6 miles
  890 Main Street
  Saint Francis, Maine 04774
  (207) 398-3211

....

FORT KENT, MAINE 04743

**Greater Fort Kent Area Chamber
of Commerce**
(207) 834-5354

fortkentchamber.com

GROCERY STORE
Paradis Shop N Save
.7 miles
  62 West Main Street. # 101
  Fort Kent, Maine 04743
  (207) 834-3020
  paradisshopnsave.com

CONVENIENCE STORE
Circle K
.7 miles
  308 West Main Street
  Fort Kent, Maine 04743
  (207) 834-3196
  circlek.com

NATURAL FOOD (CO-OP)
Market Street Co-op
.5 miles
  26 Market Street
  Fort Kent, ME 04743
  (207) 231-5065

RESTAURANTS
Several restaurant options along Main Street/
Route 161 and near the Northern Door Inn

LODGING
Northern Door Inn
1 mile
  356 West Main Street
  Fort Kent, Maine 04743
  (866) 834-3133 or (207) 834-3133
  northerndoorinn.com

CAMPING
Fort Kent Block House
.2 miles
  Primitive camping

LIBRARY
Fort Kent Public Library
.5 miles
  1 Monument Square
  Fort Kent, Maine 04743
  (207) 834-3048
  maine.gov/msl

LAUNDROMAT
Dinah's Laundromat
.7 miles
  47 Pleasant Street
  Fort Kent, Maine 04743
  (207) 834-6635

POST OFFICE
Fort Kent Post Office
1.2 miles
  152 West Main Street
  Fort Kent, Maine 04743
  (207) 834-3313

BANK
TD Bank
.7 miles
  62 West Main Street #104
  Fort Kent, Maine 04743
  (207) 834-6181
  tdbank.com

KeyBank
.9 miles
  101 West Main Street
  Fort Kent, Maine 04743
  (800) 539-2968
  key.com

ATM
There are many ATMs located at businesses
all along West Main Street.

OTHER
**U-Haul Neighborhood Dealer
at Twins Service**
.9 miles
  67 Market Street
  Fort Kent, Maine 04743
  (207) 834-2060
  uwebconnect.com/
  twinsservicefortkentmaine

Rite Aid Pharmacy
.3 miles
  84 East Main Street
  Fort Kent, Maine 04743
  (207) 834-5444
  riteaid.com
  Photo development/back-up disks

MEDICAL FACILITY
Northern Maine Medical Center
1 mile
  194 East Main Street
  Fort Kent, Maine
  (207) 834-3155
  nmmc.org

Medical Facilities

NEW YORK
Adirondack Medical Center
1.7 miles from NFCT kiosk
2233 State Route 86
Saranac Lake, N.Y. 12983
(518) 891-4141
amccares.org

CVPH Medical Center
1.3 miles from NFCT kiosk
75 Beekman Street
Plattsburgh, N.Y. 12901
(518) 561-2000
cvph.org

VERMONT
Northwestern Medical Center
10.5 miles from Swanton, Vt.
133 Fairfield Street
St. Albans, Vt. 05478
(802) 524-5911
northwesternmedicalcenter.org

North Country Hospital
2 miles from Newport Marina
189 Prouty Drive
Newport, Vt. 05855
(802) 334-7331
nchsi.org

NEW HAMPSHIRE
Weeks Medical Center/ER
10.9 miles from Groveton, N.H.
173 Middle Street
Lancaster, N.H. 03584
(603) 788-4911
weeksmedical.org

Androscoggin Valley Hospital
29 miles south of Errol, N.H.
59 Page Hill Road
Berlin, N.H. 03570
(603) 752-2200
avhnh.org

MAINE
Rangeley Family Medicine
1.4 miles from NFCT kiosk
42 Dallas Hill Road
Rangeley, Maine 04970
(207) 864-3303
rangeleychc.org

Jackman Community Health Center
.8 miles from Pomerleau Park
376 Main Street
Jackman, Maine 04945
(207) 668-7755
PCHC.com/Jackman

Charles A. Dean Memorial Hospital
20 miles south of Rockwood, Maine
364 Pritham Avenue
Greenville, Maine 04442
(207) 695-5200
cadean.org

Northern Maine Medical Center
1 mile from NFCT kiosk
194 East Main Street
Fort Kent, Maine 04743
(207) 834-3155
nmmc.org

Local Pronunciations

Guide to Phonetic Pronunciations of Regional Names

Adirondack	add-der-RON-dack
Allagash	AL-ah-gash
Ammonoosuc	am-mon-NEW-sock
Androscoggin	ann-droe-SKOG-en
Attean	A-tee-en
Berkshire	BERK-sure
Brassua	BRASS-aw
Caucomgomoc	cock-ma-go-mic
Champlain	SHAM-plane
Chesuncook	chess-SUN-cook
Demo (Road)	DEE-moe
Enosburg	E-nuss-berg
Errol	ERR-role (rhymes with Carol)
Forked	FORK-ed
Memphremagog	mem-fruh-MAY-gog
Missisquoi	miss-SIS-kwoi
Michaud	MEE-show
Mooselookmeguntic	moose-look-mah-GUN-tick
Musquacook	ma-squaw-cook
Nulhegan	null-HE-ghan
Oquossoc	o-KWA-sick
Penobscot	pen-NOB-scot
Plattsburgh	PLATS-berg
Québec	kay-beck (French) or kwuh-beck (English)
Rangeley	RANGE-lee
Raquette	RACK-et
Saranac	SAIR-rah-knack
Telos	TEA-loss
Umbagog	um-BAY-gog
Umbazooksus	um-bah-zook-sus
Umsaskis	um-sass-kiss
West Milan	west MY-lan

NFCT Kiosks or Information Panels and Registration Boxes

As of 2014

Town or Geographic Area	Kiosk or Registration Box Location
Old Forge, N.Y.	Visitor Center Boat Landing
Fifth Lake**	Carry Trail
Brown's Tract**	Carry Trail
Raquette Lake, N.Y.	Boat Launch
Long Lake, N.Y.	Village Beach/Park Area
Upper Saranac Lake**	Bartlett Carry
Saranac Lake, N.Y.	Lake Flower Dam Carry
Saranac River*	La Duke Lean-to
Union Falls Pond**	Carry Trail
Town of Saranac	Pickett's Corner Access/Boat Launch
Plattsburgh, N.Y.	Green Street Boat Launch
North Hero, Vt.	Visitor Center
Swanton, Vt.	Route 78/Depot Street Bridge Parking Area
Enosburg Falls, Vt.	Bridge of Flower and Light
Richford, Vt.	Davis Park
Potton (Mansonville), Qué	Village Welcome Sign/Riverside Access
Newport, Vt.	Waterfront Boardwalk
East Charleston, Vt.	10 Mile Square Road/Clyde River Access
Island Pond, Vt.	Lakefront Village Park
Bloomfield, Vt.	Debanville Landing
Town of Colebrook, N.H.	Riverside Parking Area (South Side of Bridge)
Connecticut River*	Samuel Benton Campsite
Groveton, N.H.	Riverside Village Park
Stark, N.H.	Stark Historic Center
West Milan*	Gord's Corner Store
Errol, N.H.	Androscoggin River Boat Access/Parking Area
Pontook Reservoir*	Pontook Boat Launch
Rangeley, Maine	Rangeley Town Cove Park
Eustis/Stratton, Maine	Route 27 Boat Launch/Confluence of South Branch Dead River and Flagstaff Lake
Dead River	Long Falls Dam
Dead River*	Spencer Rips Put-In/Campsite
Moose River*	Demo Road Bridge
Rockwood, Maine	Kineo Boat Launch
Penobscot River	Lobster Lake Loop
Chamberlain Lake	Ranger Station
Churchill Dam	Near Parking Area/Churchill Dam
Fort Kent, Maine	Riverside Park

* NFCT Registration Box Only
** NYDEC Registration Box Only

Trail Town Populations

Based on 2010 U.S. census data

Town or City	Population
Old Forge, N.Y.	756
Inlet, N.Y.	333
Raquette Lake, N.Y.	96
Long Lake, N.Y.	711
Saranac Lake, N.Y.	5,406
Clayburg/Redford	n/a
Picketts Corners, N.Y.	n/a
Plattsburgh, N.Y.	19,989
North Hero, Vt.	810
Swanton, Vt.	2368
Highgate Center, Vt.	n/a
Sheldon Springs, Vt.	n/a
Sheldon Junction, Vt.	n/a
Enosburg Falls, Vt.	1329
Richford, Vt.	1361
Glen Sutton, Qué	n/a
Mansonville, Qué[†]	1850
Perkins Landing, Qué.	n/a
Newport, Vt.	4589
Derby Center	597
Salem Lake/West Charleston, Vt.	686*
(also includes Charleston and East Charleston West)	
Island Pond, Vt.	821
Bloomfield, Vt./North Stratford N.H.	n/a
Groveton, N.H.	1118
Stark, N.H.	556*
West Milan, N.H.	n/a
Errol, N.H.	298
Oquossoc, Maine	193
Rangeley, Maine	1168
Stratton, Maine	630
Jackman, Maine	862
Rockwood, Maine	316
The Northeast Carry	n/a
Chesuncook Village, Maine	< 12
Allagash, Maine	227
St. Francis, Maine	485*
Fort Kent, Maine	2488

n/a   Unincorporated; data not available

*   Includes surrounding area within same county (not indicative of available services)

[†]   2000 Canadian census data

Helpful Web Links

NORTHERN FOREST CANOE TRAIL
NorthernForestCanoeTrail.org
The official NFCT organization website. Check here for the most recent trail updates and trail town services changes. Read other paddler blogs, post questions to the forum and apply for trip recognition.

GOOGLE EARTH
google.com/earth
An excellent resource for viewing the Trail prior to paddling it. Turn on the photos layer to see posted pictures.

AMERICAN WHITEWATER
americanwhitewater.org
A national data base of river information with links to USGS river gauges and dam release information.

UNITED STATES GEOLOGICAL SURVEY (USGS)
waterwatch.usgs.gov
Links to current streamflow conditions throughout the United States.

NOAA—NATIONAL WEATHER SERVICE
water.weather.gov/ahps
Comprehensive National Oceanic and Atmospheric Administration site listing national weather forecasts, river observations, river forecasts and flood warnings.

NATIONAL WEATHER SERVICE
weather.gov
Official U.S. weather, marine, fire and aviation forecasts, warnings, meteorological products, climate forecasts and information about meteorology.

MESSAGE BOARDS
paddling.net
npmb.com (Northeast Paddlers Message Board)
See what other paddlers are talking about or post your own questions about the NFCT.

International Scale of River Difficulty

This is the American version of a rating system used to compare river difficulty throughout the world. This system is not exact; rivers do not always fit easily into one category, and regional or individual interpretations may cause misunderstandings.

Paddlers attempting difficult runs in an unfamiliar area should act cautiously until they get a feel for the way the scale is interpreted locally. River difficulty may change each year due to fluctuations in water level, downed trees, recent floods, geological disturbances, or bad weather. Stay alert for unexpected problems!

As river difficulty increases, the danger to swimming paddlers becomes more severe. As rapids become longer and more continuous, the challenge increases. There is a difference between running an occasional class-IV rapid and dealing with an entire river of this category. Allow an extra margin of safety between skills and river ratings when the water is cold or if the river itself is remote and inaccessible.

CLASS I RAPIDS
Fast moving water with riffles and small waves. Few obstructions, all obvious and easily missed with little training. Risk to swimmers is slight; self-rescue is easy.

CLASS II RAPIDS: NOVICE
Straightforward rapids with wide, clear channels which are evident without scouting. Occasional maneuvering may be required, but rocks and medium-sized waves are easily missed by trained paddlers. Swimmers are seldom injured and group assistance, while helpful, is seldom needed. Rapids that are at the upper end of this difficulty range are designated "Class II+".

CLASS III: INTERMEDIATE
Rapids with moderate, irregular waves which may be difficult to avoid and which can swamp an open canoe. Complex maneuvers in fast current and good boat control in tight passages or around ledges are often required; large waves or strainers may be present but are easily avoided. Strong eddies and powerful current effects can be found, particularly on large-volume rivers. Scouting is advisable for inexperienced parties. Injuries while swimming are rare; self-rescue is usually easy but group assistance may be required to avoid long swims. Rapids that are at the lower or upper end of this difficulty range are designated "Class III-" or "Class III+" respectively.

CLASS IV: ADVANCED
Intense, powerful but predictable rapids requiring precise boat handling in turbulent water. Depending on the character of the river, it may feature large, unavoidable waves and holes or constricted passages demanding fast maneuvers under pressure. A fast, reliable eddy turn may be needed to initiate maneuvers, scout rapids, or rest. Rapids may require "must" moves above dangerous hazards. Scouting may be necessary the first time down. Risk of injury to swimmers is moderate to high, and water conditions may make self-rescue difficult. Group assistance for rescue is often essential but requires practiced skills. A strong eskimo roll is highly recommended. Rapids that are at the lower or upper end of this difficulty range are designated "Class IV-" or "Class IV+" respectively.

CLASS V: EXPERT
Extremely long, obstructed, or very violent rapids which expose a paddler to added risk. Drops may contain large, unavoidable waves and holes or steep, congested chutes with complex, demanding routes. Rapids may continue for long distances between pools, demanding a high level of fitness. What eddies exist may be small, turbulent, or difficult to reach. At the high end of the scale, several of these factors may be combined. Scouting is recommended but may be difficult. Swims are dangerous, and rescue is often difficult even for experts. A very reliable eskimo roll, proper equipment, extensive experience, and practiced rescue skills are essential. Because of the large range of difficulty that exists beyond Class IV, Class 5 is an open-ended, multiple-level scale designated by class 5.0, 5.1, 5.2, etc., each of these levels is an order of magnitude more difficult than the last. Example: increasing difficulty from Class 5.0 to Class 5.1 is a similar order of magnitude as increasing from Class IV to Class 5.0.

Source: www.americanwhitewater.org

Web Cams

The following websites include live webcams that are recording current conditions for NFCT water bodies. Search for the webcam links on each of these sites.

Old Forge, N.Y. – Western Terminus
oldforge.net

Inlet, N.Y.
nelsonscottages.com/

Raquette Lake, N.Y.
raquettelakenavigation.com/raquettelakenews/raquette-lake-navigation-webcam/

Upper Saranac Lake – Chapel Island
uppersaranac.com/video-cam-feed/

Lake Champlain Marina, Newport, Vt. and Island Pond, Vt.
The Recreation Network Web Cams
myrecnet.com/webcam/webcams.htm

Lake Champlain (Burlington, Vt.)
hazecam.net

North Hero Island, Vt.
heroswelcome.com

Island Pond, Vt.
islandpond.com

Rockwood, Maine - Mount Kineo
rockwoodonmoosehead.org

Chesuncook, Maine
chesuncooklakehouse.com

Lake Mooselookmeguntic
baldmountaincamps.com

Jackman, Maine
jackmanmaine.org

Index

Acknowledgements

This guidebook would not have been conceived without six cohorts who willingly and somewhat blindly agreed to join me on my 50th birthday canoeing adventure in 2011: my husband Sam Vainisi, who probably never envisioned that the wedding vows he recited to me 30 years ago, promising to support me as I pursued my goals, would quite mean this; my daughter, Kacia, who was forced to endure camping trips with her family and alone time with her mother in the Boundary Waters Canoe Area Wilderness. I count you as one of my best canoeing partners and with whom I immensely enjoy paddling—especially on this last trip alone together before your wedding; and for my friends Becky Miller, Linda Stolz, Joyce Fritz and Kay Glodowski who not only made paddling the entire trail possible for me, but added to a greater depth of memories and deepened friendships.

To the staff at Northern Forest Canoe Trail Inc., who encouraged me to go for it and were instrumental in answering my questions and clarifying information. I am particularly indebted to Kevin Mack, Sandy Tarburton and Walter Opuszynski who patiently responded to emails. Repeatedly.

Through the organization and its Facebook page, I have met other Through- and Section Paddlers, who provided guidance when planning my own Through-Paddle as well as insight and support as I conducted research for this book. Chris Gill, you are one of the Trail's greatest advocates and advisors. Your detailed emails frequently diverted me away from my tasks at hand, not at all an unwelcome interruption. Section-Paddlers Kalmia Angustifolia, Chuck Horbert, Alan Flint, Ben Malakoff, Tonya McKenna and Geoff Davis, and Through-Paddlers Laurie Chandler (2015), Eric McIntyre (2014), Megan (Little Bug) McAlonis (2014), Valerie Welch (2014), Peter Macfarlane (2013), Team 3M (2012), Mark Fromm (2012), Russ Collett (2011), Mike Lynch (2011), Cathy Mumford (2010) and Sam Brakeley (2009)—with whom I had the privilege of getting to know through emails and phone calls reliving our trips—and for all the other NFCT bloggers, know that your posts were inspiring and informative. You are all part of a growing NFCT community, of which I am a grateful member.

My heart is especially full of thanks for the connection I made with Through-Paddlers Justine Jarvis, T.K. and their four-pound Yorkshire terrier Moxie—of Team Moxie—whose chalk messages left under bridges I eagerly searched for and whose paddle strokes I followed, but never caught up to in 2011. Our trips were intertwined even though we didn't meet until after I got off the Trail, a month after finishing their own Through-Paddle.

Thanks is also due to Ranger Matt LaRoche, who graciously proofed the mileage segments pertaining to the Allagash Wilderness Waterway; to the folks at the Northwoods Stewardship Center and Andy Cappello from Newport, Vermont Parks and Recreation; to Joyce Salisbury and Bill Hanley who helped me navigate the publishing world when I had no idea where to start; to Marti Gillespie for her superb editing skills and guidance pertaining to myriad usages of the comma and to Bon Iver's Justin Vernon, whose song *Skinny Love*, became the catchy earworm that got me through the Mud Pond Carry.

Of course, I wouldn't have celebrated any 50th birthday if not for my parents Sharon and Roger Daanen. They not only gave me life, but cultivated my love of nature and adventure through early family camping trips in northern Wisconsin and road trips throughout the United States.

Kagan, you missed out on this grand adventure, but you have adventures of your own to pursue. Your mother is happy that you contributed by helping out with some research and proofing.